THE NEW RUSSIAN REVOLUTIONARIES

OGURTSOV

VAGIN

PLATONOV

BORODIN

SADO

THE NEW RUSSIAN REVOLUTIONARIES

by
John B. Dunlop

NORDLAND PUBLISHING COMPANY
Belmont, Massachusetts 02178
1976

By the Same Author

Staretz Amvrosy (1972; 1975)

*Aleksandr Solzhenitsyn: Critical Essays
and Documentary Materials* [co-editor]
(1973; 1975)

VSKhSON: Sbornik materialov [compiler] (1975)

Library of Congress Catalog Card Number 74-22865
ISBN 0-913124-09-5
© Copyright 1976 by Nordland Publishing Company
All Rights Reserved

© Copyright of the Russian text of "Programma" by YMCA-Press 1975

PRINTED IN THE UNITED STATES OF AMERICA

TO OLGA

About the Author

Dr. John B. Dunlop, Associate Professor of Russian at Oberlin College, was graduated *magna cum laude* from Harvard in 1964. He received his M.A. and Ph.D. from the Department of Slavic Languages and Literatures at Yale University. Dr. Dunlop, recipient of several academic honors and fellowships, received a Fellowship for Younger Humanists from the National Endowment for the Humanities (1974-1975) spending the year in London where he was appointed an "Academic Visitor" at the London School of Economics and Political Science. Dr. Dunlop, author of numerous articles which have appeared in *Survey, The Russian Review, The Times Literary Supplement, Transactions* and *Frontier,* is the author of *Staretz Amvrosy,* co-editor of and contributor to *Aleksandr Solzhenitsyn: Critical Essays and Documentary Materials,* and compiler of *VSKhSON: Sbornik materialov* (in Russian).

Preface

This study attempts to recount the history and assess the ideological and political significance of the largest underground revolutionary organization to be uncovered in the Soviet Union in the post-Stalin era. An understanding of the ideas of the "All-Russian Social-Christian Union for the Liberation of the People" is essential for anyone concerned with the question of contemporary ideologies potentially capable of terminating Marxism-Leninism's rule in the USSR. Due to the extensive footnotes, this volume may be of interest to the specialist as well as to the general reader intrigued by the fate of modern Russia.

On the matter of transliteration, I have elected to employ the Library of Congress system, with two exceptions: Mordovia instead of Mordoviia and Trotskyism rather than Trotskiiism.

A number of institutions have aided me in my research for this book. Oberlin College granted me an early sabbatical and Research Status for the academic year 1974-1975, and the National Endowment for the Humanities awarded me a Younger Humanist Fellowship to support my investigations into contemporary religious-based Russian nationalism. The London School of Economics and Political Science kindly appointed me an Academic Visitor for 1974-1975, while the School of Slavonic Studies of the University of London and the Centre for the Study of Religion and Communism in Keston, Kent offered me access to their valuable library holdings.

Of the many individuals who assisted my project, the following deserve to be singled out for special mention.

Peter Reddaway of the London School of Economics was of immense help at all stages of my research, and his comments upon the initial draft of this book were of great benefit. It is fair to say that without his continued encouragement this study would probably not have been brought to completion. A huge debt is also owed to my wife for her excellent draft translations of virtually all the materials appearing in this volume and for her unflagging support. The dedication page inadequately expresses my gratitude to her. Richard Haugh of Iona College gave generously of his time in reading the manuscript and in offering numerous helpful suggestions. Thanks are also due to Edith W. Clowes for translating a section of the "Program" of the revolutionary organization and to Joan O'Connell for performing the burdensome task of compiling the names index as well as helping with the proofreading.

JBD

Contents

CHAPTER I

The Sources

ON FEBRUARY 2, 1964 an important clandestine military-political organization made its appearance in Leningrad. Its declared aim: the formation of an "underground liberation army" which would "overthrow the [Soviet] dictatorship and destroy the defensive forces of the oligarchy."[1] Calling itself the All-Russian Social-Christian Union for the Liberation of the People[2] or, more commonly, VSKhSON—the Russian acronym for the organization's somewhat ponderous title,[3]— the underground union succeeded in recruiting almost thirty members before it was uncovered by the KGB in 1967. Another thirty "candidates" were being prepared for membership. By the time of its arrest, the organization had extended its influence to such disparate locations as Moscow, Tomsk, Siberia and Siauliai, Lithuania.

Once the regime had succeeded in unmasking the union in February, 1967, it became aware that it had discovered the most significant military-political organization to appear in Soviet Russia since the death of Stalin. What made VSKhSON particularly disturbing and unwelcome was its "neo-Slavophile" orientation. For the Soviet leaders probably fear few things more than an opposition based on Russian nationalism and seeking to resurrect the influence of the Russian Orthodox Church. Such an opposition will inevitably find broad-based support among the populace.

In late 1967 the four leaders of VSKhSON were tried *in camera* (in violation of Soviet legal practice) and given sentences ranging from eight to fifteen years imprisonment. In March-April, 1968 the rank-and-file were tried, and seventeen were awarded sentences ranging from ten months to seven years.[4] With the exception of the two most important leaders, who were immured in Vladimir Prison, the VSKhSON membership was then sent off to concentration camps in Mordovia.

If the regime could have had its way, not a word concerning VSKhSON would have become known either in the USSR or the West. The Soviet mass media have never made mention of the organization and presumably never will. Extremely thorough searches were carried out by the secret police at the homes of VSKhSON members and their friends and relatives in the hope that all materials relating to the union would be successfully confiscated. Despite the thoroughness and diligence of the security organs, however, key materials concerning VSKhSON began to make their way abroad as early as 1967. Shortly before their arrest, the VSKhSON leaders providentially decided to send a copy of the organization's "Program" abroad to the émigré activist Nikita Struve, editor of the Paris-based journal *Messenger of the Russian Student Christian Movement* [*Vestnik R. S. Kh. D.*].[5] This extraordinarily valuable source appears for the first time in English in Appendix II to this volume.[6]

Important coverage of VSKhSON was provided by the *samizdat*[7] bimonthly *A Chronicle of Current Events* [*Khronika tekushchikh sobytii*], a journal devoted to publicizing abuses of human rights in the Soviet Union. In its first issue, dated April 30, 1968, the *Chronicle* reported the trial of the VSKhSON rank-and-file and communicated some tantalizing details about the organization. Over the thirty-four issues which have followed—the publication was temporarily sup-

pressed by the KGB in 1972 but fully resurrected in 1974—
the *Chronicle* has kept an eagle eye on the fortunes of
VSKhSON members in the labor camps and Vladimir Prison.
It has also reported when they have completed their sentences
and been released.[8]

In late 1970, an anonymously-written *samizdat* essay bearing the cumbersome title "The All-Russian Social-Christian
Union for the Liberation of the People: Its Membership,
Program, Methodology, Ideological Positions and Reasons
for Failure" reached the West.[9] Dated "Leningrad, 1969,"
this document evidences a close-hand knowledge of
VSKhSON's history and activities (we shall subsequently
refer to its author as S., for *samizdat*). What it does not
provide, however, is information shedding light on the per-
sonalities of the military-political union's leaders and members.

Soon two resourceful individuals, working in ignorance
of each other's efforts, undertook to fill in this gap. The
first of these was Aleksandr Aleksandrovich Petrov-Agatov
(b. 1921), a colorful former member of the Union of Soviet
Writers who had previously been imprisoned from 1947-1956
and from 1960-1967.[10] Released in 1967, Petrov-Agatov succeeded in enjoying only a year of freedom—during which
time he published in several Soviet journals—before he was
again arrested and given a seven-year sentence for his
poems, which one KGB official adjudged "worse than an
atomic bomb." From the Mordovian camps Petrov-Agatov
contrived to smuggle out two *samizdat* works, "The Russia
They Don't Know"[11] and "Prison Encounters,"[12] both containing accounts of conversations held with VSKhSON members in the camps. One was hardly surprised to read in
Chronicle No. 27 that "for communicating his reminiscences
to the outside world" Petrov-Agatov had been transferred in
November, 1970 to Vladimir Prison. He remained there until
December, 1973, when he was returned to the Mordovian
camps.[13]

More systematic information on VSKhSON was provided by Vladimir Nikolaevich Osipov (b. 1938), a prolific *samizdat* author who, until his November, 1974 arrest, edited the well-known neo-Slavophile journal *Veche* and its successor *Zemlia.* Himself an alumnus of the camps—he served from 1961-1968 for earlier *samizdat* activity—Osipov had occasion to encounter some of the VSKhSON membership shortly before his release. His interest aroused, he researched the organization and in January, 1972 issued his study "The Berdiaev Circle in Leningrad."[14] This detailed account served, despite some inaccuracies and one deliberate attempt to mislead (which will be discussed in Chapter VI), to fill in many of the gaps left by previous sources. Osipov also discusses VSKhSON *en passant* in a number of his other writings.

Another document deserving mention is the anonymously-written "Information concerning Igor' Viacheslavovich Ogurtsov (b. 1937)."[15] Dated July 21, 1974, it offers important information on the biography and conditions of imprisonment of the VSKhSON leader. Hereafter its author will be cited as A. (for "anonymous").

Soviet legal materials relating to the investigation and trial of the revolutionary union represent another valuable source. It may seem astonishing that such documents are allowed to circulate in the Soviet Union, but such is occasionally the case. The defendants' lawyers, and frequently the defendants themselves, are permitted access to these materials. Osipov reports that "absolutely all facts" in his "The Berdiaev Circle . . ." are based on "the materials of the investigation and trial."[16] And Petrov-Agatov tells us that in camp he managed to obtain from a VSKhSON member the materials of the investigation and trial for perusal.[17] In "The Russia They Don't Know" he produces lengthy extracts from one of the VSKhSON leaders' statements to the court.

Considering the tendency of such materials to "gravitate" westwards, it is not surprising that certain of them have penetrated abroad. First, there is the full text of the

"Sentence" [*Prigovor*] passed by the Soviet court in the trial of the VSKhSON rank-and-file, a most helpful document which reached the West in 1973.[18] Second, there is the "summation of the investigation" [*zakliuchenie sledstviia*] in the case of the rank-and-file.[19] This latter document, which "sums up" the results of the KGB's investigations into VSKhSON, represents one of the most valuable sources available on the revolutionary union. Other legal materials mentioned by Petrov-Agatov and Osipov have yet to make their way to the West.[20]

Persons recently permitted to emigrate from the Soviet Union are another profitable source of information. I have benefited from talks with a number of such individuals, but by far the most significant information has been supplied by two former Leningrad lawyers, Iurii Handler and Yuri Luryi.[21] Handler, now living in New York, became closely acquainted with several VSKhSON members—in particular Evgenii Vagin, one of the organization's leaders with whom he spent two years in the same work brigade—in the Mordovian camps. My lengthy talk with him will be cited in the notes as "Handler Interview." Yuri Luryi, presently a resident of Toronto, served as the defense attorney for two VSKhSON rank-and-file, Bochevarov and Konstantinov, at their 1968 trial. When I learned of Luryi's arrival in Canada in late 1974, I wrote him requesting that he write an account of the trial and give his impressions of the revolutionary union. He kindly obliged with an informative twelve-page essay entitled "They Were Moved by a Painful Love of Homeland,"[22] which he intends to publish in an émigré journal in the near future. He and I also exchanged several letters on the subject of VSKhSON.

A last source which should be mentioned is Bernard Karavatskii's "Reminiscences of a Participant."[23] Karavatskii is an East European, now living in Denmark, who knew three of the VSKhSON leaders personally during the time the revolutionary organization was active in Leningrad.

Though not officially a member of the underground union, Karavatskii was fully apprised of its aims and intentions, with which he sympathized.

It should be emphasized that I have made mention of only the most significant source materials. A complete listing of sources on VSKhSON will be found in the notes to this volume. Readers of Russian have the opportunity of consulting a collection of materials on VSKhSON, compiled by myself, which was published in the late spring of 1975 by YMCA-Press in Paris.[24] This volume contains most of the important sources available on the revolutionary organization.[25]

To conclude, while one would of course appreciate seeing more information concerning VSKhSON drift westwards, we are undoubtedly fortunate in possessing the material we do. In many cases, those electing to send such information out of the Soviet Union did so at considerable risk. Aleksandr Petrov-Agatov was compelled to languish three years in Vladimir Prison largely because of his curiosity concerning the All-Russian Social-Christian Union for the Liberation of the People, and Osipov's interest in the organization may have been a contributing factor to his recent arrest. Soviet citizens choosing to write about VSKhSON or assisting source materials concerning it to reach the West could not but have been aware of the regime's displeasure at their activities. Why they nevertheless decided to take such a risk should become clear from the chapters which follow.

CHAPTER II

The Leaders

> He that dwelleth in the secret place of
> the Most High shall abide under the
> shadow of the Almighty.
>
> I will say of the Lord, He is my refuge
> and my fortress: my God, in Him will
> I trust.
>
> Surely He shall deliver thee from the
> snare of the fowler, and from the noi-
> some pestilence . . .
>
> A thousand shall fall at thy side, and
> ten thousand at thy right hand; but it
> shall not come nigh thee.
>
> (Psalm 91, *KJV*[1])

IT WAS TO THE READING OF Psalm 91 that four students at
Leningrad State University took an oath on February 2,
1964, founding an underground military-political organization aimed at overthrowing the Soviet regime.[2] As Boris
Pasternak informs us in *Doctor Zhivago,* this psalm was
traditionally sewn into the clothing of Russian soldiers during World War I to serve as a talisman.[3] Thus the VSKhSON
leaders were consciously resurrecting a time-honored Russian

19

practice. As believing Russian Orthodox Christians, they
were undoubtedly also seeking Divine protection for their
endeavor. And with good reason. These four young men,
aged twenty-six to thirty, were taking on what may well be
the most skilfully repressive totalitarian regime in the history of the globe.

Let it not be thought at the outset that these four individuals were revolutionary "dreamers," ivory-tower intellectuals divorced from reality. All four had received military
training in the Soviet armed forces; one had served in an
airborne-paratroop division.[4] Two came from military families.[5] One was the former junior wrestling champion of
Leningrad.[6]

We begin our treatment of these remarkable men with
the VSKhSON "head," Igor' Viacheslavovich Ogurtsov, who,
if he endures, will be released from imprisonment in 1982
(to commence a five-year period of court-imposed exile).
Ogurtsov was born on August 22, 1937 in the city formerly known as Stalingrad, and now as Volgograd. At an
early age, however, he moved to Leningrad and may be considered an adopted son of that northern city. His father,
Viacheslav Vasil'evich, was a naval officer and a member
of the Communist Party; his mother, née Evgeniia Mikhailovna Derevenskova, was a pianist. Apparently of Great Russian peasant stock (his name derives from the Russian word
for cucumber—*ogurets*), Ogurtsov seems to have come from
a closely-knit, patriotic family. Once he was arrested, he was
not abandoned by his parents (as frequently happens, especially in Party families, in Soviet Russia); rather, they did
all they could to obtain his early release and preserve his
health.[17]

From birth Ogurtsov seems to have been a unique individual. Vladimir Osipov writes:

> Igor' Orgutsov is an exceptional and unusual per-
> son. From childhood on he continually honed his

will, was merciless toward his own weaknesses, led an ascetic mode of existence, neither smoked nor drank, slept virtually on boards. An enormous strength of will, high intelligence, erudition, a knowledge of several foreign languages, skill at writing, an excellent knowledge of music and, at the same time, moral purity and a sensitivity toward those around him—all of this sharply singled Ogurtsov out wherever he happened to be: at home, at work, in the organization. A vegetarian, Ogurtsov did not eat meat, refused everything that smacked of luxury. At the same time, he used to pull drunks out of ditches, would never pass by a beggar without contributing, suffered at the sight of the unfortunate. Ogurtsov was a Christian and a convinced Russian patriot. A decisive influence on his world-view . . . was exerted by the great Russian thinker Nikolai Aleksandrovich Berdiaev.[8]

A. has added some details not present in Osipov's account. During Ogurtsov's years at the university, he writes, the future VSKhSON leader

occupied himself very seriously with self-education, studied philosophy, history, economics and the political structure of various countries and their constitutions, studied literature very seriously and intently, proposing to make it his basic vocation in the future. He studied architecture, art and music, played the piano, sometimes composed. His favorite composers were Skriabin, Rakhmaninov, Chopin and Verdi. He was very interested in the history of the past Great Fatherland War [World War II] and assiduously noted down the stories of his father's numerous military comrades who had served as senior officers and active participants in the war.[9]

And Bernard Karavatskii, who was personally acquainted with Ogurtsov, effuses:

> It is most difficult of all for me to write about Igor' Viacheslavovich Ogurtsov, perhaps because I did not observe, either in his character or actions, any negative traits. In short, he could be characterized as an exceptionally remarkable and gifted individual. There exist persons—purposeful, extraordinarily intelligent men—who, through their life and their ideas, introduce a new and illuminating order into the life of society. It always seemed to me that this man knew how to draw strength from unknown sources of life. His will in achieving his thought-out goals is unique. On the majority of questions his knowledge was exhaustive, and that which he did not know, he tried to learn thoroughly. In his personal library there were hundreds of the rarest books in all-possible languages. Igor' studied foreign languages, philosophy, psychology, history, military art, Yoga and scores of other subjects, and I must admit that his knowledge was staggering. Scholars who knew him maintain that Ogurtsov is a real savant. According to his mother, a piano teacher, Igor' could have become a first-rate pianist (he knows how to improvize marvellously). In his knowledge of Yoga, he has achieved that which is granted only to those who in the quest for truth are prepared to repudiate their bodies.[10]

Lest the opinions and accounts of Osipov, A. and Karavatskii appear hyperbolic, let us hear Aleksandr Petrov-Agatov, the poet and political prisoner now in his third decade of detention by the authorities:

Igor' Viacheslavovich Ogurtsov, about whom I had

63512

already heard so many good things at the 11th
[Mordovian] camp, grew, after my acquaintance
with the materials of his case, into a gigantic figure.
Intelligent, with a broad education, pure in thought,
heart, tongue and body (he is a virgin at age thirty-
five)—even from the pages of the sentence and the
stenogram of the trial Ogurtsov rose up like an
eagle, and I saw his wings spread out over Russia . . . I embrace you, my dear countryman. I kiss
the soil on which you walk, Evgeniia Mikhailovna
and Viacheslav Vasil'evich—mother and father of
Ogurtsov . . . To have such a son is a joy with which
nothing else can be compared.[11]

The well-known Soviet dissident Iurii Galanskov, who
perished tragically and prematurely at age thirty-three in the
Mordovian camps, said of Ogurtsov, with some of whose
views he was in disagreement, ". . . people like Ogurtsov
have to be preserved. He belongs to the entire nation, not
to this or that system."[12] Both Aleksandr Solzhenitsyn and
Academician Andrei Sakharov have also manifested an interest in Ogurtsov and his fate.[13]

Not all, however, are in agreement in evaluating Ogurtsov
positively. Whereas for Osipov and Petrov-Agatov he represents a gifted individual whose volitional and ascetic pro-
pensities are tempered and given direction by Christian
caritas, for others he is the virtual incarnation of Luciferian
pride, a double of Dostoevskii's Stavrogin in *The Devils.*
Such persons frequently refer to him as "the Führer" and
"Napoleon." One dissident, who spent time with Ogurtsov
in prison, called him "Anti-Christ."[14] And one of the
VSKhSON leaders, Evgenii Vagin, later voiced regret at
the "awesome," virtually hypnotic influence which Ogurtsov
had exerted on him. Once, upon seeing Sean Connery (the
actor who played James Bond) in a film, Vagin came away

amazed at how alike Connery's and Ogurtsov's mannerisms were.[15]

For reasons which should hopefully become clear over the course of this study, it is our suspicion that Ogurtsov's defenders are closer to the truth than his detractors. Strong will and self-discipline—unquestionably character traits of the VSKhSON leader—are not necessarily "demonic" qualities. What matters, of course, is how and to what end they are utilized.

To return to Ogurtsov's biography. After completing secondary school, he enrolled in the Philosophy Faculty of Leningrad State University. After two-and-a-half years of study there, however, he decided to transfer to the Eastern Faculty (philological division) of the same university. He completed his studies in 1966. Because at the time of his graduation there was little demand for those trained in semitology, he was forced to take a job at an institute for shipbuilding, where he worked as a translator and *referent* [reader].[16]

Ogurtsov seems to have conceived of the idea for VSKhSON as early as 1962. In the summer of that year he communicated the idea of the future organization to Vagin while both were doing their summer military training. By early 1964 he had also recruited fellow Eastern Faculty student Mikhail Sado and law student Boris Averichkin.

From VSKhSON's inception Mikhail Iukhanovich Sado served as deputy head of the organization. His official title was "director of personnel, responsible for security." Like that of Ogurtsov, his biography is somewhat uncommon. As he put it in his address to the court:

> I was born in 1934 in Leningrad in a family of bootblacks. My parents were illiterate. By nationality I am an Assyrian. You of course know that the Assyrians settled in Russia largely during the First World War of 1914-18 and, being closely connect-

ed, as Christians, with the Russians, they found here
a homeland for themselves. And I, as in his time
Pushkin, who traced his lineage from Ethiopia, am
unable to conceive of myself without Russia, the
Russian language and Russian culture . . ."[17]

The vice-commander of this Russian patriotic revolu-
tionary organization was thus a non-Russian by blood. And
Sado was not unique in this respect. The VSKhSON rank-
and-file also included a Bulgarian, a Lithuanian and a Tatar.[18]
Two of the organization's candidates for membership were
Armenians.[19]

In his address to the court Sado told how the Great Purge
of 1937 struck the Soviet Assyrian community with the same
decimating force as it smote the rest of the populace. All
Assyrian schools and publications were closed. The entire
Assyrian intelligentsia and the majority of Assyrian men over
thirty were arrested, including Sado's father, grandfather and
two maternal uncles. Only his father survived, after serving
a sixteen year sentence (he was arrested when Mikhail was
three and released when he was nineteen). All of Sado's
relatives were rehabilitated during Khrushchev's de-Stalinization campaign of 1956-57. In addition to a boyhood and
adolescence spent with his father being in prison, Sado (and
his mother) had to endure the horrors of the Leningrad
blockade during World War II. Because of the blockade, he
was unable to commence his schooling until age ten.

In 1951 Sado entered the Communist Youth League
[*Komsomol*], and the following year he became wrestling
champion of Leningrad. The subjects which attracted him
most in school were history and literature. But much of the
intrinsic interest of these disciplines was eroded by their complete saturation in ideology. "During literature lessons we
were fed Stalin in huge portions . . . During history lessons
we were assured that without Stalin the October Revolution
could not have succeeded and that for everything, literally

everything including life itself, we were indebted only to Stalin."[20] Told in school of the fantastic harvests being reaped by Soviet agriculture, Sado was surprised to see the real state of the collective farms when he visited the Kuban' and the Ukraine. Yet whatever doubts he may have experienced were those of a believer. Like all the members of VSKhSON, Sado was almost religiously attracted to Communism during the period 1952-1956.[21] The gap between Soviet propaganda and reality served only on occasion to perplex and puzzle him.

In the fall of 1954, the twenty-year-old Sado was called up into the army and assigned to an airborne-paratroop detachment. "I took part in a number of maneuvers. I was put on alert during the events in Hungary. I saw an atomic explosion."[22] During maneuvers conducted in Iaroslavl' and Kostroma provinces, he was continually struck by the "hopeless poverty" of the Russian countryside and apalled at the mindless destruction of the once-beautiful Russian country churches. "Churches, chapels and monasteries were in total disrepair and falling apart. Many churches had become fuel warehouses, storerooms and workshops. I felt unbearable pain at this desecration of Russian culture."[23]

A far greater shock for Sado was the death of Stalin— the cornerstone of the Soviet theocracy: ". . . I was sure that something incredible would happen when Stalin died."[24] With several of his schoolmates, Sado travelled to Moscow to see the dictator's funeral. "The impression of this funeral, where people crushed each other, was like a vision of hell and has remained with me all my life."[25] Soviet poet Evgenii Evtushenko has described in his *Precocious Autobiography* the grisly scene at Stalin's funeral in which scores were trampled to death by a panic-stricken crowd. It seemed as if Stalin were taking a last portion of victims with him.[26]

De-Stalinization left an even greater impression on Sado. In 1956 he and his fellow soldiers were read the Central Committee decision condemning Stalin's "cult of the personality." When Sado returned to Leningrad after being demobilized in 1957, "... there was talk of nothing but the anti-Party group of Malenkov, Molotov, Kaganovich and others ... My soul was uneasy, for these very persons who were now being anathematized had stood next to Stalin for many years and our history was composed of their names. 'What is happening?' I asked myself. But there was no time to figure it out. I had to prepare for my university entrance examinations."[27]

At Leningrad State University—subsequently to be cited as LGU, the accepted Soviet acronym[28]—new cultural and political shocks awaited Sado:

> Every new development in the country after the unmasking of the cult of the personality was greeted very emotionally by the students, who indulged in stormy self-expression. Remarque, Hemingway and Dudintsev's *Not by Bread Alone* were read with extreme eagerness. Discussions of the last-named book were often sharp and tumultuous.[29] The morbid attitude of the students to the cult of the personality was demonstrated by the fact that all debates sooner or later led to this question. And criticism of the cult very often ended in a demand for the severe punishment of all who were guilty of the repressions. Such literature as Raskolnikov's "Letter to Stalin," E. Ginzburg's *Journey Into the Whirlwind*, A. Solzhenitsyn's *One Day in the Life of Ivan Denisovich*, etc. could not but make an impression.[30] I was personally gripped by this tragedy. The tragedy of an epoch. Unfortunately, all of us soon realized that this was not the end of the tragedy but only its beginning. The cult of Stalin was already being replaced by the cult of Khrushchev.[31]

With the obvious exception of his non-Russian nationality, Sado's life-experience may be seen as emblematic of that of the entire VSKhSON membership. First a quasi-religious acceptance of the Stalin theocracy, sporadically undercut by nagging doubts caused by the disjunction between Soviet myth and reality. Then shock at the death of the seemingly deathless Leader (perfectly understandable, one wonders what will happen in China when Mao is no more). Then the almost unendurable jolt of Khrushchev's eminently unsecret "secret speech" to the Twentieth Party Congress in 1956 and the ensuing de-Stalinization. But there was more to follow. The enormous web of Soviet concentration camps was exposed with great artistic power by Solzhenitsyn in the November, 1962 *Novyi mir* and by others, such as Evgeniia Ginzburg, in *samizdat*. The perfect society was shown to have been a holocaust comparable to Hitler's Germany. Most of Sado's educated contemporaries seem to have hoped that the Khrushchev reforms would continue apace, leading to a more democratic society. Sado and Ogurtsov felt otherwise. For them the Khrushchev reforms were ephemeral and offered absolutely no guarantees against a return of the Terror. In early 1964 they resolved to take up the sword.

Sado married before he joined the organization, while he was a student at LGU. He and his wife, Dzhina, subsequently had two daughters of whom Sado is reportedly extremely fond. Despite his handsome appearance, which makes him naturally attractive to women, he has been an exemplary family man.[32]

Karavatskii, who met Sado frequently, offers this mildly critical assessment of the VSKhSON deputy leader:

> Mikhail Sado ... is a colorful personality. Extraordinarily strong physically, a sportsman and parachutist, he was the oldest of the three [main leaders of the organization]. An innate tendency toward conspiracy found itself an excellent outlet in

the organization, in which he performed the duty of director of counter-intelligence. One will always remember his eyes, dark and expressive, and his penetrating gaze. Those who had occasion to wrestle with him were often paralyzed by his stare ...

By character, Sado differs a great deal from Ogurtsov, since Mikhail was not inclined to hold orthodox views and was always prepared to make exceptions to the rules he held to ...

Mikhail Sado was the active organizer of VSKhSON, its dynamic force.[33]

While a student at LGU, Sado was, it seems, offered employment by the KGB, as Petrov-Agatov reports with his usual *panache:*

This happened shortly before he finished the university. Mikhail Iukhanovich was summoned to the 'Big House', to the directory of the Leningrad Committee of State Security [KGB]. The man who received him ... was refinement and courtesy itself; the young, self-satisfied face of the stranger melted in compliments. 'We need to have several lines translated from the Arabic, Mikhail Iukhanovich. No-one in Leningrad can do it better than you'.

Sado did the translation.

'Excellent! Excellent!' smiled the half-moon which had descended to earth.

'And if it wouldn't inconvenience you, could you please translate this from the Hebrew. After all, you know Hebrew too ... Just a few lines. Be so kind'.

Mikhail Iukhanovich did the translation from Hebrew.

'Well, incidentally ...' smiled the moon.

That 'incidentally' lasted more than an hour.

The elegant intelligence officer with military bearing and the manners of an experienced agent offered Sado a job in the security forces.

'We'll send you to the Middle East ... You yourself understand that at present it's an *extremely* sensitive area ... A brilliant career opens up before you. You won't have to live only on bird's milk'.

'Thank you, but I prefer only one kind of milk. The milk of truth. And it's in Christianity ... As far as my career is concerned, ... [the poet] Blok once said, "A poet doesn't have a career. He has a fate ..." A scholar is the same thing as a poet'.

The moon laughed, splashing forth cold rays.

'Mysticism ... mysticism, Mikhail Iukhanovich ... And you are of course joking. But what prevents you from engaging in Christianity? That's even very much to the point. Religions have always been faithful helpers of intelligence officers'.

'Let me out!' Sado ended the talk. 'I ask you, spare me this conversation'.[34]

To sum up, Sado strikes one as warmer and more "human" than Ogurtsov, though not as brilliant or as ethically steadfast as the VSKhSON "head." By nature a kindly man, Sado was perhaps not steely enough to be in charge of the underground union's security arrangements, though his courage is unquestionable. But then it was his kindliness (as well as his and Orgutsov's Christian "personalism") which ensured that VSKhSON members wavering in their revolutionary zeal or even seeking to leave the organization did not end up at the bottom of the Neva River. The man who would only half-jokingly introduce himself to his prison cellmates as "Mikhail Sado, future Minister of Interior of Free Russia"[35] abhorred all unnecessary violence and hoped for as bloodless a coup as possible. Describing Sado's activity in the organization, Petrov-Agatov writes, "No, Mikhail Iukhanovich is not a saint. Far from a saint. He is a sinful soul. He had to do 'dirty' business as well. He obtained money for the secret Union, without which it could not exist. Dirty, of course, does not mean black [evil]. Sado never killed anyone, never deceived anyone, never poisoned anyone. But he is a man and does not feed on manna from heaven."[36]

It is somehow fitting that the director of VSKhSON's "ideological division," Evgenii Aleksandrovich Vagin, should have been a Dostoevskii specialist. For if it is true that Dostoevskii's influence in the period preceding the Bolshevik Revolution was far less than that of the materialists and atheistic socialists against whom he polemicized so ardently in *The Devils, Notes from the Underground* and other of his works, it is equally true that his influence has been markedly on the rise in Soviet Russia since the death of Stalin, who, correctly fearing the writer's appeal, generally forbade his appearance in print. Vagin was reportedly tapped to edit the first volume of a much-touted Soviet complete works of Dostoevskii (when this volume eventually appeared in 1972, Vagin's name was, predictably, absent, despite the considerable work he had put into it).[37]

Evgenii Vagin was born in 1938 in the ancient Russian city of Pskov into a family of teachers.[38] A gifted student, he graduated from secondary school with a gold medal; this meant he could enter university without having to take entrance exams. At the insistence of his father, Vagin first enrolled in chemistry, but his lack of talent (or interest) became immediately clear and he was rejected. He then followed his natural inclinations and enrolled in literature at the LGU Faculty of Philology. Vagin's relations with his father seem, in general, to have been quite strained; when, for example, his father decided to enter the Communist Party, Evgenii reportedly wrote him a "sharp letter."[39]

After completing both his undergraduate and graduate studies at LGU, Vagin was offered a post at the prestigeous Pushkin House Institute of Literature in Leningrad. There he worked on a dissertation on Dostoevskii and researched both Russian and foreign literatures (he knows French well and has a reading knowledge of English).

Like many Soviet youths in the humanities, Vagin was not inclined to overestimate the merits of the regime. When, in the summer of 1962, Igor' Ogurtsov communicated to him the idea of the future revolutionary organization, he proved more than receptive. Vagin's enthusiasm for the ideas of Dostoevskii, Berdiaev and Konstantin Leont'ev rendered him fertile soil for Ogurtsov's religio-nationalist ideas. There was also the virtually hypnotic effect which the intelligent, ascetic, athletic Ogurtsov had on him. Vagin succumbed almost without struggle to the future VSKhSON "head's" efforts to recruit him.[40]

After entering the revolutionary organization, Vagin decided to marry (his wife's name is Rima), and the couple had a daughter, Anastasiia. This marriage was the cause of an altercation with Ogurtsov, who felt that, for reasons of

psychology and security, unmarried members of the underground union should *remain* celibate.[41]

Karavatskii, who was clearly impressed with Vagin, has
this to say about him:

> I used to meet him [Vagin] at Ogurtsov's apart-
> ment, to which he would come with a stack of for-
> eign newspapers and journals and make a very de-
> tailed survey of current events. One was struck by
> his erudition, his knowledge of languages, the ex-
> traordinary tenacity of his mind, his ability to grasp
> what was most important and to make correct con-
> clusions. Vagin everywhere enjoyed respect and love
> for his sincerity, scholarship, the objectivity of his
> judgments, his wit and his extraordinary purity of
> heart. After Evgenii's arrest, his wife was left with
> a young child on her hands and went to live with
> her mother in Pskov.[42]

Petrov-Agatov has devoted several pages of his "Prison
Encounters" to Vagin. Some excerpts:

> Evgenii Aleksandrovich made a most pleasant im-
> pression on me. Tall, well-proportioned, reflective,
> he exuded, even in prison garb, an air of nobility,
> intelligence and refinement of manners. Can one
> exude refinement of manners? Judging from Vagin,
> one can. In the company of [the writer Andrei]
> Siniavskii ... I passed not less than two hours in
> conversation with Evgenii Aleksandrovich. We
> talked about literature, art and politics. For all
> Vagin's humility, it is impossible not to observe his
> erudition and high intellect. One felt that here was
> a man who had not picked a world-view, some-
> thing which has recently become fashionable, but
> had *worked one out* in himself ... I felt that

Evgenii Aleksandrovich was very, very Russian and,
like all the members of this secret organization,
excessively conventional and traditional [in his
views].[43]

Petrov-Agatov also describes an Easter meal held by the
VSKhSON members of camp 11. As the senior member
present, Vagin headed the festivities:

All the *Peterburzhtsy* at the 11th camp had without exception gathered for the Easter meal. They
had also invited Andrei Donatovich [Siniavskii]
and myself. Besides coffee and cookies, there was
nothing on the table.

Evgenii Aleksandrovich, as it were leading the table,
thrice pronounced, 'Christ is risen!'

All stood up, made the sign of the cross and answered, 'Indeed He is risen!'

Outside it was spring. The earth was thawing.
Hearts also could not help but melt . . .

Vagin gave a short speech. Its sense was that those
gathered here were the salt of Russia. And he believes in the rebirth of the country, of the nation.
And he also believes in those seated at the table.

I don't know why, but I wanted to weep. As before,
I loved Vagin and those gathered here and did not
for a moment doubt that . . . all those seated at the
table were destined to build a new Russia, but all
the same I wanted to weep . . . I am not a prophet
and do not know the destinies of men. But I already
knew that those at the table were the best people in
today's Russia. But they were not yet the salt of the

earth. At the Easter table there had gathered ...
brethren.

'They *can* become the salt', I thought, 'if they suffer much, if they overcome themselves and learn to
love'.[44]

From the available sources, one envisions Vagin as an
unquestionably gifted but somewhat narrow and cerebral individual, not of the stature of an Ogurtsov or Sado. It is
perhaps not surprising that at the trial of the leaders Vagin
did not emulate the fortitude of the other two and con-
fessed his "crimes," thereby earning a reduced sentence of
eight years imprisonment.[45] It would not, however, be just
to imply that Vagin has been broken by his arrest and incarceration. According to Osipov, he manifested considerable steadfastness in the camps by refusing to attend compulsory political indoctrination sessions.[46]

The fourth and last VSKhSON leader, Boris Anatol'evich
Averichkin (b. 1938), served as the organization's archivist.
Osipov tells us that, for security reasons, only Ogurtsov
knew of his existence.[47] This was to protect the organization's archives from seizure in case of disaster. Ogurtsov and
Averichkin are reported to have known each other since boyhood; Averichkin was most likely the first future VSKhSON
member to fall under Ogurtsov's influence.[48] All sources
testify to Averichkin's "closed," uncommunicative character,
probably the reason Ogurtsov chose him as archivist. Like
Vagin, Averichkin did not distinguish himself at his trial and
received a reduced sentence. Petrov-Agatov briefly describes
him in his "Prison Encounters": "... Boris Anatol'evich
Averichkin, the grandson of one of the first Soviet admirals,
with a reserved expression on a face framed by a thick, dark,
fire-red beard. Very nice, still a boy, with tender cheeks and
attractive square eyes."[49] Both Averichkin and Vagin were
released from the camps in early 1975.[50]

In Chapter III we shall have a look at the revolutionary rank-and-file whom the VSKhSON leaders succeeded in recruiting into their clandestine union.

CHAPTER III

The Revolutionary Rank-and-File

IT WAS THE BROAD mass of the Soviet populace which gave
birth to the rank-and-file (and leaders) of the All-Russian
Social-Christian Union for the Liberation of the People. As
Mikhail Sado expressed it in his address to the court, "These
[the members of VSKhSON] are all children of Soviet
workers, employees, intelligentsia, officers. All were born in
Russia, all studied in Soviet schools and institutions of higher
learning."[1] And S. notes, "... almost all members of the organization came from orthodox Soviet families..."[2] Surely
the social origin of the VSKhSON membership is one reason
the regime has sought to pass over the organization's existence in silence.

The VSKhSON rank-and-file member who received the
harshest sentence—seven years—was Viacheslav Mikhailovich
Platonov. Reportedly, the regime even briefly considered
trying him together with the VSKhSON leaders.[3] Platonov
was born in 1941 into a Leningrad working class family. In
1958 he enrolled in the Eastern Faculty of LGU, where he
distinguished himself in his studies. In 1962 he was chosen
to participate in a scholarly expedition to Ethiopia, where he
did research at Emperor Haile Selassie I University. The following year he commenced his graduate studies, which were

37

completed in 1966. While a graduate student, he also served as a teaching assistant in the Department of African Studies and published several articles. At the same time, he worked on and completed a dissertation entitled "Ethiopian Historiography: Chronicles of the 14th-15th Centuries." He was scheduled to defend his thesis in the spring of 1967, but his arrest in February of that year postponed this stage of his scholarly career.[4]

Platonov's role in VSKhSON was an extremely active one. At his trial he reportedly exclaimed, "Only in the organization did I feel myself a human being!"[5] Probably because of his education and zeal, he was selected to be a member of the revolutionary union's "ideological division," headed by Evgenii Vagin. Platonov was unmarried.

The other rank-and-file member of the ideological division, Nikolai Viktorovich Ivanov (b. 1937), also received a quite severe sentence. An instructor in art history at LGU, he had previously completed his undergraduate work in 1961 and his graduate studies in 1964. His devotion to learning was so intense, Petrov-Agatov informs us, that he would lug *nine* suitcases about from camp to camp containing "not clothes, of course, and not food, but books, only books . . ."[6] Unlike the vast majority of VSKhSON members, Ivanov apparently had some noble blood, being an "aristocratic offshoot" of the Pushchin family.[7] His father, however, was a convinced Communist, who suffered a stroke (his third) upon hearing of his son's arrest.[8] After reporting that Ivanov was a favorite of Mikhail Sado, Petrov-Agatov adds some laudatory comments of his own: "Ivanov delighted me. He is an inexhaustible fount of knowledge. It turns out that he has been working for a long time on a dissertation on Orthodoxy. Everything connected with [religious] faith in Russia, with ancient and contemporary art—he knows to the minutest details."[9] Like Viacheslav Platonov, Ivanov is a bachelor.

In October, 1965 an individual who was to be one of

VSKhSON's most active participants entered the organization. Leonid Ivanovich Borodin was born in 1938 in the city of Irkutsk, Siberia into a family of teachers. Upon graduating from secondary school, he sampled and then rejected a career in the police, enrolling instead at Irkutsk University. In 1956, the year of Khrushchev's "secret speech," he was expelled from the university (and the *Komsomol*) for belonging to a clandestine student group called "The Free Word" and for listening to an illegal radio station.[10] He was not, however, tried on criminal charges; this was probably because of his youth. In 1962 Borodin graduated from the D. Banzarov Pedagogical Institute with a concentration in history. He is also reported to have worked on a dissertation entitled "Berdiaev's Philosophical Views," although one can hardly believe that such a topic could be defended in the Soviet Union.[11] After graduating from teachers' college, he attained a post at and eventually became principal of the Serebriansk High School in Luga District, Leningrad Province, where he appears to have been quite successful. Osipov writes that he enjoyed "the undivided love of the pupils . . . Tactful and benevolent, he succeeded in quashing the inner conflicts among the teachers and carried the collective along with his enthusiasm and love of work."[12] And, Osipov adds humorously, "no-one ever suspected that in the bust of Lenin, located in the school hall, the principal was keeping the documents of VSKhSON."[13]

A successful recruiter and member of VSKhSON's "counter-intelligence" unit, Borodin took his revolutionary activity seriously. He "went several times to see 'The Saloniki Patriots' [presumably, a film or play about Greek Communists] to prepare himself for death, and he could conceive of dying only in battle."[14]

Certain negative traits of Borodin—at least in the eyes of the VSKhSON leaders—should be mentioned. Before joining the organization, he had in 1964 formed his own party, called "the Democratic Party."[15] This party either simply ran

out of steam or was abolished by Borodin when he entered
VSKhSON in 1965. But Borodin had acquired the habits of
a leader (his own party, principal of a high school) and may
have chafed at his subordinate, though responsible, role in
VSKhSON. It is rumored that he may have intrigued to replace Ogurtsov as "head" of the organization.[16] In any case,
it is a fact that he was subjected to a VSKhSON "court of
honor" [*sud chesti*] and censured (but not punished) for his
voluntarism.[17] After his arrest, Borodin cooperated with the
authorities but then regained his firmness in the camps.[18]
Like Ivanov, he was awarded a sentence of six years.

Borodin is a not entirely ungifted poet.[19] The fragments
of his verse which Petrov-Agatov produces in "The Russia
They Don't Know" impress one with their sincere, kenotic
love for Russia and their fervent religiosity:

> At the walls of a defiled church
> I take an oath to Russia on my sword.
> But I meet the approaching boor
> With only a cross on my shoulders.
>
> I am sinful and guilty.
> I had only dreams.
> But I should be glad to be crucified
> If only thou [Russia] might be free.[20]

In the camps Borodin suffered from a painful stomach
ulcer of the same variety as killed Iurii Galanskov at age
thirty-three. It is not surprising therefore that suffering represents a constant refrain in his poetry:

> O God! I cannot sleep.
> Enter through the twilight smoke
> As a golden radiance
> Into my coffin.

> And let Thy love multiply
> My sufferings . . ."[21]

Petrov-Agatov encountered Borodin in a camp hospital where he had been sent for treatment of his ulcer:

> No, it was not in Moscow and not in Leningrad that I met him. Our paths crossed in Mordovia, behind barbed wire in a camp for political prisoners. And not just in a camp for politicals but in the hospital of that camp . . . This frail man of medium height was very ill. Both he and the history of his illness bespoke a stomach ulcer. But I had the impression that there was no stomach ulcer. Rather it seemed that they had brought in a burning heart which was flaming out in all directions . . . He did not burn in parts, he was all aflame. And inside, in his womb, he was unbearably hot. He writhed from the unbearable pains. Writhed but did not moan or cry out. And when the pain would let up just a bit, he would read his poems . . ."[22]

At the time of his arrest, Borodin was separated from his first wife (they had one child). After his release from prison, he married Larisa Evseevna Simanovich, a Russian Jew.[23]

A few words concerning the three VSKhSON members selected to be "squad" commanders. Vladimir Fedorovich Ivoilov (b. 1938) entered the organization at the same time as his friend Borodin. Ivoilov graduated from the LGU Faculty of Economics in 1966 with a concentration in political economy. After graduation, he was sent by the state to Tomsk to be instructor in his field at the Tomsk Polytechnical Institute. Once settled there, he set about establishing a VKShSON branch in the Siberian city. Like Ivanov and Borodin, Ivoilov was given a six-year sentence.

Mikhail Borisovich Konosov (b. 1937) began but did not complete his higher education. He was employed as a fitter at the Leningrad Gas Company and, at the same time, was enrolled as a correspondence student at the Gor'kii Institute of Literature in Moscow. Konosov was unquestionably the most successful of the VSKhSON squad commanders and was engaged in expanding his unit to a "platoon" when the organization was broken by the KGB.

Like Borodin, Konosov was a poet. Before his arrest he published in Soviet newspapers and journals.[24] As were most of the VSKhSON members in leadership roles, he was Russian Orthodox in his religious views. And he was married (his wife's name was Liudmila).

Petrov-Agatov gives a somewhat ironical sketch of Konosov, "Konosov, a poet, who admitted that it would be better to address him not only by his first name but by his patronymic as well. He seemed to be very kind and open but tried to give the impression of being deep in concentration and perspicacious."[25] Konosov did not distinguish himself at the investigation and trial, and Ogurtsov is supposed to be quite irritated at him for his behavior.[26]

Georgii Nikolaevich Bochevarov (b. 1935), the third of the VSKhSON squad leaders, entered the organization in late 1964. He is the son of a Bulgarian Communist who fled to the Soviet Union to avoid being put to death by a Fascist court. Unfortunately, "Stalin put into effect the Fascist court's sentence. The elder Bochevarov was executed as 'an enemy of the people'."[27] Petrov-Agatov claims that a street in Sofia, the Bulgarian capital, is named after Bochevarov's revolutionary father.[28] Yuri Luryi, Bochevarov's defense attorney at the trial of the VSKhSON rank-and-file, has this to say about his client:

> Georgii Bochevarov finished the Eastern Faculty of Leningrad University. He is the son of a Bulgarian Communist and professional revolutionary. In the

beginning of the thirties, his father was sentenced to death in Bulgaria and fled to the USSR, where he worked during the last years of his life as a professor of political economy in one of the institutes of the city of Kuibyshev. There he was arrested and shot. But when that period arrived which in the USSR is bitterly and in whispers jokingly referred to as 'the era of the late Rehabilitance,' the deceased Bochevarov-*père* was deemed to have been guilty of nothing. Once Bochevarov-*fils* told me that he is tortured to this day by the memory of how he used to believe in the guilt of his father and of how he once permitted himself to reproach his mother for having married an 'enemy of the people.' The recovery of his sight began during his first student years. He read and thought a great deal, and his acquaintance with Igor' Ogurtsov and Mikhail Sado brought Georgii to the decision to devote his life to the salvation of his homeland.[29]

After graduation from LGU in 1965, Bochevarov went to work as an engineer—like Ogurtsov he seems not to have been able to find a job in his speciality, Eastern Studies—and continued his activities in VSKhSON, first as a member of the organization's counter-intelligence unit and then as a squad commander. There is evidence that Bochevarov was, like Borodin, an independent-minded member of VSKhSON, one given to disputing the views of the leaders.[30] Osipov tells us that Bochevarov had a serious difference of opinion with Ogurtsov and Sado and that his squad was eventually disbanded. Bochevarov cooperated with the investigating authorities after his arrest and received a surprisingly light sentence of two years and six months.[32] Still, his behavior in the camps and since his release could hardly be described as docile.[33]

Of the remaining rank-and-file sentenced in early 1968,

one notes a heavy "technical" representation: six engineers (Baranov, Buzin, Ivlev, Miklashevich, Nagornyi and Ustinovich), a technician (Zabak) and a mechanic (Shuvalov). The humanities are represented by Sudarev (high school English teacher) and Konstantinov (librarian). Veretenov was an economist.[34]

Some other significant data on the seventeen rank-and-file members who received sentences: thirteen of them had been born in the period 1935-1939, i.e. were in their late twenties or early thirties at the time of arrest. This means that they had reached maturity during the period of ideological flux accompanying the Khrushchev "reforms" and de-Stalinization. As far as their education is concerned, two had completed graduate work and eleven, a university or higher technical education. Three had begun but not finished their higher education, while only one had not completed his secondary education. This information suggests that the revolutionary commitment of the VSKhSON rank-and-file was no transient outpouring of youthful maximalism. They were a mature, well-educated lot with good jobs (by Soviet standards). Finally, the fact that over half the members were married and over a third had children is not unimportant. For such men to become revolutionaries, especially under Soviet totalitarian conditions, required serious dedication indeed.

Among the VSKhSON members not sentenced, one finds an instructor at LGU (Fakhrutdinov), a student at the Leningrad Theatrical Institute (Shestakov) and an employee at the Leningrad Institute of Optics (Petrov). Of the twenty-three known candidates for membership in the revolutionary union, a large number, not surprisingly, were students, mostly at LGU (Abramov, Andreev, Balaian, Ekimov, Kalinin, Lisin, Paevskii, Raginian, Virolainen). The others whose professions are known represent a *pot-pourri:* a teacher (Anufriev), an economist (El'kin), a museum supervisor (Osipovich) and a fitter (Stateev). Two of the more startling candidates are S. N. Kulakov, the son of a Leningrad Vice-Admiral and deputy-commander for political affairs of a naval district (and perhaps of a base), and D. V. Frederiks, a grandson of the former Court Minister of Tsar Nicholas II.[35]

Geographically, VSKhSON was of course centered in Leningrad, but it did extend its influence to a number of other locations: Moscow (candidate Orlov-Chistov), Siauliai, Lithuania (presumably Iovaisha), Valaam Island near Finland (Konstantinov), Irkutsk (Goncharov), the Pamir region (Kozichev), Tomsk (Ivoilov and candidates Anufriev and Stateev), Krasnodar (candidates S. N. and E. N. Alekhin) and, reportedly, Volgograd and Petrozavodsk.[36] Several VSKhSON members (Borodin, Veretenov) lived outside the city of Leningrad at addresses in Leningrad Province.

To conclude, it was an interesting assortment of Soviet citizens pulled in by the KGB's nets in 1967. And the more the regime learned about the organization, the more it had cause for concern. Small wonder, then, that the state took over a year to prepare the trial of the VSKhSON rank-and-file.

CHAPTER IV

The Uses of Literature

THE SOVIET COURT which tried the VSKhSON rank-and-file decided that they had actively "prepared, multiplied, disseminated and kept anti-Soviet, tendentious and reactionary religious literature."[1] Indeed literature played such a major role in the organization's activities that Vladimir Osipov, seeking to downplay its military-political intentions, felt it plausible to state, "Although a sentence concerning 'the armed overthrow of the Communist enslavement' stood in the program, statute and conspiracy manual [of VSKhSON], in practice nothing was done or contemplated in this direction ... To change the awareness of people with the help of non-Marxist literature—this, and not some fantastic 'plot', was the authentic aim of Ogurtsov."[2] Osipov's "disinformation" to the contrary, the situation was actually more complex: VSKhSON needed a fund of literature for recruitment, the "education" of its own members and the enlightenment of the populace when the time came. The organization's military and literary plans were interwined and inseparable.

In treating VSKhSON's literary activities, it would seem logical for us to begin with the first step—the acquisition of literature. This did not present overly much of a problem, since Leningrad State University, especially in the early and mid-sixties, teemed with "anti-Soviet" literature. Books, articles and transcripts of foreign radio broadcasts could be bought or borrowed from LGU instructors and students, as well as from Leningrad intellectuals. The "summation of the investigation" [*zakliuchenie sledstviia*] offers some examples of how this was done:

> In the spring of 1966 . . . [Nikolai Ivanov] gave Sado for filming a typewritten translation of separate chapters of N. Struve's *Christians in Contemporary Russia,* published in 1963 in France. The book was received for temporary use from Leningrad State University teacher S. N. Savel'ev.[3]

> Also in 1966, [Ivanov] contributed to the anti-Soviet organization's fund tendentious materials multiplied by [VSKhSON candidate] Abramov on a typewriter, including the 'stenogram' of the Moscow trial of the anti-Soviets Daniel' and Siniavskii, written down during a broadcast by the British propagandistic radio station 'B.B.C.'.[4]

> In 1965, before entering 'VSKhSON', the accused Ivoilov acquired from a student, a citizen of the PNR [Polish People's Republic], for ten rubles two books published in the West. He gave one of them, F. Northrop's anti-Soviet *The Meeting of East and West* (New York, 1946), along with other hostile materials to Sudarev in May, 1966. The other book, E. Wilson's *To the Finland Station,* of revisionist content, he gave to Borodin in the fall of 1965 to read . . . It was seized from Borodin's apartment [by the KGB in February, 1967] in the hiding place where he had concealed it.[5]

The VSKhSON membership also actively engaged in acquiring materials directly related to their military-political plans. Thus, besides collecting "hostile" and "tendentious" literature, Ivoilov also obtained West German military specialist Eike Middeldorf's *Tactical Handbook.*[6] Ustinovich acquired and gave to VSKhSON head Ogurtsov Curzio Malaparte's *Coup D'État: The Technique of Revolution.*[7] And Evgenii Vagin obtained the memoirs of White Army generals Denikin and Wrangel and Aleksandr Kerenskii's *The Kornilov Affair.*[8]

A valuable contact was formed by Ogurtsov with a Polish citizen named Zavadsky, a relative of a Polish government official. From him Ogurtsov "received literature published in the West," and to him he gave "a film with [Evgeniia] Ginzburg's *Journey into the Whirlwind.*"[9] As the reader has undoubtedly noted, Eastern bloc citizens living in the Soviet Union were a valuable source of Western literature.

Through LGU instructor Il'ias Fakhrutdinov, who was a member of VKShSON for several months before voluntarily leaving the organization out of disagreement with its goals, Ogurtsov made contact with helpful foreigners such as the Russian émigré Ekaterina L'vova, a French citizen. It was L'vova who spirited the VSKhSON "program" out of the Soviet Union.[10]

All new literature of potential use to the organization was read and evaluated. Since many of the works selected were in foreign languages, "several translators systematically worked through foreign literature."[11] The most active translators among the revolutionary union's membership seem to have been Vagin, Platonov, Bochevarov, Sudarev and Klochkov.[12] Some examples of their sedulity:

In November, 1964, on instructions from Sado, [Platonov] translated from the English separate parts of B. Russell's book *Bolshevism: Practice and Theory...*[13]

In 1965-1966, [Bochevarov] contributed to 'VSKhSON' for propaganda use translations done by him of books published in the West: G. Muller's *The Use (Application) of the Past,* J. Clarkson's *History of Russia,* R. Pipes' *The Formation of the Soviet Union* and F. Maclean's *Escape to Adventure.*[14]

In 1965-1966, [Sudarev] completed translations for 'VSKhSON' of anti-Soviet and tendentious books and articles for which, in February, 1966, he received the thanks of the 'head' of the anti-Soviet organization, Ogurtsov.[15]

VSKhSON also encouraged its members to exercise their own literary talents. As S. puts it, "There was created a significant fund of their own literature, attesting to the creative activity of the participants in the organization."[16] The three most important organization documents were its "program," "statute" [*ustav*] and "conspiracy manual" [*nastavlenie po konspiratsii No. I*]. The first two were the work of the VSKhSON leaders (Ogurtsov would appear to be the principal author of the "program"[17]); Borodin was one of the authors of the conspiracy handbook.[18]

Konosov contributed a number of writings to the revolutionary union's "fund." In the spring of 1965, he submitted two poems entitled "Admiral Kolchak" and "Hungarian Lyric," while in September of the same year he contributed an article "The Lessons of Novocherkassk."[19] In January, 1967, he drafted a "leaflet to the workers" to be used during the organization's projected activities in the fall of that year.[20]

VSKhSON member Sudarev penned two articles: "Concerning the Victims" and "A Specter Is Haunting Europe."[21] Bochevarov wrote pieces with such titles as "The Contemporary Situation in the Communist Parties of Europe," "Leninism, Trotskyism and Stalinism" and "The Reasons for the Origin of the Cult of Stalin." He also completed part one of a "Short History of the CPSU [Communist Party of the Soviet Union]."[22]

Once VSKhSON had acquired, translated or written a book or article deemed appropriate to its needs, it was faced with the problem of how to reproduce it. By printing press? But in the Soviet Union, as Julius Telesin, a dissident who recently emigrated to the West, has expressed it, "printing presses ... 'belong to the people.' "[23] As for photocopying machines, in Telesin's words, "To be sure, there are a large number of photocopying machines in the Soviet Union but they are not sold to private persons, hired out, or set up for private use. They belong to state organizations and their entire output is strictly controlled. Each of them is guarded like a military object by persons who protect it vigilantly from any 'ideological diversion.' "[24] Mimeographs and hectographs belong to the same category.[25]

Under Stalin, even typewriters were regarded as potential enemies of the people and had to be officially registered.[26] After the dictator's death, however, laxity set in, and during the 1960s typewriters, typing and carbon paper could easily be obtained in Soviet shops without arousing suspicion. The difficulty involved in typing longer works is not difficult to imagine. It takes many hours and, unless one is very careful, errors can find their way into the text. If one hires a typist, one needs adequate funds and risks a denunciation to the authorities. The first typed copy of a text cannot be circulated because the KGB can trace the typewriter from it; the ninth and tenth carbons are apt to be barely legible. Several other factors can render the finished product difficult to read. "A work is, of course, easier to read when it is not typed very closely ... On the other hand, single-space typing creates its own conveniences—less work for the person typing it (fewer sheets need to be inserted in the typewriter), less paper is used, and the finished work takes up less space."[27] There is also a "fear factor" present as the typist jitteringly taps out a document of dubious pleasure to the regime.

That VSKhSON used this classic method of *samizdat* reproduction is clear from the sources. Osipov tells us that the organization possessed "around fifteen typewriters."[28] One example of how they were put to use:

> In July, 1966, [Ivanov] received from Vagin a typewriter belonging to 'VSKhSON', brand-name 'Mersedes', and obligated himself to multiply on it for the organization the [Papal] encyclical 'Mater et Magister' and other tendentious literature, but in January, 1967 he gave this machine to [candidate] Abramov, charging him to multiply literature needed by the participants of 'VSKhSON' for their anti-Soviet propaganda.[29]

More widespread, however, was the reproduction of literature by means of photography. Compared with typing, this method has both advantages and drawbacks. As Telesin observes, "The other method of reproducing texts—by photography—is technically more complex. Film and paper for this can be obtained, although sometimes with difficulty, but not everyone knows how to take, develop and print photographs. Moreover, the text that is being photographed has to be clean; and the eighth carbon of a typed version is of no use. One other drawback: photographic paper is thicker than ordinary paper, and a large photocopied work takes up much more room than a typescript ... The advantages of the photographic method are its greater speed (in skilful hands) and the absence of errors and distortions."[30] A recent *samizdat* do-it-yourself manual by K.

Glukhov [pseud.], entitled "Photography as a Method of Multiplying Textual Documentation," reports that "photographing and developing a book of 150-300 pages takes 3-6 hours and costs about 2-3 rubles for film and chemicals."[31]

The sources attest to considerable employment of this method by VSKhSON:

> In 1964 Ogurtsov and Sado photographed Berdiaev's book *The New Middle Ages*.[32]

> In December of 1964, [Ustinovich] received from Ogurtsov the task of filming the texts of the [VSKhSON] program and other anti-Soviet literature of the illegal organization. He also received 10 rubles of 'VSKhSON' funds to obtain the necessary photo-equipment. He bought a lamp, reagents and other materials.[33]

> In November, 1966, the accused Konosov charged the accused Buzin, Miklashevich, Nagornyi and their confederate Petrov to prepare a photocopy of I. Solonevich's *Escape from Russian Chains* from a film received from Ogurtsov.[34]

> In the summer of 1966, [Platonov] gave his consent to the 'VSKhSON' leaders to organize in his apartment a photolaboratory for the multiplication of anti-Soviet and other literature from the 'VSKhSON' fund. To this end, he received from Vagin a roll of microfilm and literature designated for filming...[35]

On at least one occasion, VSKhSON members who worked as engineers and technicians daringly tried to do some filming at their place of work: "...the accused Nagornyi and Zabak during the period of the end of 1966 and the beginning of 1967 attempted to print part of Solonevich's *Escape from Russian Chains* and Fedotov's book *The Christian in a Revolution* in the photo-booth of the branch laboratory of electronics and semi-conductors of the Leningrad Institute of Exact Mechanics and Optics . . ."[36] Encountering some difficulty (perhaps Soviet security precautions), they then transferred their work to Petrov's apartment "for which he [Nagornyi] brought his enlarger, brand-name 'Leningrad-2', to the latter's [Petrov's] apartment."[37]

Once VSKhSON had reproduced its literature, it then faced a problem familiar to any dweller in a totalitarian society—where to conceal it? Like most Soviet citizens, the organization's members lived in cramped quarters with few potential hiding places available. This, together with the KGB's known diligence in conducting searches, must have been a disquieting factor. In 1972, to take just one example of KGB thoroughness, the security forces searched the apartment of Roal'd Mukhamed'iarov, a dissident suspected of having contact with the *Chronicle of Current Events.* "The KGB scoured about his apartment for four full hours. The search was conducted in the most meticulous manner. Finally, under the grating in a vent in the kitchen they discovered the latest numbers of the *Chronicle,* and the search was immediately terminated."[38]

The sources demonstrate that finding adequate *tainiki* [hiding places] was a constant concern of the VSKhSON membership:

As the 'commander' of a 'squad', [Ivoilov] in his meetings with the accused Sudarev and Ivlev, including the one at his apartment in February, 1966, discussed the question of seeking out places of concealment for 'VSKhSON' literature. Not having succeeded in preparing such places, he hid anti-Soviet literature in his room, suspending it in a sack behind the window, and in the furnace room of his place of work.[39]

Miklashevich concealed literature in the attic of his home.[40] Konstantinov kept his at his mother's apartment.[41] And Ivanov, shortly before his arrest, transferred his to the apartment of a female acquaintance.[42]

As has already been stated, the purpose of VSKhSON's fund of literature was twofold: (1) to facilitate the recruitment of new members; (2) to "re-educate" those already recruited into the organization. Some materials were reserved for members only, e.g. the VSKhSON conspiracy manual and Malaparte's *Coup D'État*. Most, however, were suitable for both candidates and members. The following are a few of the many examples provided by the sources of how this literature was used:

> In the period December, 1965-June, 1966, [Ivoilov] actively inclined his acquaintance G. B. El'kin, an economist at one of the construction firms of the city of Leningrad, toward hostile activity within 'VSKhSON'. In conversation with him, he systematically defamed the Soviet state and social system, supplied him with M. Djilas' *The New Class*, T. Meray's *Thirteen Days* ... and G. Rauch's *History of Soviet Russia*, all in photocopies, and other works. He gave him for familiarization the program and statute of 'VSKhSON' and proposed that he enter the illegal anti-Soviet organization, which he declined.[43]

> In the period 1966-1967, [Ivanov] disseminated among his acquaintances anti-Soviet literature. In particular, he acquainted A. I. Osipovich, E. P. Abramov, D. V. Frederiks and his brother M. V. Ivanov with the 'VSKhSON' program. He acquaint-

ed Osipovich, Iu. D. Margolis and V. I. Sandler
with M. Djilas' *The New Class* and Osipovich,
Abramov and Margolis with Solonevich's book
Escape from Russian Chains.[44]

In the spring of 1965, trying to determine the
political views of his comrade [at work] S. I.
Radchenko, in order later to work on him with the
aim of recruiting him into 'VSKhSON', [Ivlev]
gave him M. Djilas' *The New Class* and also other
literature to read. He ceased his hostile attempts
only when Radchenko reacted negatively to the
anti-Soviet content of the above-named book
[Djilas].[45]

Six works received such widespread use by the revolutionary organization that they could perhaps be termed
"VSKhSON classics." These books were:

1. Milovan Djilas, *The New Class*
2. Tibor Meray, *Thirteen Days That Shook the Kremlin*
3. Georg von Rauch, *A History of Soviet Russia*
4. Ivan Solonevich, *Escape from Russian Chains*[46]
5. Nikolai Berdiaev, *The New Middle Ages*
6. Nikolai Berdiaev, *The Russian Idea*

Full bibliographical information on these titles may be
found in Appendix III ("The VSKhSON Library"). What
shall interest us here is why the underground union chose
these particular works as its "classics." A brief summary of
their contents will hopefully suggest the answer.

Since its initial appearance in 1957, Milovan Djilas' *The
New Class* has attracted broad and deserved attention.
Written by the former vice-president of Communist Yugoslavia, the book demonstrates that the Bolshevik revolutionaries who seized power in 1917 laid the foundations for
the emergence of a ruling class more ruthless and oppressive

than the tsarist aristocracy. This new ruling class is the Communist political bureaucracy, which has entrenched itself in Eastern Europe as well as in the USSR. For Djilas, Communist societies are divided into "the monopolists of administration, who constitute a narrow and closed stratum" and the "mass of producers (farmers, workers and intelligentsia) who have no rights."[47] The power of this new class is "the most complete known to history."[48] Its members relish their prestige and power and would never willingly surrender them.[49] Because of the actions of this class, "Communist regimes are a form of latent civil war between the government and the people."[50] Sensing "continuing and lively opposition" on the part of the populace, the new class "aspires to reduce this opposition by naked force."[51] As an ideology Communism has largely run its course and therefore enjoys considerably reduced support among the masses it rules. "The Communist oligarchs no longer know what the masses think or feel. The regimes feel insecure in a sea of deep and dark discontent."[52]

Although Djilas is a gradualist, his book can and did have a *revolutionary* impact on Soviet youth. It is not surprising that *The New Class* was VSKhSON's single most effective means of recruitment. The regime of course has long been aware of the threat constituted by this passionately honest and skilfully-written book. In 1963 it declared dissident Vladimir Bukovskii "insane" for possessing two photocopies of the work (Bukovskii was released after spending 18 grueling months in a prison psychiatric hospital).[53]

Tibor Meray's *Thirteen Days That Shook the Kremlin* is the work of a Hungarian socialist and patriot who describes Hungary's brief interlude of freedom in 1956. What this study offered VSKhSON members and candidates was a positive vision of what *could* happen in Russia if the Communist grip on the country were loosened. The book succeeds in capturing the excitement and idealism of Hungary of 1956: "... the intellectuals who met at the university tried

to draft a platform . . . The direction of industries and factories must be given to freely-elected Workers' Councils.
A free system of agriculture must be guaranteed, and the
system of mandatory deliveries to the state must be abolished.
There must be complete freedom of press and of public as-
semblage."[54] The attempt of the Hungarians to find a middle
road between Western capitalism and Eastern Communism
must also have appealed to VSKhSON (the organization's
"program," as we shall see in Chapter XI, exhibits a quest
for such a middle path): "Among the polyphony of themes,
the insistence on the continuation of 'socialist gains' became
more and more dominant. Delegation after delegation voiced
firm opposition to any attempt to restore the old bourgeois
system. The peasants proclaimed that they would never surrender their land to the landowners; the industrial workers
insisted on keeping control of the factories."[55] Meray's book
was also bound to produce a sense of shame in a Russian
reader, ". . . at the moment when the Revolution was being
consolidated and when the desire to protect the socialist
bases of Hungarian life was increasing, Soviet troops were
spreading out across the country preparatory to strangling
the Revolution in the very name of those socialist ideas."[56]
It is undoubtedly to atone for such crimes that the VSKhSON
program pledges to assist Eastern Europe attain its liberation
from Communism.

A History of Soviet Russia, written by West German
scholar Georg von Rauch, is "a summarized survey of the
events of the years 1917-1956, described in chronological
order."[57] Its appeal to VSKhSON was probably twofold.
First, its calm, scholarly elaboration of events in a manner
free from ideological cant gives a quite damning picture of
the Soviet regime from the Revolution to 1956. Second, the
author clearly sympathizes with the Soviet populace for the
great trials it has undergone, and he refuses to accept that
the Bolshevik experience reveals any deep-seated flaw in the
Russian national character, "I am entirely opposed to the

view that Russia's evolution toward Bolshevism was in any way predetermined. I do not hold that present conditions are a natural consequence of a Russian predisposition for autocratic, despotic forms of government."[58] Von Rauch's religio-philosophical approach to Bolshevism may also have appealed to VSKhSON: "Bolshevism is really a phenomenon of the era of the masses, a gigantic two-faced affair, one a product of the rationalization and mechanization of human culture, the other an expression of the irrational forces and demonic instincts of the human soul which were thought to have been banished by idealism and humanism."[59]

Rauch's study also discusses previous oppositional forces in the Soviet Union and seeks to explain the reasons for their failure. On the Whites he writes, "They [the Whites] lost because they had no constructive program for the future, no plan reflecting the political and social aspirations of the masses. They lost because they could not come forward with any idea which, beyond the slogans of the negation of Bolshevism and Tsarist restoration, could have aroused the enthusiasm of the people."[60] General Andrei Vlasov, who directed a Russian force under the Germans during World War II, was wiser, ". . . his [Vlasov's] program of a 'single and indivisible Russia' differed considerably from the rigid centralism and the unitary concept of the Tsarist empire and the White Guard Russians of the Civil War of 1919. He made no claims to Poland and Finland and it seemed as if the independence of the Baltic nations was something that could be discussed with him. Moreover his program for an 'indivisible Russia' left room for certain autonomous federalist aspirations of the non-Russian groups."[61] There is evidence that the VSKhSON leaders arrived at similar views to those attributed to Vlasov by von Rauch.[62] In the "positive" section of their "program," so as not to repeat the error of the Whites, they endeavor to offer a constructive program for the future, reflecting the political and social aspirations of the Russian masses.

Ivan Solonevich's *Escape from Russian Chains* is a spirited anti-Bolshevik classic, written in the mid-thirties by a Belorussian lawyer and athlete devoted to the idea of "one Russia." As well as giving a gripping account of the author's flight to Finland, the book devotes considerable space to reporting the politics of the Soviet populace, especially the youth. Solonevich is particularly interested in views on alternative political systems which might replace Bolshevism. "During the years when I made up my mind to escape," he writes, "I regarded myself as a scout, who must gather all available data concerning the strength and weakness of the enemy."[63] He notes that some in Russia desire a technocracy. "Take any plant or factory," a student tells him, "and throw out the Party cell. What is left? The workman and the engineer. The Party cell's only aim in life is to bother everyone ... We shall throw them [the Communists] out, but we will not let the landlords in ..."[64] "Listen," another youth informs him, "I will tell you what the younger generation of Russia feels. We must overthrow the whole Soviet system ... What we want is land for the peasant; while the workman needs a free Trade Union ..."[65] On economic matters, Solonevich sees Russian youth inclining "toward a compromise between state and private ownership."[66]

A dedicated Russian patriot, Solonevich mourns the enthrallment of his people, "The pronounced contrast between the compassion accorded us [by the Finnish border guards] and the inhuman cruelties I had witnessed and experienced in Soviet Russia, overwhelmed my heart with humiliation."[67] And he is led to lament, "... my unfortunate, martyred country, will she ever be redeemed from the bitter degradation of hailing the supreme ability of men who are blockheads, and singing praises to the clemency of ruthless executioners?"[68] It is not difficult to see why Solonevich, with his combative, yet compassionate, love for Russia, appealed to VSKhSON.

The works of the philosopher Nikolai Berdiaev (1874-

1948) were highly valued by the revolutionary organization. Two of them—*The Russian Idea* and *The New Middle Ages*—were widely employed in recruitment work. The former represents a quest for the underlying "idea" informing Russian history. Berdiaev searches for it by examining the country's leading intellectual and spiritual currents. His conclusion:

> Russian thought and the Russian quest at the beginning of the nineteenth century and the beginning of the twentieth bear witness to the existence of a Russian Idea, which corresponds to the character and vocation of the Russian people. The Russian people belong to the religious type and are religious in their spiritual make-up. Religious unrest is characteristic even of the unbelievers among them. Russian atheism, nihilism, materialism have acquired a religious coloring ... The refined skepticism of the French is alien to the Russians; they are believers even when they profess materialist communism ... The Russian Idea is eschatological, it is oriented to the end; it is this which accounts for Russian maximalism. But in Russian thought the eschatological idea takes the form of striving after universal salvation.[69]

Berdiaev's view (greatly influenced of course by Dostoevskii) of the inherent religiosity and maximalism of the Russian is given expression in the VSKhSON "program." A number of other aspects of the "Russian Idea" discussed by him are also accepted by the "program," e.g. that Russians "in their ultimate depth have always been anti-hierarchical, almost anarchist,"[70] that "the Russian Idea is the idea of community and the brotherhood of men and peoples,"[71] that "Russia's moral values are defined by an attitude towards man, and not towards abstract principles of property or of the State,"[72] and that "the Russian people, in accordance with its eternal Idea has no love for the ordering of this earthly city and struggles towards a city that is to come, towards the new Jerusalem."[73]

The New Middle Ages, a provocative work that has surprisingly never been translated into English, was first published in Berlin in 1924. It contains Berdiaev's program for Russia's emergence from the Bolshevik yoke. In his words, "The *New Middle Ages* was written in a positive form...," i.e. is more than a critique of Bolshevism but also attempts to provide an alternative vision of the ordering of society.[74] As will be shown in Chapter XI, a number of Berdiaev's ideas expressed in *The New Middle Ages* were incorporated into the "positive" section of the VSKhSON "program."

Osipov informs us that the Djilas, Meray, Rauch and Solonevich books, plus Solonevich's *Russia in Chains*[75] and Curzio Malaparte's *Coup D'État,* used by VSKhSON as a tactical manual, were sent by the Leningrad KGB to central headquarters in Moscow for examination [*ekspertiza*]. All were judged "indisputably anti-Soviet."[76] The probable reason for the Berdiaev books' not being sent was that the Moscow KGB's attitude toward the philosopher's works, long a thorn in Soviet hides, was well-known.

A few words concerning what might be called VSKhSON's "emerging classics," i.e. those works approved for recruitment and educational work by the organization's leaders.[77] A number of these writings deal with religious and spiritual questions. Thus, for example, Nikita Struve's *Christians in Contemporary Russia* traces the history of the Russian Church under the Communists and discusses the fierce anti-religious persecution of 1959-1964. Ivan Il'in's *The Path of Spiritual Renewal,* written by a well-known émigré philosopher, contains an interesting and religiously-motivated defense of nationalism and patriotism. And G. P. Fedotov's *The Christian in a Revolution* and Semen Frank's

The Spiritual Foundations of Society, both studies by noted émigré scholars, offered VSKhSON additional food for thought.

Most of the "emerging classics" not concentrating on religio-spiritual questions represent investigations into the economic and social structure of modern society. (Some, such as Fedotov's book, deal with both religious and socio-economic problems.) Of particular significance is Wilhelm Röpke's *Civitas Humana: A Humane Order of Society.* VSKhSON's esteem of this book—the organization also approved Röpke's *A Humane Economy: The Social Framework of the Free Market*—indicates that the revolutionaries may have been moving in new directions in their quest to avoid the pitfalls of capitalism and Communism. Röpke's book will be discussed in Chapter XI.

Let us now pass on to a question that intrigued early commentators of VSKhSON. Why did this revolutionary underground union spend so much time reading and reproducing literature? Why such a heavy stress on "self-education" [*samoobrazovanie*]? The answer, I suspect, is to be found in Berdiaev's writings, particularly in *The New Middle Ages.* "Bolshevism," Berdiaev writes, "must first of all be overcome from within, spiritually, and after that politically."[78] And he continues:

> No, the problem of Bolshevism is not an external and mechanical problem which may be resolved by military might; it is first of all an inner and spiritual problem. It is impossible by exclusively military means to free Russia and the Russian people from the Bolsheviks, as though they were a band of robbers who had bound up the people ... We need faith and an idea. The salvation of the presently perishing societies will come from unions and organizations having a firm base, inspired by faith. From them will be formed a new fabric of society.[79]

Reading this, one can understand why the commanders
of VSKhSON "squads" were concerned to keep their troops
and candidates for recruitment supplied with literature sub-
jecting the Soviet system to reasoned critique and also
sketching an alternative vision of society. The quotations
which follow demonstrate this concern:

> In March, 1966, seeking possibilities to provide his
> 'squad' with anti-Soviet literature, [Ivoilov] re-
> ceived from Sado, through the accused Ustinovich,
> a film with the text of T. Meray's *Thirteen
> Days* . . . and G. Rauch's *History of Soviet Russia*
> and also 7 rubles for obtaining photo-materials. He
> delivered the film and the photo-materials he had
> purchased to [the village of] Serebrianka, where,
> together with Borodin and [candidate] El'kin, he
> printed two copies of T. Meray's book . . . and one
> copy of G. Rauch's . . .[80]

> [In November, 1966] for the use in the propaganda
> activity of his unit, [squad commander Konosov]
> received from Vagin a photocopy of Rauch's *His-
> tory of Soviet Russia,* printed in Russian in the
> USA, and in January, 1967 for the same purpose
> received from Ogurtsov a photocopy of I. Il'in's
> *The Path of Spiritual Renewal,* published in Rus-
> sian in France.[81]

> On February 1, 1967, in the vestibule of the sub-
> way station 'Peace Square' [Konosov] had a con-
> spiratorial meeting with the accused Zabak, heard
> his report concerning his anti-Soviet activity and
> gave him a photocopy of the letter of the [Moscow]
> priests N. Eshliman and G. Iakunin for use in the
> ideological preparation of candidates for member-
> ship in 'VSKhSON'.[83]

The VSKhSON squad commanders also sought to expand the holdings of literature written by members of the organization, particularly tactical literature:

> The accused Konosov, on instructions from Ogurtsov, organized in early 1966 a meeting of his 'squad' at Sado's apartment ... Speaking out at this meeting, he insisted on the drafting of a 'methodological handbook' which would contain instructions concerning the methods and ways of preparing persons already recruited into 'VSKhSON'. He also insisted on the publication of 'information bulletins' by the anti-Soviet organization ... [83]

The formation of a new and promising VSKhSON *filial* in Tomsk by Ivoilov presented the problem of how to convey the organization's literature there from Leningrad. In January, 1967 Borodin made a long train journey, on VSKhSON funds, to Tomsk to confer with Ivoilov and Veretenov (who resided for a short time in the Siberian city before taking a job in Leningrad Province):

> In January, 1967, [Veretenov] took part, with the accused Borodin and Ivoilov, in a discussion of the question of how to deliver to Tomsk the 'VSKhSON' documents necessary for the carrying out of recruitment and the reception of new participants into the anti-Soviet organization. [Veretenov] gave his consent to receive, upon his departure for Leningrad, and send to Tomsk the program and other literature of 'VSKhSON'. He agreed with Borodin on a time and place to receive them. In order to ensure the safe delivery of these materials, he planned to send them to Tomsk by post, after having agreed with his acquaintance V. M. Solodovnikova that he could

send parcels to her address [in Tomsk] from Leningrad.[84]

A major aspiration of VSKhSON was to have its own printing press. Printed materials look more impressive than typed ones and can boost the morale of a revolutionary organization. Still, the obstacles involved in obtaining and operating an illegal printing press in the Soviet Union are truly formidable. By 1965, however, Leonid Borodin had somehow managed to obtain 41.5 kilograms of printer's type, which he submitted to VSKhSON for its underground press.[85] The type was transported by Borodin, Ustinovich and Kozichev to Ustinovich's apartment for keeping; later it was given to Averichkin, the VSKhSON archivist, for concealment.[86] Next, the organization succeeded in finding a printing press in a state of disrepair which it intended to fix.[87] All that was needed further were printer's ink and paper:

In the fall of 1966, with the aim of preparing the 'VSKhSON' journal for publication, the accused Konosov, carrying out the instructions of Ogurtsov, commissioned Baranov, Nagornyi and Zabak to obtain printer's ink and convey it to Vagin. Carrying out this commission, the accused Baranov in October, 1966 acquired a packet of printing paper and a can of printer's ink. At the instructions of the same Konosov, these were transferred during a conspiratorial meeting outside the First Leningrad Medical Institute to the accused Nagornyi who, together with the accused Zabak, carried them to Vagin, who was waiting for them on Ruzovskaia Street.

In preparation for the transfer of these materials, Nagornyi twice met conspiratorially with Vagin, once at the Kazan' Cathedral and once at the Naval Museum. [Both times] he instructed Zabak to stand watch to ensure that the place of meeting was safe.[88]

For this delicate operation both Nagornyi and Zabak received the official thanks of the VSKhSON leadership.[89]

As the revolutionary union's ranks grew more plenteous and its plans more ambitious, it was decided to form an "ideological division" [*ideologicheskii otdel*] to carry out the "systematization, crystallization and intensification of recruitment work,"[90] to supervise the education of already-recruited VSKhSON members and to prepare the publication of "battle bulletins." The sub-unit was created in November, 1966: "The accused Ivanov, at Sado's suggestion, took part in November, 1966 in an illegal meeting at Ogurtsov's apartment and under the latter's [Ogurtsov's] direction. Ogurtsov declared the formation of an 'ideological division' of 'VSKhSON', which was to be headed by Vagin, who was also present at the meeting..."[91] Besides Vagin and Ivanov, Viacheslav Platonov, also in attendance, was assigned to the division. Later, in January, 1967, Sudarev was co-opted as an assistant to Ivanov.[92]

At the November meeting, Ogurtsov stressed that more order had to be introduced into the multiplication of the organization's fund of "anti-Soviet, revisionist and other religious and reactionary literature" (the KGB's words, of course, not Ogurtsov's) to ensure their efficient use in recruitment activities and in VSKhSON's projected journal and battle bulletins. By January, 1967 the division had moved into high gear. On the twelfth of that month:

> The accused Platonov and Ivanov, as representatives of the 'ideological division' of the anti-Soviet organization, met together with Vagin at a meeting conducted ... by Ogurtsov at his apartment. They agreed to carry out his demand for the activization of 'ideological work' in 'VSKhSON', i.e. the com-

pletion of preparatory work for the publication of
printed materials—the so-called 'battle bulletins' and
complete sets of anti-Soviet and other hostile literature for use in the propagandistic activity of the
sub-units of the organization.[93]

Two days later a second meeting was held:

> At the next regular meeting of the 'ideologists'
> of the illegal organization, on January 14, 1967,
> which took place under Vagin's leadership at
> Platonov's apartment, the accused Ivanov and
> Platonov occupied themselves with sorting out the
> 'VSKhSON' literature which had been brought by
> Ivanov to the meeting. They engaged in determin-
> ing the time, order and means of reproducing it
> for use in publishing the first 'battle bulletin' and
> in creating complete sets of anti-Soviet and other
> hostile literature for the propaganda work of the
> 'squads'.[94]

The activization of the "ideological division," following
as it did the acceleration of VSKhSON's military-political
plans, meant that the revolutionary union was fast becoming a threat. The comparatively harsh sentences meted out
to Platonov and Ivanov demonstrate the authorities' distaste
for the "division." From the regime's point of view,
VSKhSON was unmasked just in time.

CHAPTER V

Recruitment

RECRUITMENT REPRESENTED the life-blood of VSKhSON. Without constantly expanding numbers, the revolutionary organization would be unable to realize its military-political aims and its morale would inevitably suffer. For these reasons, the *Ustav* [Statute] of the union insisted that each VSKhSON member had to recruit at least one more.[1] Besides being necessary, however, recruitment was also exceptionally difficult. The far-flung nets of the KGB and the willingness of a number of Soviet citizens to turn informer were not to be taken lightly. The organization had to be prepared for the arrest of one of its recruiters at any moment. Moreover, recruitment took time and was frequently frustrating. Yet, despite such obstacles, VSKhSON persevered.

The efforts of squad commander Ivoilov to recruit LGU history student Andreev may be taken as typical. Having determined that Andreev was a good prospect, Ivoilov began providing him with "anti-Soviet" literature, and, in the disapproving words of the KGB, "expressing slanderous judgments defaming the Soviet state and social system." In addition, he told Andreev "of his own participation in the illegal anti-Soviet organization [VSKhSON] in the capacity of 'squad' commander and acquainted him with its structure,

69

aims, plans and methods of struggle ...'"[2] By his boldness
Ivoilov was presumably seeking to infect Andreev with revolutionary fervor and a sense of commitment. But Andreev
appears to have hesitated, perhaps suspecting Ivoilov of
being a *provocateur,* but much more likely simply weighing
the cost of involvement in VSKhSON. Seeking to win
Andreev over, Ivoilov promised him he could be a "preacher"
[*propovednik*] in the organization (Andreev seems to have
had strong religious convictions). And to assure him of
VSKhSON's real existence he put Andreev in touch with fel-
low-member Borodin. For all his efforts, Ivoilov failed to
obtain Andreev's definite consent; on the other hand, he
managed to keep his interest and avert a refusal. Once he
had moved to Tomsk, Ivoilov continued to write Andreev
employing a pseudonym.[3]

Ivoilov's putting Andreev in touch with Borodin reflect-
ed common VSKhSON practice. Besides enabling the candidate for membership to sense that an organization actually
existed, it permitted "a fresh set of eyes" to judge the candidate's *prigodnost'* or suitability for the union. One other
example: "[Borodin] personally and with the help of
[VSKhSON members] Goncharov and Veretenov studied
the political views of Maksimov with the object of determining his suitability for participation in 'VSKhSON'."[4]

In general, recruitment efforts seem to have followed
this pattern:

1. The candidate would be "studied."

2. Then he would be approached by a VSKhSON
   member who would sharply criticize the Soviet
   system in conversation.

3. Meeting with a favorable reaction, the
   VSKhSON member would then offer the candidate "anti-Soviet" literature geared to his in-

terests and psychological make-up. Thus, one
candidate might be given Djilas for a starter
and another, Berdiaev.

4. If the candidate continued to seem promising,
    the VSKhSON member would acquaint him
    with the underground union's aims and methods.
    At this stage, a candidate would sometimes be
    offered a chance to perform auxiliary services
    for the organization, such as typing and photo-
    copying various materials.

5. The candidate would be shown the VSKhSON
    "program" and offered to join the revolutionary
    body.

Some concrete examples:

In 1965-1966, intending to recruit new persons into
'VSKhSON', [Bochevarov] persistently worked on
his acquaintances S. N. Kulakov, V. P. Goncharov
and A. K. Spaile in an anti-Soviet spirit. In conversations with them he tried to convince them of
the necessity of struggle against the existing state
and social system in the USSR, told them of his
belonging to the illegal anti-Soviet organization and
offered them to take part in its criminal activities.
He also expressed slanderous judgments defaming
the Soviet state and social system.[5]

In 1965-1966, [Buzin] brought to light persons
close to his views with the intention of recruiting
them into the anti-Soviet organization. He worked
on A. N. Orlov-Chistov and V. A. Kragin in anti-
Soviet fashion, systematically expressing anti-Soviet
slanderous judgments defaming the Soviet state and

social system. Obtaining Orlov-Chistov's consent to
enter 'VSKhSON', he gave him the assignment to
bring to light and recruit other persons of similar
views into the organization.[6]

Frequently, VSKhSON members took journeys, financed
by the organization's funds, to interview prospective members living in cities other than Leningrad who had been
picked out as promising candidates by other participants in
the revolutionary union:

> In August, 1965, on instructions from the
> 'VSKhSON' leaders, [Platonov] travelled to the
> city of Krasnodar with the aim of determining the
> 'suitability' [*prigodnost'*] for acceptance into the
> anti-Soviet organziation of S. P. Alekhin, E. P.
> Alekhin and Iu. B. Arkhangel'skii, all of whom had
> previously been selected by his confederate S. S.
> Ustinovich. In a meeting there with one of them,
> S. P. Alekhin, he explained the positions of the
> 'VSKhSON' program and expressed judgments hos-
> tile to the Soviet regime.[7]

> In January, 1967, on instructions from the
> 'VSKhSON' leader Ogurtsov, [Ivanov] left for
> Moscow where he met twice, observing the rules
> of conspiracy, with A. N. Orlov-Chistov, seeking
> to determine his 'suitability' for reception into
> 'VSKhSON' and activity within that organization.[8]

> [After journeying to Tomsk in January, 1967 on
> instructions from the VSKhSON leaders], Borodin
> gave Ivoilov the necessary attributes for the recep-
> tion of new participants into 'VSKhSON' and met
> with Anufriev, a candidate for 'VSKhSON' selected

by Ivoilov. He also gave instructions to Veretenov
to study [candidate] Stateev . . .[9]

As these quotations indicate, VSKhSON leaders Ogurtsov
and Sado kept close tabs on the recruitment activities of the
membership. Even the underground union's top recruiter,
Konosov, who "personally participated in the anti-Soviet
preparation of Baranov, Nagornyi, Shuvalov, Zabak, Petrov,
Paevskii, Nikitin, Lisin and Fomchenko," regularly informed
Ogurtsov, to whom he was directly subordinate, "concerning
the progress of his activity."[10] When members of the organization moved from Leningrad to other locations, they were
encouraged to form new cells in these places. Thus Kozichev
was asked to recruit in the Pamir region and Goncharov, in
Irkutsk.[11]

The question arises as to whether VSKhSON tried to
recruit any particular categories of people, and the answer
is clearly yes. First, because many of the organization's members were current or former students, it is not surprising
that many of its candidates came from an academic milieu:
"In the period 1964-1966, [Ustinovich] worked in an anti-
Soviet spirit on and inclined to enter 'VSKhSON' the Leningrad State University students D. G. Balaian, V. R. Kalinin,
A. Zhamakochan, V. T. Mostiev, Iu. I. Virolainen and R. V.
Raginian . . ."[12]

Another category actively recruited were former political
"deviants":

Bringing to light persons of similar views, with the
aim of later recruiting them into 'VSKhSON', the
accused Ivoilov in the fall of 1966 made contact
through his acquaintances with a group of persons
who had formerly been expelled from Tomsk State
University for anti-social, politically harmful actions. He made the acquaintance of a member of
this group, Iu. E. Anufriev, told him of the ex-

istence of the illegal anti-Soviet organization 'VSKhSON' and acquainted him with the basic positions of its program.[13]

A final category VSKhSON seems to have recruited were those with outspoken Christian convictions: "In 1966, with the aim of furthering recruitment into 'VSKhSON', [Ivoilov] proposed to [VSKhSON member] Ivlev that he make the acquaintance of LGU student S. A. Grib, about whose enthusiasm for the ideas of Christianity he had learned from the newspapers. However, Ivlev, fearing discovery, did not consent."[14]

As this last quotation would suggest, VSKhSON's recruitment activities were, at least at times, remarkably unsophisticated. Drawing attention to the revolutionary organization's recruitment of Stanislav Konstantinov, whom he defended at the trial of the VSKhSON rank-and-file, Attorney Yuri Luryi questions whether the union's "intelligence" unit was doing its job:

My second client, Stanislav Konstantinov, found himself in VSKhSON under several curious circumstances. Not a bad fellow, he had the weakness of concocting various fantasies, especially those which would render him mysterious in the eyes of his interlocutor. In the year before his arrest, Stanislav had worked on an excursion ship sailing from Leningrad to Valaam Island and served as a guide and librarian. Somehow he learned that at the home of certain of his acquaintances there had been preserved an old, broken rusty 'Mauser' which had belonged to their grandfather. He literally begged them to sell him this revolver and, once having obtained it, felt himself an extraordinarily romantic figure. In conversation with one of his friends (VSKhSON member Ustinovich) he invented the tale of the existence, in one of the districts of Leningrad province, of a secret, well-armed political organization, whose leader he was. But Konstantinov did not know of VSKhSON's existence or that Ustinovich was one of the organization's members. Ustinovich told Mikhail Sado about Konstantinov. There followed a banal, humorous story. Sado made Konstantinov's acquaintance and, failing to see through him, began insistently to offer him a union of his 'organization' with VSKhSON and a sharing of their weapons. Konstantinov could not bring himself to admit that his entire 'organization' had been the product of his own imagination. Not knowing how to extract himself from his predicament, he began to invent further. Finally, under pressure from Sado and Ustinovich, he formally entered VSKhSON, then 'shared' arms with it by giving Sado his 'Mauser'. After this, until the time of his arrest, he did not show his head to anyone and expended masses of energy in order not to meet a member of VSKhSON on the street or in another place. However, although he succeeded in hiding from Sado, he did not manage to conceal himself from the KGB.[15]

What happened to a VSKhSON candidate once he consented to enter the clandestine organization? From the sources, we know that VSKhSON had a solemn ritual of reception requiring the following materials: (1) a written oath [*prisiaga*] form to be signed; (2) a questionnaire [*anketa*] to be filled out; (3) order planks [*ordenskie planki*] and (4) a Bible.[16] The new recruit was received by at least two VSKhSON members, one of whom was the person who had obtained his consent to enter the organization. A representative case: "Having received [Veretenov's] consent, Ivoilov, together with Borodin, accepted him into

'VSKhSON' on March 12, 1966 in the office of the principal of the Serebriansk High School. The documents which
he filled out were given by Ivoilov to the 'head' of the organization, Ogurtsov.'"[17] Vladimir Osipov has criticized
VSKhSON for keeping such documents.[18] However, while it
is true that they certainly proved to be of help to the KGB
when it discovered the organization's archive, it is likewise
probably true that they provided a psychological lift for the
new VSKhSON member, made him feel he was entering a
serious, well-organized body. In general, the revolutionary
union's concern with ritual and solemnity should not be dismissed as adolescent self-romanticization or posing. The drab
uniformity and enervating dullness of Soviet life can make
ceremony and solemnity almost visceral necessities. Moreover, VSKhSON rituals enabled the organization's members
to establish important spiritual ties with the ethos of pre-
Bolshevik Russia.

During the solemn rite of entrance, the VSKhSON initiate exclaimed "I swear!" [*Klianus'*] to the aims of the union,
while Psalm 91 was being read. The "sentence" passed by
the Soviet court against the organization's rank-and-file
states that during the reception new members "took an
oath and swore '... not sparing their strength, property and
their very lives to dedicate themselves to a struggle with
the Soviet regime for the establishment of a bourgeois regime.' "[19] While the concluding prepositional phrase is certainly an interpolation—what Soviet young men would dedicate their "very lives" to establishing a "bourgeois regime"?—
the remainder of the language in the citation may well have
stood in the text of the oath. In addition to swearing to dedicate themselves to the overthrow of the regime, new members also selected a conspiratorial name. Thus Platonov
became "Andrei Timofeevich Belozerskii," Bochevarov,
"Nikolai Ivanovich Burmak" and Zabak, "Sergei Konstan-
tinovich Poleshchuk."[20] It is possible that some of the names
selected were intended to have symbolic associations:

Ustinovich chose Arkhangel'skii (from *archangel*), Ivanov, Nadezhdin (from *hope*) and Sudarev, V'iugin (from *blizzard*).[21] According to the VSKhSON Statute, new members were supposed to tithe, i.e. give 10% of their earnings as dues to the organization. Some members seem to have approached giving this amount, e.g. Platonov, Ustinovich and Bochevarov.[22] In any case, all new recruits knew they were assuming substantial financial obligations when they entered VSKhSON. As the "sentence" against the rank-and-file demonstrates, considerable dues were paid in during the three years of the organization's existence:

[Konosov] paid around 25 rubles of his own money as dues and, after collecting dues from other persons, gave Ogurtsov around 150 rubles.[23]

[Platonov], carrying out the requirements of the Statute, paid 70 rubles in dues and also collected dues from Klochkov.[24]

[Buzin] paid dues amounting to 87 rubles.[25]

[Zabak] paid 3 rubles in dues every month.[26]

To consent to enter VSKhSON was thus a serious decision. Yet in the three years of the organization's existence twenty-eight individuals made this choice and a number of candidates were preparing to make it. Perhaps it was the very seriousness of the step which appealed to prospective members. In S's words, "The accepted system of mutual relations between [VSKhSON] participants, the strict, solemn symbolism, devoid of any hysterical pathos, the ritual of acceptance into the organization, the method of work with candidates, the clear-cut hierarchy—all served the organization's goal of being a religious order."[27] To serve and perhaps save Russia—this was the goal for which twenty-eight young men were willing to dedicate their "strength, property and very lives."

CHAPTER VI

Toward a Coup D'État

THE LAST YEARS OF Khrushchev's reign, during which VSKhSON was conceived and founded, were a period of considerable tumult. Although there can be little doubt that the revolutionary union's leaders overestimated the mood of crisis in the country,[1] the situation was in fact more critical than is generally realized in the West. When on June 1, 1962 *Pravda* announced that the retail price of meat was to be increased thirty percent and that of butter twenty-five— a staggering price rise coinciding with a state-sponsored "economy drive" which had already reduced the take-home pay of the workers by approximately ten percent—widespread rebellion broke out among Soviet workers.[2] Novocherkassk, a city of 100,000, erupted in over a week of riots costing hundreds of lives. Sit-down strikes, mass demonstrations in factories and street protests flared up in Groznyi, Krasnodar, Donetsk, Iaroslavl', Zhdanov, Gor'kii, Moscow and elsewhere. Similarly, the disastrous harvest of 1963 led to a panic-buying of food resulting in serious shortages. A massive sit-down strike occurred in Krivoi Rog, and similar strikes broke out in Leningrad, Omsk, several cities in the Urals and elsewhere. According to officially published Soviet polls, there was extremely widespread dissatisfaction among

79

workers with their conditions of employment and living conditions. With this information in mind, one is better able to understand Mikhail Sado's description of the Khrushchev period in his address to the court:

> The cult of Stalin was already beginning to be replaced by the cult of Khrushchev. And conditions in the country were growing steadily worse.

> Servitude, adventurism, mismanagement, injustice cried out from every corner.

> Industrial production had bogged down. The overexpenditure of raw materials was a common occurrence. Embezzlement and bribery reached colossal proportions. Fish were dying out in the rivers and wildlife in the forest. There was complete chaos in agriculture . . .

> Dissatisfaction was growing. The price of meat and dairy products went up; wheat began to be imported from abroad. And this by Russia! There ensued adventures of various kinds with a monetary reform and government loans.

> A tense atmosphere was created in the country leading to mass protests against the Soviet regime in Novocherkassk, Karaganda, Tblisi, Krasnodar and other places.

> I was sure that we were on the threshold of an internal catastrophe which would explode at any moment and throw the country into internal chaos.[3]

When Ogurtsov, Sado, Vagin and Averichkin founded the All-Russian Social-Christian Union for the Liberation of the People in February, 1964, they were convinced that it was only a matter of time until the regime's policies brought the country to total ruin. VSKhSON was brought into existence not only to overthrow the Communists but also to rescue Russia.

Bernard Karavatskii has given us a helpful glimpse of the early theoretical deliberations of the VSKhSON leaders. "Before beginning to create the organization," he writes:

> Ogurtsov, Vagin, Sado and their friends discussed for many months and years the purely moral question of whether, in general, they had the right to rise up with weapons in their hands, i.e. whether they had the right to kill...Igor' Viacheslavovich Ogurtsov, the founder of the organization, did not permit anyone during the entire period of VSKhSON's existence to commit deeds incompatible with the ethics of Christianity. 'The end does *not* justify the means, and, once a man has soiled himself, he grows accustomed to dirt', was Ogurtsov's reaction to various projects for obtaining money, so necessary for the existence of any organization. He was deeply convinced that the power of the organization he had created lay precisely in its moral purity. The experience of history [Ogurtsov felt] has shown that all organizations and parties which have set out on a hybrid political-criminal path by employing amoral means have degenerated in their very incipiency into bands grasping for power at any price.[4]

Originally VSKhSON planned to wait approximately fifteen years (i.e. until around 1980) before making a bid for power. "The numbers of the organization were to reach approximately 10,000 at the moment action was to be taken. Fifteen years were given to all its [VSKhSON's] participants to prepare for the final goal or meet death [in battle]."[5]

According to Karavatskii, the revolutionary union rejected as completely "unrealistic" the idea that "the Communists will themselves come to democracy." It therefore had only two tactical alternatives before it: "a revolution, which would bring catastrophic results with it, and a *coup d'état,* which has been carried out more than once in various countries with divers success."[6] VSKhSON, Karavatskii continues

> selected the second path as the one promising the fewer casualties and the better results. The *coup d'état* was, to the extent possible, to take place simultaneously in both Russia and the adjacent countries. It was assumed that it would be enough to arrest the chief members of the government in order to paralyze the entire apparatus of oppression, which was deprived of initiative and had become accustomed exclusively to carrying out orders from above.[7]

The coup was to be carried out by "a group of high-ranking officers of the Soviet army dissatisfied with the existing system of state administration."[8] Once having taken power, however, this "junta" would relinquish control of all but the army, permitting economics to be in the hands of economists, science in the hands of scientists, etc., while "questions of ideology would be left to each individual citizen."[9]

For the newly-formed underground union the period February, 1964-November, 1965 was one of building. VSKhSON engaged in slow, methodical preparation for the task ahead: the eventual toppling of the regime. These years also witnessed the removal of Khrushchev from office and the accession to power of the Brezhnev-Kosygin "collective leadership." As the first winds of what came to be known as "creeping re-Stalinization" began to blow,

VSKhSON must have been reinforced in its conviction that no true amelioration was possible within the system and that Khrushchev's limited "reforms" had been merely tactical and ephemeral. On the other hand, the collective leadership's gradual tightening of totalitarian controls, with the attendant intimidation of the populace and reactivization of a vast web of informers, rendered VSKhSON's goal of eventually recruiting an underground army of 10,000 increasingly utopian.

During the period 1964-1965, we see VSKhSON concentrating on recruitment and the locating, translation and reproduction of literature. It should be remembered that none of the members could afford to be "full-time" revolutionaries; all were either students preparing for exams or working men called upon to put in a full day's work at construction bureau, research institute or university. Moreover, many were married men with family responsibilities. I do not wish, however, to give the impression that VSKhSON "dabbled" in revolution during this period. The leadership and the most committed of the rank-and-file seem to have devoted every free minute to their "anti-Soviet" designs.

By December, 1965, the organization's ranks had swelled to eighteen. At this point it was decided to form "battle squads" [*boevye gruppy*], the first step in a progression—squad, section, platoon, batallion, corps—which was eventually to provide the forces for a *coup d'état*.[10] Two squads were constituted at this time. One was headed by LGU economics senior Vladimir Ivoilov ("commander") and consisted of LGU philological student Sudarev ("ideologist and counter-intelligence specialist"), chemical engineer Ivlev and Kozichev (profession unknown).[11]

The second was commanded by gas fitter and correspondence student Mikhail Konosov and included engineers Miklashevich ("counter-intelligence") and Buzin, both employed at the Central Scientific Institute of Fuel Apparatuses.[12] The squad commanders were subordinated to Ogurtsov and the counter-intelligence representatives to Sado. At approximately the same time, a special counter-intelligence unit seems to have been formed, under Sado's supervision, consisting of high school principal Borodin, former LGU Eastern Faculty student Bochevarov and Goncharov (profession unknown).[13] Borodin was apparently the deputy commander of this unit.[14] VSKhSON's security unit soon went into action, and at the end of 1965 we find Borodin, "with the aim of detecting any shadowing," noting down and then giving to Ivoilov the license numbers of 25 automobiles standing outside the central office of the Leningrad KGB.[15] Borodin, it will be remembered, had previously spent some time at a school for Soviet militia.

Immediately upon their formation, the squads adopted conspiratorial methods. Ivoilov, for example:

> carried out meetings with the participants of his 'squad' in previously specified locations at a designated time ... In conversations with participants at his apartment he turned on his taperecorder to avert any possible eavesdropping. He also noted down and communicated to his confederates the license numbers of automobiles which, he supposed, were watching him, etc.[16]

The formation of squads was an important step. It must have made military goals seem more attainable. Not surprisingly, the question of the obtaining and concealment of arms began to assume increasing importance for the organization. The radicalizing process begun by the formation of the squads was, however, soon accelerated by an event which almost destroyed VSKhSON: the betrayal of Aleksandr Gidoni. What happened is recorded by the "summation of the investigation":

> In February-March, 1966, the accused Ivoilov, hav-

ing learned of the arrival in Leningrad for the defense of his dissertation of his acquaintance A. G. Gidoni, whose former conviction for anti-Soviet activity was known to him, informed him of the existence of the illegal anti-Soviet organization 'VSKhSON', of his participation in it and acquainted him with its aims, tasks ... plans and means of achieving them. Together with the accused Borodin, Ivoilov attempted to persuade him to enter the organization, to offer financial assistance and to seek out suitable persons for recruitment into the organization. With these aims, Ivoilov gave Gidoni M. Djilas' *The New Class,* T. Meray's *Thirteen Days ...,* N. Berdiaev's *The Russian Idea* and *New Middle Ages* in photocopies and other works to read. Suspecting Gidoni of having informed the security organs that he was a participant in an anti-Soviet organization, he ceased further work with him."[17]

According to Osipov, VSKhSON should have known better than to attempt the recruitment of Gidoni: "Incidentally, concerning traitors: the name of the informer Gidoni was widely known in the Mordovian political [concentration] camps. Gidoni was freed and began to make a career. We all knew him. But the boys from the Leningrad 'organization' VSKhSON did not. Fate brought Gidoni together with them, and the betrayer who had been unmasked in the camps knew how once again to betray people. I remember how contritely Leonid Borodin and Vladimir Ivoilov shook their heads when told this."[18]

Had Gidoni tendered his informer's statement [*donos*] during Stalinist times, the secret police would probably not have bothered to check its varacity. Ivoilov, Borodin and the others named by Gidoni would automatically have been fed into the "*Gulag* Archipelago," along with many of their friends and relatives. But in early 1966 the effects of Khrushchev's flirtation with "socialist legality" were still to be felt, and the KGB pressed Gidoni for *material evidence* of an anti-Soviet organization which he was unable to provide.[19] Still, although the KGB evidently suspected Gidoni of prevarication, it put no obstacles in the way of his defending his dissertation and taking up a teaching post at Petrozavodsk University.[20]

Fortunately for VSKhSON, it learned almost immediately that the KGB had been tipped off:

In the end of March, 1966, being informed by [a friend, V. E.] Konkin that his criminal activity as a member of 'VSKhSON' had fallen into the field of vision of the security organs, the accused Ivoilov immediately wrote the 'VSKhSON' leadership a report, delivered by the accused Sudarev, in which he communicated the information received from Konkin and expressed fear concerning his possible unmasking as a participant in the organization. With the aim of assisting the 'VSKhSON' leaders to determine the accuracy of this information, he then organized at his apartment a meeting of Sado and Konkin. He received instructions from Ogurtsov and Sado temporarily, until Konkin's information could be checked out, to cease the recruitment of new members, to conceal his anti-Soviet literature in a better place and to inform the 'VSKhSON' leaders regularly of new developments through Sudarev, who, during March-June, 1966, served as the link between the 'VSKhSON' leaders and the squad 'commander'. Ivoilov personally delivered some of the information he continued to receive from Konkin. He also asked that the anti-Soviet recruitment of 'VSKhSON' candidate El'kin be con-

tinued by means of attaching a new participant to
him . . ."[21]

VSKhSON now knew that it had nurtured a viper. But
who was it? At first, suspicions centered on candidate
Veretenov, who later became a member of the organization.

> Having learned from V. E. Konkin that Leningrad
> inhabitant L. Ia. Karpov, who was being tried by
> a social court for unworthy behavior, had in con-
> versation with him named one of the students who
> came up to him after the trial as a person connected
> with the KGB organs and suspecting him to be
> Veretenov, who was due to be received into
> 'VSKhSON', [Ivoilov] in February-March, 1966,
> checked this material: he received from Goncharov
> a photograph of Veretenov, prepared by him and
> Borodin for this purpose, and showed it to Karpov
> who failed to recognize Veretenov.[22]

Once Veretenov had been eliminated as a suspect, attention focused upon Gidoni, and we find Ivoilov asking the
VSKhSON leaders to check "whether or not his acquaintance
Gidoni was connected with the KGB."[23] At the same time, a
series of precautions were taken to avert discovery and arrest [*proval*]. "In April, 1966, [Sudarev], with the aim of
concealing the real circumstances behind his acquaintance
with Ivoilov, which actually was formed in Sado's apartment
in connection with his participation in 'VSKhSON', worked
out, in case of a possible summons from the security organs,
an 'alibi' [*legenda*] according to which he was to state that
their relations had begun after an accidental encounter in
the library of Leningrad State University prompted by their
mutual attraction to the ideas of Christianity."[24] Ivoilov and
Borodin were supposed to explain their meetings by a mutual interest in the concept "God-man."[25] During June-July,

1966, VSKhSON members Sudarev, Ivoilov, Borodin, Ustinovich and Veretenov were summoned to the KGB for "prophylactic" chats.[26] Sudarev and, one assumes, the others as well employed their prepared "alibis."[27] All of them "hid their own and their confederates' participation in VSKhSON."[28] Warned of the "intolerability and punishability of anti-Soviet propaganda and hostile organizational work," all promised "never to engage in it." However, the KGB report concludes, "in the future, until their arrest, they did not cease their anti-Soviet activity."[29]

Believers in the omnipotence and omniscience of the KGB will feel certain that, after Gidoni's report, the security organs knew all and were merely biding their time till the following February (when the arrests occurred) with the aim of catching a maximum number of revolutionaries in their nets. Personally I reject such an interpretation, for which there is not a shred of evidence in the sources. The quantity of students and intellectuals summoned to the KGB for "prophylactic" chats must be considerable. An incautious word or the perusal of an "anti-Soviet," "revisionist" or "tendentious" book can be sufficient grounds for such an invitation. The aim of such conversations is simply to discourage further interest or enthusiasm for forbidden subjects. No doubt some surveillance was employed by the KGB on Ivoilov, Borodin *et al.*, but it apparently failed to turn anything up. The secret police did not take Gidoni's information seriously, and the "alibis" and security precautions of the VSKhSON membership seem to have been enough to dampen any suspicions which might have been entertained. In short, the Social-Christians survived this first serious threat to their existence.

Gidoni's betrayal was only one of many problems confronting VSKhSON. Due to the slow growth of the organization and an understandable fear factor, a number of rank-and-file wanted to leave the organization but refrained from doing so since they feared the "contempt" of the others.[30]

One member for several months in 1965, the Tatar Il'ias Fakhrutdinov, an instructor at LGU, actually did leave it. And here is an example of wavering:

> In 1966, [Ivoilov] personally and through other participants tried to influence Kozichev, who was trying to avoid participation in the criminal activity of 'VSKhSON'. He attempted to convince him to continue in the anti-Soviet organization and enlisted the help of the accused Sudarev to exert influence on him. Sudarev was introduced to Kozichev as a 'VSKhSON' 'inspector'. With the same aim, Ivoilov organized a meeting of Kozichev with the accused Ivlev ... who, in February of the same year of 1966, reported to the leaders of 'VSKhSON' on Kozichev's conduct.[31]

Sudarev himself had experienced some indecision in the fall of 1965 but was convinced to remain in the revolutionary organization by Ivlev, acting on instructions from Sado.[32] Osipov reports that both Miklashevich and Buzin had their moments of doubt.[33] Those seriously seeking to disengage themselves from VSKhSON usually had the possibility of taking employment in a distant area. Thus Kozichev moved to the Pamir region near China and Goncharov, to Irkutsk.

If lack of enthusiasm could be a problem, so could misdirected zeal. As mentioned earlier, Borodin of the counter-inelligence unit had to be summoned on one occasion to a "court of honor" [*sud chesti*] for his voluntarism:

> In June, 1966, [Ivoilov] took part in a discussion of the conduct of Borodin organized by Ogurtsov and Sado. Borodin was charged with making unwarranted contacts with several persons, with holding up the return of anti-Soviet literature and with appearing at inopportune times when summoned

by the leadership of 'VSKhSON'. Ivoilov supported the position of the leaders of the organization
and condemned the actions of Borodin.[34]

There is evidence that VSKhSON member Vladimir
Goncharov was tried at the same time as Borodin.[35]
Goncharov, however, eventually ceased activity in the organization, while Borodin seems to have "repented" and once
again gained the favor of the leaders. As we have seen,
VSKhSON also had difficulties with Bochevarov, who "alone
of all the members disagreed with the organization and tried
to transfer it to the rails of loyalty [to the government] but
met with refusal from Ogurtsov and Sado and, faced with a
lack of legal possibilities, stayed in its ranks."[36]

Somewhat unsettling for VSKhSON must have been the
news of the arrest in mid-1965 of an underground group
of young Leningrad neo-Marxists, headed by Valerii Ronkin
and Sergei Khakhaev. Although considerably smaller (nine
persons were arrested) and far less revolutionary than
VSKhSON, the "Union of Communards," as they were
called, succeeded in publishing several issues of a clandestine *samizdat* journal entitled *Kolokol* [*The Bell*], which
continued the numeration of Aleksandr Herzen's famous
19th century publication of the same name.[37] In the fall of
1965, VSKhSON member Ivlev, on instructions from Sado,
tried to find out "the reasons for the discovery [*proval*] of
the anti-Soviet group of Ronkin-Khakhaev" but failed to
learn anything "concrete."[38] Then Goncharov of the counter-
intelligence unit tried his hand: "In the period of the end
of 1965-beginning of 1966, [Ivoilov] commissioned Goncharov to write for the leaders of 'VSKhSON' a survey of
the unmasking of the anti-Soviet group of Ronkin, which he
did, presenting an article . . . with a tendentious account of
the trial in the case."[39] The article pleased the leaders and
was designated for inclusion in the projected VSKhSON
journal.[40]

To return to the repercussions of Gidoni's attempted betrayal, it seems to have served to speed up the revolutionary union's already accelerating military plans. As early as October, 1965, Konosov had received from Sado the *Nastavlenie No. I VSKhSON,* a conspiracy manual, and set about acquiring military literature "to provide for the military preparation of his confederates."[41] At the end of 1965, as we have seen, two "battle squads" were formed, headed by Konosov and Ivoilov. In the beginning of 1966, we find Bochevarov, on instructions from Sado, trying to get from S. N. Kulakov, the son of a Leningrad vice-admiral (whom we mentioned in Chapter III), "the names, addresses and telephone numbers of the generals, admirals and other representatives of the Leningrad high command, for the purpose of using this information to arrest this category of people during the perpetration by 'VSKhSON' of an armed uprising."[42] This information seems to suggest that by early 1966 VSKhSON may have been reconsidering its original plan of striking only in 1979-1980. The Brezhnev-Kosygin regime's ominous tightening of controls and the great difficulties involved in recruiting large numbers of new members would undoubtedly have been important factors behind such a reconsideration.

Faced with the prospect of failure generated by Gidoni's betrayal, VSKhSON seems to have moved into a quasi-apocalyptic frame of mind. In April, 1966, we find squad leader Konosov informing his subordinates Baranov, Miklashevich and Buzin "of the danger of the unmasking of their underground activity and the necessity, in connection with this, to be prepared to go illegal . . ."[43] He also warned them "to observe strictly the rules of conspiracy."[44] In the same month of April, Konosov was elevated by Ogurtsov to the rank of "commander of a section [*otdelenie*]" and "organizer of a platoon [*vzvod*]" and instructed to bring the number of his unit up to 18.[45]

The following month, May, 1966, a meeting was

held at Platonov's apartment during which Sado designated Bochevarov commander of a new squad to consist
of Platonov, Klochkov and Konstantinov.[46] Thus VSKhSON
now possessed three squads, although one, Ivoilov's, had
temporarily ceased recruiting. Bochevarov's new squad members were told "to seek out possibilities for acquiring firearms for the organization and to find safe places to conceal them."[47] During the spring and summer of 1966, plans
moved ahead in this crucial area of acquiring, concealing
and transporting weapons. Miklashevich gave his consent to
Konosov's suggestion that he offer, if necessary, a company
car from his place of work "for the transportation of arms."[48]
And he tried to get a job at an auto-plant in order to have
permanent access to "auto-transport."[49] Buzin agreed to
Konosov's proposal that he use his father-in-law's garage for
the storage of arms and expressed a willingness, if necessary,
to offer a company car for the transport of weapons.[50]
During the same period, Nagornyi, learning from Konosov
of the planned acquisition of firearms for their unit, proposed that hiding-places be prepared for them in the Peterhof
district.[51]

At approximaetly the same time, squad leader Ivoilov,
aiming at an "armed action" leading to the "overthrow of
the socialist system," demanded of his unit that places for
the concealment of weapons be located, that military literature be acquired and studied, that the squad's level of military preparedness be raised and that its members all learn
to drive.[52] VSKhSON obtained its first potential firearm
when Konstantinov was pressured by Ustinovich into sur-
rendering a defective pistol, which he had "illegally" acquired in 1964, and nine bullets to the organization. For this
he received the special thanks of VSKhSON head Ogurtsov.[53]

Obtaining weapons in a tightly-controlled totalitarian
state is, understandably, no easy task. The following is an
example of one way in which VSKhSON planned to pursue
this end: "In one of his meetings with Vagin in 1966,

[Borodin] agreed to move to the city of Tula in order to establish ties with the local gunsmiths, with the aim of acquiring arms for the anti-Soviet organization 'VSKhSON'."[54]

By late 1966, the revolutionary union's plans had proceeded further. The formation of an "ideological division" under Vagin (discussed in Chapter IV) had increased the organization's efficiency of operation. A printing press was being readied for action. And a definite decision seems to have been reached to carry out some kind of military-political activities in Leningrad, apparently on the occasion of the 50th anniversary of the Soviet regime in October, 1967.[55] The Konosov "section" and proto-platoon, consisting of Nagornyi (deputy commander), Miklashevich, Buzin, Baranov, Zabak, Petrov and Shuvalov,[56] seems to have been intended to play a major role:

> In December, 1966, the accused Konosov, on his own initiative, instructed Nagornyi to study, along with Zabak, the deployment and system of defense of the building of the Executive Committee of the Leningrad Municipal Soviet of Workers' Deputies, which had been designated by the 'VSKhSON' leadership as one of the projected objects of armed seizure. Carrying out this order, the accused Nagornyi inspected the building from the outside.[57]

At the end of 1966, Konosov and Ogurtsov "played war games on the theme: 'a platoon on the attack in the conditions of a large city'."[58] During this period, Konosov was assisted by his deputy commander (and cousin)[59] Valerii Nagornyi, who seems largely to have directed the activities of Zabak, Petrov and Shuvalov.[60] At the end of 1966 and beginning of 1967, we find him organizing conspiratorial meetings for Konosov with these individuals at his apartment, Petrov's and the "Peace Square" metro station.[61]

What kind of military action was VSKhSON contem-

plating in Leningrad for October, 1967? Nothing less, it
seems, than a coup. As early as the summer of 1966, Konosov
had discussed with Nagornyi "the tactics of *coup d'état*
[*taktika gosudarstvennogo perevorota*], declaring that it
could be successfully carried out in the conditions of the
city of Leningrad."[62] A relatively small number of men, it
was felt, would be sufficient to effect such a coup because,
as Curzio Malaparte writes in his *Coup D'État: The Technique of Revolution,* one of VSKhSON's tactical "handbooks," "Not the masses make a revolution, but a mere
handful of men prepared for any emergency, well-drilled
in the tactics of insurrection, trained to strike hard and
quickly at the vital organs of the state's technical services."[63]
But once Leningrad had been taken, then what? Since the
sources do not provide an answer to this tantalizing question, one is required to speculate. Perhaps VSKhSON expected the fall of Leningrad to a Russian nationalist revolutionary organization enjoying popular support to serve as
a catalyst for a general overthrow of the regime. Here the
Hungarian Revolution of 1956, which, according to the
VSKhSON "Program," represented "the prelude for the
liberation of all peoples enslaved by Communism," could have
been taken as a model. Because of the lack of support for
the Hungarian Communist regime among the populace, the
revolution of 1956 (prior to the Soviet invasion) was remarkably bloodless. Only a "small number of agents of the
secret police turned out to be defenders of the Party oligarchy." (VSKhSON "Program") Perhaps the VSKhSON leaders felt that a similar situation would obtain in Soviet
Russia.

A second possible explanation is that the VSKhSON
members who were to seize Leningrad were intended to
sacrifice themselves for the future of Russia. Although they
would be killed, the memory of their feat would serve as a
seed from which might spring a free Russia. A major strand
of Russian Christianity has traditionally stressed that the

highest realization of the self is in voluntary self-sacrifice
for the sake of one's brethren. One thinks of Russia's first
canonized saints, the "passion-bearers" Boris and Gleb (d.
1015),[64] of Dostoevskii's numerous pronouncements on the
subject[65] and of Solzhenitsyn's words to Patriarch Pimen of
the Moscow Patriarchate, "He who is deprived of all material
strength always achieves victory in *sacrifice*."[66] According to
Evgenii Vagin, Ogurtsov told him after their arrest and trial
that he knew VSKhSON would fail. The members of the
organization, Ogurtsov felt, were to be a "spark" [*iskra*]
and "example" [*primer*]. He also used the words "sacrifice" [*zhertva*] and "flash" [*vspyshka*]. Vagin thinks that
Ogurtsov misled his followers in this respect, since many of
them thought they were going to win.[67] My suspicion, however, is that Ogurtsov "hoped against hope" that VSKhSON
would win but was prepared, unlike the majority of the membership, for the worst.

But this is all speculation. For the moment, until some
new sources reach the West, we remain ignorant of
VSKhSON's precise expectations for its projected coup in
October, 1967.

Let us now take a look at VSKhSON as it was on the
eve of its arrest in February, 1967. Squad leader Ivoilov
and fellow economist Veretenov had, upon their graduation
from LGU in 1966, been sent by the state to Tomsk to serve
as instructors in a polytechnical institute. Since both had
been summoned to the KGB for "prophylactic chats" in
June-July, 1966, they may not have regretted the transfer to
Siberia. In Tomsk they would have a freer hand and could
set up a VSKhSON branch, which is what they set about
doing. Ivoilov's Leningrad-based squad seems to have been
disbanded. In January, 1967, we find the squad's "ideologist
and counter-intelligence specialist," Sudarev, being transferred to the "ideological division" to serve as an assistant
to Nikolai Ivanov. According to Osipov, the squad headed
by Bochevarov was also disbanded, perhaps due to

Bochevarov's policy disagreements with the VSKhSON leadership.[68] Of the six members of the Ivoilov and Bochevarov squads (i.e. Sudarev, Ivlev, Kozichev, Platonov, Klochkov and Konstantinov), two, Platonov and Sudarev, were attached to the VSKhSON ideological division, and three—Kozichev, Klochkov and Konstantinov—seem to have tried to drop out of the organization.[69] Ivlev remained active, but in what capacity we do not know. To sum up, by February, 1967, the active VSKhSON units included Konosov's section (and proto-platoon), the ideological division and a counter-intelligence unit (consisting of Borodin and others—perhaps Ustinovich and Ivlev). A promising *filial* was developing in Tomsk—two candidates were being prepared for entrance into the organization—and the VSKhSON printing press was being readied for action. And plans for a military coup in Leningrad in October, 1967 were in the early stages.

The reader who has been consulting the footnotes will have remarked that in our chronicling of the revolutionary union's military-political activities we have relied heavily on the "summation of the investigation" [*zakliuchenie sledstviia*] and, to a lesser extent, on the "sentence" [*prigovor*] passed by the Soviet court against the VSKhSON rank-and-file. Is such reliance justified in the light of the regime's well-known tendency to be somewhat cavalier with historical fact? In this case, I believe, it is. First, it should be noted that the impression these documents give that VSKhSON was poised to move out of the planning stage finds implicit confirmation in certain of the non-regime sources, such as S. and Petrov-Agatov.[70] Second, the information they provide on VSKhSON's recruitment activities, plans for a printing press, acquisition of literature, etc. is shown to be trustworthy by the other, non-regime sources.

The fact that VSKhSON was arrested before having obtained weapons has led some commentators to argue that it should not be taken seriously as a military-political organization. Thus Attorney Yuri Luryi, relying for the most part on information received from his client Georgii Bochevarov, tends to downplay VSKhSON's significance as a revolutionary body: "Not one leaflet, not one demonstration, no foreign connections—nothing! ... In this so-called '*military-political* organization' there were no arms. The only exception was an old *broken* revolver."[71] As Luryi sees it, the KGB was interested in inflating the significance of VSKhSON, "They had to create the impression that a large, active, military (or at least militarized) organization had been created. Not sparing their lives—so the version would go—the heroic *chekisty* [secret police] had caught this powerful organization and thereby saved the socialist state. And now, naturally, they could count on large rewards, medals and elevation in rank."[72]

For all our respect for Luryi's skill in fathoming the KGB mind, we find ourselves unable to agree with him on this point. As shall be shown in Chapter VII, the authorities eventually decided to hold a fairly "low-key" trial of the VSKhSON membership. Seven of the union's rank-and-file and all thirty of its candidates for membership were spared sentences. Moreover, the text of the "sentence" against the 17 passes over in silence a number of the more sensational passages in the "summation of the investigation" concerning VSKhSON's projected seizure of government buildings or its plans to arrest military brass. And not a single word about heroic *chekisty* saving the USSR ever appeared in the Soviet press. One therefore concludes that, rather than attempting to inflate the significance of VSKhSON, the regime tried to *downplay* it. This was because the authorities eventually realized how dangerous the organization's *ideas* actually were.

Another commentator who has attempted to make light of VSKhSON's military-political significance is Vladimir Osipov. In his "The Berdiaev Circle in Leningrad" he writes that, "all practical acts of the Leningraders [VSKhSON] were limited to the reading and reproduction of books" and that any military activities contemplated were projected "twenty years ahead."[73] Osipov repeats this assertion in other of his writings. One example: "All of VSKhSON's activity was limited, strictly speaking, to the reading and discussion of books. But there was unfortunately also a formal (and fantastic!) side to the matter: a statute and program. The white-heat of intellectual conversations over a cup of coffee destroyed these most honest fellows."[74]

Since Osipov claims to have read the materials of the investigation and trial of VSKhSON,[75] he must either disbelieve what they say about the underground union's military plans and preparations (but why then does he keep silent about the matter?) or he must wish for some reason of his own to mislead *samizdat* and Western readers. I suspect the latter to be the case. The reason behind Osipov's desire to "disinform" his readership is almost certainly his strong and sincere conviction that "a popular revolution is in general undesirable" in Russia because "the moral condition of the people is now significantly *lower* than during the period of the civil war troubles."[76] Revolution, Osipov feels, would be a cataclysmic disaster for the demoralized Russian populace and cannot even theoretically be considered as a solution to the nation's predicament. If Osipov actually thinks VSKhSON intended a revolution, then he is of course wrong. The Social-Christians, as we have seen, specifically rejected such a course in favor of a maximally bloodless *coup d'état*. It is probable, however, that his strictures also refer to a coup. Whatever the case, our strong suspicion is that Osipov, out of humanitarian motives, has chosen to distort the true nature of VSKhSON's military plans and intentions.

A few words in closing about the psychology of the VSKhSON membership. As Osipov has pointed out, a definite plus for the organization was its internal "discipline" and sense of order.[77] The strong religious convictions of the VSKhSON leadership and many of the most active rank-and-file added an extra dimension to this discipline, render-

ing the revolutionary body what S. has called a "religious
order."[78] Moreover, as the same commentator points out, the
organization witnessed a "gradual Christianization" of its
membership as "many members of the union, who had at
one time only experienced a sympathy for the ethical side
of Christian teaching later accepted it [Christianity] in all
its fullness and value . . ."[79] Despite this gradual Christianization, however, they "did not lose those qualities necessary
for participants in an illegal military organization."[80] This
was because:

> The organization itself was to become an initial
> cell, a certain prototype of the future [non-Com-
> munist] society. Its internal spiritual constitution
> was to be determined by Christian principles, while
> at the same time it preserved its military-political
> character, as required by its main goal [the over-
> throw of the regime]. In sum, it was a plan for the
> creation of a militant religious order, capable not
> only of heading the anti-Communist movement in
> Russia but also of offering her [Russia] another
> form of existence.[81]

S's interpretation is endorsed by Osipov:

> The Social-Christian union was not simply a polit-
> ical organization. It was also a kind of brotherhood,
> of *zemliachestvo* [an association of fellow-country-
> men]. Christians and patriots united together as if
> to preserve the warmth of ideas from the gloom
> and cold of the indifferent. 'Only in the organiza-
> tion did I feel myself a human being!' exclaimed
> Viacheslav Platonov at the trial. Imagine the ego-
> ism, calculation, venality and cowardice which are
> all about, and yet, in spite of this, [there apppears

on the scene] a union of the unmercenary, men of
ideas and conscience.[82]

Although it seems difficult to believe, the VSKhSON
membership appears to have suffered from an overconfidence
which led to conspiratorial sloppiness: "Despite the existence
of comparatively literate instructions and handbooks on practical conspiracy, its [conspiracy's] most elementary requirements were not observed either by the rank-and-file or by
the leaders of the organization as well, and not so much
because of carelessness or irresponsibility, as due to under-
estimation of the opponent."[83] VSKhSON paid dearly for
this overconfidence when the KGB moved in during
February, 1967.

CHAPTER VII

Arrest and Trial

VLADIMIR OSIPOV'S "The Berdiaev Circle in Leningrad" offers us a detailed account of the way in which the KGB succeeded in breaking VSKhSON. The court "sentence" against the rank-and-file provides us with the dates of arrest of the members of the revolutionary organization and generally tends to corroborate Osipov's version, while demonstrating that, as usual, he has allowed minor factual errors to creep into his reportage.[1]

The downfall [*proval*] occurred in the "section" of Mikhail Konosov, the one, it will be remembered, which was to have greeted the 50th anniversary of the Soviet regime in unusual fashion. On February 4, 1967, Vladimir Fedorovich Petrov, a member of the unit since November, 1966, chose to submit a written desposition to Major General Shumilov of the Leningrad KGB in which he apprised the general "of the existence of VSKhSON, of his membership in the organization and named those whom he knew."[2]

We do not know overly much about Petrov, except that he seems to have worked as a technician at the Leningrad Institute of Exact Mechanics and Optics, where Nagornyi, Shuvalov and Zabak were likewise employed. It is also known that he was engaged to be married and that his fiancée re-

101

jected him when she learned he had betrayed his friends.[3] The
"summation of the investigation" shows that Petrov was an
active member for the three months he was in the organization. Meetings were held at his apartment,[4] he participated
in the photographic reproduction of "anti-Soviet" materials,[5]
he contributed five rubles a month in dues,[6] etc.

The sources provide us with some useful snippets of information concerning Petrov's motivations for betrayal. S.,
for example, devotes a lengthy passage to him (and we beg
the reader's indulgence for the "Teutonic" phraseology):

> The immediate cause for the downfall of the Social-
> Christian union was precisely its recruitment policy
> of viewing a politically negative attitude [toward
> the regime] as being a *sufficient* level of self-con-
> sciousness for a person to be permitted to partic-
> ipate in an illegal struggle, with, of course, con-
> tinuing individual work to assist each person to
> assimilate and master the organization's positive
> idea. That is to say, while being prepared for en-
> trance [into VSKhSON], a candidate was *de facto*
> brought into the structure of the organization and
> then often of necessity required to 'stretch himself
> up' to to the necessary level. The idea behind this
> practice was that a negative awareness's only ten-
> dency is to assimilate the opposite [i.e. of Com-
> munism] and that it can in no way return to the
> point of departure [Communism]. However, as ex-
> perience has shown, a negative feeling can totally
> represent what is actually only a variation of the
> negated idea [Communism], due to a sense of the
> incompatibility between what exists and should
> exist. What was suppressed during the period of
> disillusionment can reappear only during a prac-
> tical confrontation with new ideas. Such was, in

particular, the history of the betrayal which resulted
in the destruction of the Social-Christian union.[7]

In other words, Petrov, once a convinced Communist,
was so disgusted with the discrepancy between Communism's
seemingly elevated goals and its actual practices that he
was willing to join an underground union dedicated to
the overthrow of the regime. Once, however, confronted
with VSKhSON's "positive" message, i.e. Social-Christianity,
his dormant instincts revived and he decided to pen his
denunciation to Major-General Shumilov. Thus, according to
S., it was revived conviction rather than simple cowardice
which led Petrov to betray the organization.[8]

Osipov appears to support such an interpretation when he
writes, "Only Petrov was an ardent atheist. During his entrance [into VSKhSON] he exclaimed, 'What the devil do
I need your God for!' "[9] While one suspects that this incident may be apocryphal, its statement that Petrov was a
vehement atheist could well be true. If so, it backs up what
S. tells us.

Petrov's denunciation was written on February 4th. In it
he named those VSKhSON members with whom he was acquainted: Konosov, Nagornyi, Shuvalov and Zabak. Osipov
writes that the following day Zabak was seized on the street,
and—luckily for the KGB—he just happened to have a copy
of the VSKhSON "program" in his pocket. This provided
the security organs with the "material evidence" they needed
to arrest the remaining persons named by Petrov.[10] There followed a kind of domino effect:

On February 6-7, Konosov, Shuvalov and Nagornyi
were also arrested. Konosov, that 'wandering min-
strel of the White [Army] movement', at his first
interrogation denied the fact of the existence of
the organization and of his participation in it. On
the next day, February 8th, he was shown the testi-

mony of Nagornyi, who with 'open heart' told all. Pressed to the wall by his cousin's testimony, by the program found on Zabak and also by the promises of investigator Kapustin to apply compulsory medical [i.e. psychiatric] treatment to him, Konosov admitted his participation in the organization, the fact of its existence and named his immediate commander — Ogurtsov. Konosov communicated Ogurtsov's address and also named Sado and Vagin and gave their addresses.[11]

The *"Prigovor"* [Sentence] states that Zabak, Konosov and Nagornyi were arrested on February 7th and Shuvalov (the fourth name communicated to the KGB by Petrov) on the 8th. Hence, while Osipov's dates appear to be a bit off, he has probably provided a correct sequence of events. Assuming his account is basically accurate, it would seem that Nagornyi was the only one of the four arrestees to crack completely during the initial interrogation. Since Nagornyi had been one of VSKhSON's most active members, twice decorated by the VSKhSON leaders for his zeal and appointed to the responsible post of deputy-commander of Konosov's unit, it appears odd that he collapsed so easily. Perhaps his youthful age (23) and his wife and small child were factors. But Nagornyi did not know the names of the VSKhSON leaders; they had to be extracted from Konosov, and extracted they were under threat of torture.

According to the "Sentence," Baranov, a member of Konosov's unit, was picked up on the 10th. The next arrests did not occur until the 15th, when the VSKhSON leaders were seized. Apparently the KGB had Ogurtsov, Sado and Vagin under intensive observation until that date. Very unhelpful for the leaders was the fact that Konosov's wife Liudmila, in Osipov's words, "forgot" to call her friends the Vagins and tell them of her husband's arrest.[12] Eventually, however, the VSKhSON membership realized that disaster was imminent. Ogurtsov took the organization's literature and hurried off to visit Boris Averichkin, the VSKhSON archivist. Since only Ogurtsov knew Averichkin's identity and had confidence in his own ability to stand up to the KGB, he probably felt that at least VSKhSON's documents would survive the approaching storm. Unfortunately, he failed to notice the KGB "tail" behind him and unwittingly led the security organs to a rich find—the VSKhSON archive.[13]

Other members of the organization were engaged in similar frenetic activity:

> In the middle of February, 1967, having received a warning from Sado of the danger of an unmasking [of VSKhSON], the accused Ivanov passed this on to his confederates Vagin and Shestakov and hid the 'VSKhSON' literature which had been at his apartment at the home of his female acquaintance V. S. Baliakina, whence it was seized [by the KGB].[14]

From this text we learn that the VSKhSON leaders discovered that they were in danger only around the middle of February, i.e. almost a week after the initial arrests. Madame Konosov's failure to inform the Vagins was therefore crucial, and Osipov understandably terms her role "vile" [*gnusnaia*].[15]

On February 15th, the four leaders of VSKhSON were arrested, as was Miklashevich of Konosov's unit. Once under arrest, Boris Averichkin, the organization's archivist, immediately decided to cooperate with the authorities (presumably out of fear) and decoded the list of VSKhSON participants he was keeping; he also communicated their addresses, places of work, etc.[16] Having gained access, apparently without much effort, to VSKhSON's archive, the KGB now had a complete list of the organization's members and more than adequate biographical information on them.

Osipov states that the rest of the VSKhSON rank-and-file were seized on the 17th.[17] According to the "Sentence," such was not the case, although a goodly haul was indeed brought in on that day (Platonov, Ivanov, Ustinovich, Bochevarov and Sudarev). The following day Borodin and Ivlev were taken into custody. The KGB seems now to have been in a hurry, probably to keep the alerted VSKhSON membership from dropping out of sight.

Out in distant Tomsk, Ivoilov learned of the opening of criminal proceedings against his associates and "took measures to conceal their and his own criminal activity."[18] On February 22nd, the Tomsk KGB arrived uninvited at the door and conducted an initial search. They, however, failed to find the copies of the VSKhSON oath, questionnaire and emblems which Ivoilov had concealed in some undoubtedly ingenious hiding place. After his guests had departed, Ivoilov destroyed the oath and questionnaire forms but decided to keep the emblems. On February 23rd, he was summoned to the Tomsk KGB where he gave evidence in accord with the "alibis" previously worked out by his squad. On March 9th, however, Ivoilov was arrested, and a month later, on April 4th, the KGB returned to his apartment, one assumes with crowbars and other instruments, and succeeded in turning up the VSKhSON emblems.[19]

Nine days previously, on March 1st, Stanislav Konstantinov, a librarian dwelling on Valaam Island near Finland, had been seized. That left only two of the VSKhSON membership—Buzin and Veretenov—at liberty. From the "summation of the investigation" we know that Veretenov showed up on February 19th at the apartment of Borodin's relatives to receive some VSKhSON materials for the Tomsk *filial*. There he seems to have learned of Borodin's arrest the day before.[20] Did he then go into hiding? Perhaps together with Buzin? Or were they purposely allowed to go free so they might be shadowed by the KGB? The sources do not tell us, but it is interesting that both were arrested 3½ months later on the same day: June 2, 1967.[21]

Strange as it may seem, the "Sentence" informs us that four VSKhSON members were released several days after their arrest. Bochevarov and Sudarev, who had been arrested on the 17th, were released on the 20th. Ivlev, arrested on the 18th, was released on the 21st, and Konstantinov, seized on March 1st, was set free on the 4th.[22] They were held and then let go under Article 122 of the Code of Criminal Procedure ("Detention of Persons Suspected of Committing a Crime") which reads in part:

> An agency of inquiry shall be obliged to draw up a record of any instance of detaining a person suspected of committing a crime, with indication of the grounds and reasons for detention, and shall be obliged to give notice thereof to a procurator within twenty-four hours. The procurator shall be obliged, within forty-eight hours from the moment of receiving notification of a detention, to sanction confinement under guard or to free the person detained.[23]

Hence the procurator decided to release Bochevarov, Sudarev, Ivlev and Konstantinov. There certainly were "grounds and reasons" for their detention; yet they were let go. Why? Bochevarov's defense attorney, Yuri Luryi, thinks that his client and the others were released for "operational ends," i.e. so that the KGB could keep them under surveillance and observe them establishing ties with persons unfamiliar to the security forces. Personally, I find this theory quite convincing.

Upon being arrested, the majority of the VSKhSON members behaved in far from exemplary fashion. As Osipov writes:

> Various VSKhSON members, finding themselves in prison, behaved in cowardly fashion. Personally to

repent and to tell about oneself while not involv-
ing others, that, in the final analysis, is an individual affair. But thoroughly to dwell on the 'crimes'
of one's comrades—then why take an oath? Of
course the behavior of several VSKhSON members
during the investigation was no worse than that of
the Decembrists or Petrashevtsy. Just leaf through
the testimonies of the Trubetskois and Ryleevs
[both Decembrists]. A nightmare! It would seem
that in both cases people took too heavy a burden
on their shoulders. The burden turned out to be
above their strength, and there flowed forth 'open-
hearted' testimonies. I myself remember the fear I
experienced in the Lubianka [Prison] in October,
1961. A sharp, unexpected (arrest is always 'unexpected') 180 degree turn of fate, the thought of the
approaching seven years of horror and perhaps
even worse ... Imagine what the VSKhSON-tsy,
dispersed in their separate cells, must have felt,
those honest fellows practically being accused of a
military coup! One cannot take a truck onto one's
back. There are no iron men, and there should not
be any iron organizations.[24]

Petrov-Agatov confirms that a number of Social-Christians "somewhat compromised themselves during the investigation."[25] And the "summation of the investigation" tells
us that both Bochevarov and Borodin admitted themselves
guilty as charged and "assisted the exposure of the criminal
activity of the leaders and other participants of the anti-
Soviet organization."[26] No doubt many of the other members
acted similarly. As has been previously mentioned, Evgenii
Vagin feels that Ogurtsov is partly responsible for the un-
edifying behavior of the VSKhSON rank-and-file, since he
imbued them with the idea that they could *win* and did not
prepare them sufficiently for the much more likely defeat.[27]

How did the VSKhSON leaders behave under interrogation? Averichkin, the archivist, apparently did not distinguish himself. Vagin, director of the "ideological division," denied the existence of VSKhSON and his participation in it for several days after his arrest, but "becoming acquainted with the abundance of depositions of the remaining [VSKhSON] participants against their leaders," he decided to confess.[28] Afterwards, he, like Averichkin, seems to have cooperated with the investigators.

The two major *personae* of the organization somewhat redeemed its honor. Mikhail Sado underwent "sixty grueling interrogations."[29] For a fortnight after his arrest he "denied the existence of the organization and his participation in it."

When shown the testimonies of the others against him, he denied their authenticity. Concerning the VSKhSON program, a copy of which had been seized at his home, Sado declared that he had drawn it up himself with the intention of publishing it in the future, and he continued to deny the existence of the organization. But, in the beginning of March [1967], blockaded by evidence, he too was forced to confess.[30]

But it was Ogurtsov's behavior which gave the regime pause. Like Vagin, he denied the existence of VSKhSON and his participation in it for several days but then, realizing that this was foolish in light of the voluminous evidence against him, admitted both. But he confronted his interrogators with a firmness of conviction and resolution which seem to have changed their attitude toward the revolutionary union. Previously, the initial head of the investigation is supposed to have predicted, "Ogurtsov will get five years..."[31] Probably the authorities figured that a trial of the leaders and perhaps several of the more active rank-and-file would serve as sufficient warning to preclude the emergence of similar organizations in the future. Despite its dangerous intentions, VSKhSON had had no ties with foreign intelligence, was not a minority nationalist movement and possessed only one non-functioning Mauser as arms.[32] Ogurtsov's depositions, however, forced the investigators radically to reassess their opinion of the revolutionary organization. As Osipov puts it:

> As distinguished from the majority of the VSKhSON-tsy, Igor' Viacheslavovich Ogurtsov exhibited unparalleled courage and steadfastness. I do not know a man equal to him in personal qualities. But, extremely unfortunately, Ogurtsov in his depositions during the investigation presented the affair as far more serious than had been contemplated by any of its participants ... After Ogurtsov's depositions, the behavior of the *chekisty* [secret police] changed sharply. The director of the investigation division, Syshchikov, hurriedly informed Moscow of the seriousness of the organization which had been uncovered. Moscow replaced Kapustin [the first investigator] with Investigator of Especially Important Affairs Movchan.[33]

By claiming that Ogurtsov presented VSKhSON's aims as "far more serious" than had been contemplated by the organization, Osipov is continuing his work of "disinformation." What Ogurtsov seems to have done was simply to tell the truth about what he had actually planned.[34] In so doing, he was of course knowingly condemning himself to a severe prison sentence and possible execution. As he later told Evgenii Vagin, it was his belief that only a sincere program and sincere revolutionaries would attract the Russian people. He had to be a model of steadfastness for others.[35]

Petrov-Agatov, who was able to familiarize himself with the materials of Ogurtsov's case, has written with deep respect of the VSKhSON "head's" behavior under investigation: "To this prisoner [Ogurtsov] both Assistant Attorney General Terekhov and a representative of the Central Committee came to pay their respects. They tried to convince him to renounce his opinions. Meeting with refusal, they threatened him with execution. But he did not flinch. To the great honor of Russia he did not flinch and took the white nights of Petersburg with him to the dungeons of Vladimir."[36] Not every political prisoner receives a visit from the Assistant Attorney General. The regime clearly wanted to break Ogurtsov and thereby crush the spirit of his organization and of any admirers he might have outside it. But Terekhov and the Central Committee member failed dismally. In Petrov-Agatov's words, Ogurtsov "behaved blamelessly at the investigation and trial and showed himself a model of courage and steadfastness."[37]

Once the regime became convinced that it was dealing with an organization constituting—in the person of its leader and in its ideas—a genuine threat, it decided to stage a larger trial than had originally been contemplated. This decision was apparently taken in July, 1967, for we find Bochevarov, Sudarev, Ivlev and Konstantinov, who had earlier been released after questioning, being re-arrested on the 12th of that month. At about this same time, some thirty candidates for membership in VSKhSON were arrested for "failure to inform" [*nedonositel'stvo*].[38] According to Osipov, they were to have been tried together with the rank-and-file, i.e. a trial of almost *sixty persons* was contemplated. The KGB then busied itself with conducting an exhaustive investigation of VSKhSON. S. informs us that the materials of the investigation, which have now been locked up "in inaccessible safes, for eternity," amounted to "more than 100 volumes."[39] "One hundred volumes!" he exclaims, "One more tragic page in Russia's history."[40] And Osipov tells us that several LGU professors—Chagin, Kon, Tiul'panov and "someone else"—were assigned to examine the VSKhSON "program." Their conclusion: "No textual borrowings from Western sources were discovered in the program."[41] All of the VSKhSON literature, both that written by its members and the books and articles used by it, was carefully scrutinized and classified by the Leningrad KGB. As we have already seen, six books (the Djilas, Rauch, Meray, Malaparte and two Solonevich works) were sent to Moscow where they were adjudged "indisputably anti-Soviet."[42] By late November, 1967, the regime was ready to try the four leaders of the revolutionary organization.

There is evidence that Viacheslav Platonov, the most active of the rank-and-file, was at first to have been tried together with Ogurtsov, Sado, Vagin and Averichkin.[43] This plan, however, was discarded, and the four leaders were tried *in camera* in a trial lasting about ten days, which concluded on December 3rd or 4th. The accused were charged under Article 64 of the Criminal Code, the relevant portion of which reads:

> *Article 64. Treason.* Treason, that is, an act intentionally committed by a citizen of the USSR to the detriment of the state independence, the territorial inviolability, or the military might of the USSR: going over to the side of the enemy, espionage, transmission of a state or military secret to a foreign state, flight abroad or refusal to return from abroad to the USSR, rendering aid to a foreign state in carrying out hostile activity against the USSR, or a conspiracy for the purpose of seizing power, shall be punished by deprivation of freedom for a term of ten to fifteen years with confiscation of property with or without additional exile for a term of two to five years, or by death with confiscation of property.[44]

Specialists in Soviet law feel it was an error to try the

four leaders under Article 64. To be sure, there was "a con-spiracy for the purpose of seizing power," the one seemingly relevant passage in the article. But *in deeds* virtually nothing was accomplished toward this end. Hence the leaders were being tried for their intentions rather than their deeds. Fur-thermore, the *in camera* proceedings were a violation of Soviet legality.

Former Leningrad defense attorney Yuri Luryi has this to say about the prosecutor and judge at the trial: "The state prosecutor was Sergei Efimovich Solov'ev, the procu-rator of Leningrad. In the presiding chair [i.e. as judge] sat Solov'ev's former assistant, Nikolai Aleksandrovich Ermakov. Formerly, Sergei Solov'ev had been chairman of the court and Nikolai Ermakov had been a member of this court and secretary of the Party bureau, i.e. the 'right hand' of his chief. Upon moving up from his judgeship to a higher post—that of procurator of Leningrad,—Solov'ev recommend-ed his former Party assistant for his old position. This tandem conducted the trial of Ogurtsov, Sado, Vagin and Averichkin with complete unanimity. The court's sentence corresponded exactly to the wishes of the procurator."[45] Of the lawyers representing the accused, only the name of Ogurtsov's attorney, Semen Aleksandrovich Kheifets, is men-tioned by the sources.[46]

At the trial Ogurtsov, while admitting himself "guilty" of several points in the charge, flatly refused to recognize himself culpable of *izmena rodine* [betrayal of the home-land], the principal accusation against him. And he actively defended the VSKhSON program.[47] Concerning Ogurtsov's final address to the court, Luryi writes, "From the accounts of others and from a reading of the protocol of the court session, there remain in my memory very strong impressions of Ogurtsov's last statement to the court. It was filled with courage, dignity, depth of judgment, and some day it *will* be read by all. He ridiculed the prosecutor and all his shabby 'logic'. He reminded his audience that Lenin had once been

kept in one of the cells next to his during a trial. Comparing
the 'extent of actions committed,' he recalled the sentence
that a *tsarist* prosecutor had demanded for Lenin and compared it to what his *Soviet* colleague was seeking in accusing Igor'. He also compared the time, situation and stability
of the two regimes.''[48]

Mikhail Sado also refused to admit himself a "traitor"
but, unlike Ogurtsov, maintained that the organization had
been on the road to dispersement and had *de facto* ceased to
exist at the time of arrest.[49] He also seems to have denied
that VSKhSON had any concrete military intentions.[50] Vagin
and Averichkin "admitted themselves guilty of treason and
expressed repentance."[51] Like Sado, Vagin denied that the
organization had entertained any military plans.[52] Interest-
ingly, the four leaders' defense attorneys seem to have exerted themselves to such a degree that they were suspected
by the KGB of having a "favorable attitude toward the
prisoners."[53]

In early December the court passed sentence. Ogurtsov
was given the *maximum* sentence possible under Article 64
(with the exception of execution): fifteen years imprisonment to be followed by five years in exile. Moreover, it was
stipulated that the first seven years of the sentence should
be spent in Vladimir Prison. Sado was given thirteen years
imprisonment, with the initial three years to be spent in
Vladimir Prison. Vagin and Averichkin were sentenced to
eight years in the camps, receiving "a punishment less than
the lowest limit provided by law."[54] One reason for the comparatively light sentences received by Vagin and Averichkin
was later revealed by Prosecutor Katukova, who asserted
that "only Ogurtsov and perhaps Sado" were dangerous to
the regime, while the others "only fell under their influence."[55]

Although the trial of the leaders was held in strictest
secrecy, news of it did leak out and create a ripple of interest among Soviet intellectuals. The French paper *Le Monde*

published a somewhat garbled account of the trial as early as December 7, 1967. It reported that the trial had been "interrupted." Actually the regime was simply preparing for the trial of the rank-and-file, which occurred 3½ months later.

The first decision which had to be made by the authorities was whether or not to try the thirty VSKhSON "candidates." Probably because it feared the publicity a trial of almost sixty persons would generate, the regime decided in January, 1968, not to try the candidates. Undoubtedly the candidates did receive some form of punishment, such as loss of a job or being demoted at work. (A recent émigré to the West informed me of a case in which an individual who merely accepted an "anti-Soviet" book from a VSKhSON member was sacked from his job.) Of the rank-and-file, it was decided not to try seven: Fakhrutdinov, Goncharov, Iovaisha, Klochkov, Kozichev, Shestakov and Petrov. The last-named, of course, thoroughly earned his reprieve by his informer's report to Major-General Shumilov. The others seem to have been either rather inactive members (Klochkov, Iovaisha) or formerly active ones who succeeded in leaving the organization (Fakhrutdinov) or at least tried to (Goncharov, Kozichev). Shestakov, as has already been pointed out, had been in the revolutionary union only slightly over a month when it was broken by the KGB. Another important factor: none of the seven seems to have recruited another member into VSKhSON.

The trial of the seventeen took place from March 14-April 5, 1968. The defendants were charged under Articles 70 and 72 of the Criminal Code. Article 70 treats "Anti-Soviet Agitation and Propaganda."[56] Article 72 deserves to be quoted in full:

Article 72. Organizational Activity Directed to Commission of Especially Dangerous Crimes Against the State and Also Participation in Anti-Soviet

Organizations. Organizational activity directed to the preparation or commission of especially dangerous crimes against the state, or to the creation of an organization which has as its purpose the commission of such crimes, or participation in an anti-Soviet organization, shall be punished in accordance with Articles 64-71 of the present Code.[57]

It is obvious that Article 72, rather than Article 64, under which the four VSKhSON leaders were incorrectly tried, covers the organization's activities, which were merely *"directed* to the preparation or commission" of the overthrow of the regime. For Ogurtsov to have been given the maximum sentence foreseen under Article 64 was indeed a mockery of Soviet legality.[58]

VSKhSON member Stanislav Konstantinov, the owner of the Mauser, was also charged under Article 218-1, "Stealing of a Firearm, Ammunition or Explosives," which carries a maximum sentence of seven years imprisonment. Actually, as we have seen, he merely purchased an unregistered pistol from another person. If anyone stole the pistol, it was that person, Citizen G. P. Bal'dysh.[59]

At the trial fourteen lawyers represented the accused.[60] Both the judge (N. S. Isakova) and prosecutor (I. V. Katukova) were women. Yuri Luryi has this to say about Isakova:

> The judge's chair was occupied by the first deputy of the chairman of the Leningrad Municipal Court, Nina Sidorovna Isakova. A highly-qualified jurist, Isakova represents a vivid example of a successful Soviet judicial employee. This unmarried, childless woman possesses a clear mind and firm will. Expediency, embodied in instructions *from above,* is more important and sacred to her than any legal principle. But at the present time one must know

how, while performing lawlessness, to impart a law-like form to it, so that outwardly all should appear decorous. O, this is a great art, and Miss Nina Isakova possesses it better than many of her colleagues. Thus, while observing all outward forms, she condemned an *adolescent* to death. The sixteen-year-old Neiland was executed, notwithstanding the fact that in the Soviet Union 'persons who have not reached 18 years of age before committing a crime cannot be given a death sentence'. (Article 22 of the Foundations of Criminal Jurisprudence of the Union of SSR and Union Republics.)[61]

And this about Katukova:

The state prosecutor's bench was occupied at this trial by the senior assistant procurator of Leningrad for the supervision of KGB investigation, Inessa Vasil'evna Katukova. Katukova is a very beautiful woman, and this would especially strike one and seem inappropriate when, garbed in a procurator's dress coat, she would call upon the court to pass harsh sentences. Always knowing the case material to perfection, Inessa Katukova was the indispensable assistant of her chief, Procurator Sergei Solov'ev, whenever he would personally support the accusation in a political case. Three years later, during a trial known to the whole world which received the name 'the case of the Leningrad hijackers', my client Eduard Kuznetsov would tell me, 'Solov'ev is a blockhead, but Katukova is a bright girl! See how she nudges him in the side whenever he rambles too much?' Soon this pretty 'bright girl' would stand together with Solov'ev and demand the death sentence for Eduard Kuznetsov and Mark Dymshchits. But here, at the trial of the

17, the articles of the Criminal Code provide a punishment of not more than seven years for the defendants, and toward the end of the trial Inessa Katukova will, with unruffled calm, demand for all 17 Russian patriots deprivation of liberty amounting to a total of 60 years.[62]

The trial of the seventeen witnessed the following infringements of Soviet legality: (1) certain of the defendants were held too long pending trial; (2) passes were required to attend the supposedly "open" proceedings, which were held in a half-empty courtroom; (3) the majority of the witnesses were ordered removed from the hall immediately after giving their testimonies.[63] Two Soviet lawyers, Iurii Handler and Nikolai Danilov, tried unsuccessfully to attend the trial. They then wrote a letter of protest to Attorney General Rudenko, dated April 4, 1968. Their letter reads in part:

> Since March 14, 1968, a trial of 17 Soviet citizens, who were arrested in February, 1967 and charged under articles 70 and 72 of the Criminal Code of the RSFSR, has been in process in the Leningrad Municipal Court. To date, the press, radio and television have offered no information concerning either the reasons for their arrest or the proceedings of the trial. This case was not posted in the Leningrad Municipal Court on the list of cases to be heard and examined and continues unposted to the present time, although the trial has already been in progress for three weeks. Only persons with special passes and the nearest kin of the accused, who are on a list, are permitted into the courtroom. Despite the fact that there are always a number of free chairs in the hall, entrance to the trial re-

mains closed for those not possessing special passes
or being close relatives of the accused.

Such a situation seems to us to be an infringement
of one of the basic principles of Soviet legal procedure—the principle of publicity [*glasnost'*], which
is absolutely necessary in any political trial. It is
noteworthy that in the neighboring courtrooms [of
the Leningrad Municipal Court], in which criminal
cases are being heard, publicity is fully observed.

We are not here concerned with the guilt or innocence of the accused, since we are deprived of
even the possibility of forming an opinion about
this, but with the absence or limitation of publicity
and of access to courtroom sessions which have
characterized all the political trials of recent years
in Leningrad (the case of Ronkin and others in
1965, the case of Ogurtsov and others in 1967,
the present trial). Taking into consideration our
country's past, one cannot but experience deep anx-
iety at this.[64]

For their unseemly concern with questions of Soviet legality, attorneys Handler and Danilov were arrested in August, 1968, together with several of their friends. At a trial
in December, 1968, Handler was sentenced to three years in
a concentration camp. One of the charges against him was
that he had "attempted to penetrate" the trial of the
VSKhSON rank-and-file (which was supposedly open!).
Danilov was spared a trial, since he was declared "insane"
and incarcerated in a prison mental hospital.[65] After his release from the camps, Handler was permitted to emigrate
and is now living in the United States.

To return to the trial, Yuri Luryi gives us this first-hand
description:

Presently in Hall 48, on the second floor of building 16 on the shore of the Fontanka, where the
Leningrad Municipal Court is located, the participants in the trial are taking their seats before the
beginning of the court session. The prosecutor is,
together with the judge and assessors, seated at an
elevation. The defense attorneys, two steps lower
down, are seated at their little tables in any order
they wish. The accused are seated as the KGB
special guard wishes. Besides the usual armed soldiers from an escort regiment (a specially trained
regiment of the Internal Forces), trained 'specialists'
from a KGB prison are present, and it is they who
carry out the seating of the accused. Only they can
decide how each accused is to be seated on the
benches, who should sit next to whom and who
should be kept at a distance from whom. Without
their permission and supervision, you cannot walk
up to your client during a break and have a talk
with him. Each day at the beginning of the session
they collect from the accused copies of the summation of the charge against them and, having checked
to make sure that nothing has been placed in them,
for example a letter, they give these copies to us,
the attorneys. At the end of the day the same process is carried out in reverse. Incidentally, in this
regard the lawyers are in no way different from
their clients: it was also forbidden for us to take
our notes out of the court in order to work with
them at home in a relaxed and familiar atmosphere.
Every day at the end of a session we had to surrender our dossier to the 'special department'; the
next morning we would receive it back during session. One should say that such a system strongly
hinders the defense attorneys, but no-one paid any
attention to our timid objections.

By the way, while the Ogurtsov trial bore the stamp 'secret' and was heard in closed session, the case of the 17 VSKhSON members was formally heard in an open courtroom. I did not say 'formally' by accident. In reality even we, the defense attorneys, entered the hall by showing special passes consisting of pieces of pink cardboard with certain incomprehensible marks on them. If such a piece of cardboard should fall into the hands of a foreign correspondent, he would be unable to guess what it was. And even if he were told, it would be impossible to prove. There is not on this piece of cardboard a single letter stating that before you is a pass to the Leningrad closed church of 'open justice'. The relatives of the accused and a select public entered the hall with the same passes. I specially interested myself in learning how they give out these passes. It turns out that the KGB gives these cardboards to district committees of the CPSU in limited quantities, and they then distribute them among various enterprises and institutions via their Party leaders, who are specially instructed whom they can give such a pass to, and whom not. But the greater part of the public entered the courtroom not by these pink passes but by special red booklets. These individuals were notable for their well-cut suits, bearing and heightened attention to all the rest present. They performed the role of a claque, and, depending on the circumstances, either expressed popular indignation or emitted sarcastic chuckles at the expense of one of the accused or his lawyer.[66]

At the trial, one of the VSKhSON leaders was conspicuously absent as a witness. Osipov writes:

The unrepentant leader, Ogurtsov, was not called as a witness in order to avert his exerting a 'harmful' influence on the others. Sado defended the accused and continued to maintain that the organization was approaching disintegration [at the time of arrest] and demanded that all the accused be freed, since they had already served time under investigation. At Sado's appearance in the courtroom, all 17 got up to greet one of their leaders. Before the summoning of witness Vagin, Judge Isakova asked irritably, 'Well, are you going to stand up again?' Nevertheless, many got out of their seats to greet Vagin as well.[67]

Yuri Luryi gives this account of Sado's entrance into the courtroom:

I was sitting with my back to the accused and watching how Mikhail Sado was being brought in under guard for interrogation as a witness. Suddenly I heard an incomprehensible sound behind me. I looked back and turned to stone: all seventeen men had stood up to greet their leader and friend. Both those who had repented and those who had not; those who had admitted their guilt and those who had not; those who feared punishment and those prepared for it—all of them, paying no attention to the court, the guard or the KGB supervisors, by standing up before their leader and senior comrade, in accordance with a *ritual* of the already-destroyed VSKhSON, were showing him that they were with him in their hearts and that they had remained the same despite prison bars. Such will I remember them all my life.[68]

Reporting on the trial, *Chronicle of Current Events* No. 1

observed, "All the accused admitted themselves guilty (obviously in the sense of admitting the facts of the charge), but not all repented ... It is known for certain that no-one was charged with ties with NTS [a Russian émigré organization based in West Germany], nor with currency operations, nor with the possession of arms."[69] There appear to be two slight errors marring this basically accurate account. The relatively harsh sentences awarded to four members of the rank-and-file seem to have suggested to the *Chronicle* correspondent that they failed to "repent" at the trial. Actually, if the "sentence" of the trial is to be believed, only Veretenov expressed "incomplete repentance."[70] And, as far as possession of arms is concerned, there was of course Konstantinov's rusty, broken Mauser, manufactured in 1898.[71]

On April 4-5, 1968, the court announced its sentence. Yuri Luryi offers these cautionary comments concerning this Soviet legal document:

It should be remarked that several of the accused denied their participation in such matters as the dissemination of literature or the recruitment of new members into the union. Several defense attorneys very successfully carried out the defense of these accused, disputing, with argumentation, the charge on many points and, frequently, on all points except formal membership in VSKhSON. But the one-eyed Themis closed her ears and remained completely deaf to all the conclusions of the defense. And in the 'sentence' it is impossible to find even a hint of the fact that several charges were contested, that concrete arguments were advanced against concrete charges. This represents a very coarse infringement of the principle of justice. The fact of the matter is that in the USSR they do not pass a verdict of guilt or innocence but a 'sentence'. And the sentence is passed not by a jury but by the court, headed by a presiding professional judge and including two assessors. *De facto,* the sentence is passed by the judge *alone;* as a rule, the assessors respectfully and easily agree with him and sign the sentence he has written.[72]

Here are lengthy excerpts from the text of the sentence:

SENTENCE

In the Name of the Russian Soviet Federative Socialist Republic, 4-5 April, 1968

The court collegiate for criminal affairs of the Leningrad Municipal Court, consisting of:

Presiding—*N. S. Isakova,* Deputy Chairman of the Leningrad Municipal Court

People's Witnesses—*M. L. Ivanov* and *I. P. Krainov*

Secretary—*K. I. Likhomanov*

With the participation of the senior assistant procurator of the city of Leningrad, the senior justice councillor Comrade *I. V. Katukova*

And the assistant procurator of the city of Leningrad, the junior justice councillor Comrade *E. A. Gusev* and

The attorneys *I. L. Kachurina, Z. S. Gol'denberg, V. I. Vvedenskii, Iu. I. Lur'i, E. V. Altukhov, P. P. Vasil'ev, V. M. Tikhonov, S. L. Astanovitskii, Iu. I. Buzinier, B. V. Bril', M. A. Ronin, A. I. Tsubin, A. V. Gurevich, R. V. Shatrov*

Examined in the city of Leningrad in open court session the case against:

[Here follow the names, dates and places of birth, nationality, education, place of employment, marital status and address of 16 of the accused. See Appendix I for most of this information.]

For crimes foreseen under Articles 70, part 1 and 72 of the Criminal Code of the RSFSR and

Konstantinov, Stanislav Vladimirovich

[There follows the same biographical information concerning him.]

accused of crimes foreseen under Articles 70, part 1, 72 and 218, part 1 [218 refers to the stealing of a weapon].

The court collegiate, having examined the materials of the preliminary investigation and having analyzed them in the course of judicial examination

ESTABLISHED

the guilt of the accused [17 names] for participating in the illegal anti-Soviet organization 'The All-Russian Social-Christian Union for the Liberation of the People' (VSKhSON), founded by their confederates *I. V. Ogurtsov, M. Iu. Sado, E. A. Vagin* and *B. A. Averichkin* with the aim of overthrowing the Soviet state and social system by armed means. They agreed with the program and statute of this organization and systematically engaged in hostile organizational activity.

They actively carried out anti-Soviet propaganda, prepared, multiplied, disseminated and kept anti-Soviet, tendentious and reactionary religious literature.

Having assumed positions hostile to the socialist system in the USSR and having entered into a criminal compact with their confederates, they, during the period 1964-1966, entered at various times into the anti-Soviet organization VSKhSON, took an oath and swore '. . . not sparing their strength, property and very lives to dedicate themselves to the struggle with the Soviet regime for the establishment of a bourgeois regime'. During their entrance into VSKhSON, they filled out questionnaires and selected conspiratorial names.

Having agreed with the anti-Soviet demands of the program and statute, the accused, until the moment of their unmasking, acted in a direction leading to the practical realization of their criminal designs.

In accordance with the structure of VSKhSON which had been worked out, they entered into various sub-units of this illegal organization, which consisted of 'divisions' and 'squads', united into 'sections', 'platoons', 'companies', 'battalions' and 'corps'.

At assemblages and during personal encounters, they repeatedly discussed plans and methods for struggle with the Soviet regime, questions of the activization of recruitment of new members, the creation of a VSKhSON printing press, the acquisition of arms, the expansion of the VSKhSON fund of anti-Soviet literature and the payment of dues.

The accused acquired apparatuses of multiplication—typewriters, cameras, enlargers and other objects. The dues, moreover, were used to pay expenses connected with the journeys of VSKhSON members to other cities to recruit new members and to acquaint themselves with the activity of individual members of the organization.

In matters of conspiracy, the accused followed the instructions of the *Nastavlenie No. 1 VSKhSON*.

In distinguishing the criminal actions committed by each of the accused, the court established that:

[Here follows a detailed summary of the 'criminal actions' of each of the 17 accused. Recruitment efforts, 'literary' activities and payment of dues are the major categories.]

The accused [17 names] fully admitted their guilt in performing the above-enumerated criminal actions.

The court collegiate considers that the guilt of the accused in committing the actions incriminated to them has been fully substantiated by the materials of the case.

Through the testimonies of the accused, given by them in detail during both the preliminary investigation and the trial, concerning the circumstances of the actions performed by them, it was established that each of them, upon entering as a member into the anti-Soviet organization and participating in its further activity, directed, together with his confederates, his efforts in organized fashion toward the overthrow of the existing state and social system of the USSR.

They devoted their chief attention to questions of the growth of the organization through the recruitment of new members and to questions of the multiplication, keeping and dissemination, with propagandistic aims, of anti-Soviet, tendentious and reactionary religious literature.

They carried out the reception [of new members] into the organization by observing an established ritual, by the filling out of questionnaires, the taking of oaths and the selection of conspiratorial names. They created a material base through funds paid in as dues. As a rule, they entered into one of the sub-units of VSKhSON and engaged in the preparation and creation of a printing press, in military preparation and in questions connected with the obtaining and concealing of weapons.

These testimonies of the accused are borne out also by those of witnesses *Klochkov, Shestakov, Iovaisha, Kozichev, Goncharov* and others, who were recruited at one time into the anti-Soviet organization, and also the testimonies of the witnesses [the names of 18 candidates for membership in VSKhSON follow] and others, who were being prepared with the same end in mind [i.e. recruitment into VSKhSON].

The testimonies of witnesses *Sado* and *Vagin,* who were convicted in another case, confirmed the existence of VSKhSON and the participation of the accused in it.

The court has no reason not to trust the testimonies of the above-named witnesses, with the exception of the testimonies of *Sado* and *Vagin* concerning the absence of an intent by the organization's members to overthrow the Soviet system by armed means. Their testimonies and those of the accused in this area are refuted by the VSKhSON program and also other case materials: the structural ordering of the organization on the model of military sub-units, the discussion at assemblages and during personal encounters by *Platonov, Konosov, Buzin, Nagornyi* and *Miklashevich* of matters relating to the obtaining of arms and places of concealment for them, and by the acquisition of military literature by the accused *Konosov* and *Ivoilov,* and by other evidence.

Moreover, the guilt of the accused is established by the protocols of the inspection, confiscation and seizure of a significant quantity of program documents of an anti-Soviet and religious content and also anti-Soviet books printed in the West [which were found] both in the original and in photocopies. [Their guilt is also established] by material evidence: typewriters, cameras and other photo apparatuses, as well as by the conclusions of the criminal experts employed by the judiciary. And by the testimonies of witnesses [6 names] concerning the sale of a 'Mauser' pistol to Konstantinov and the dissemination by him of a book by M. Djilas.

On the basis of the above, the court collegiate considers that the actions of [16 names—Konstantinov's is missing, but this is undoubtedly an error] are qualified correctly according to Article 70, part 1, 72 and 218, part 1 of the Criminal Code of the RSFSR.

Moving on to a discussion of the measure of punishment to be meted out to the accused, the court collegiate takes into account the seriousness of the crimes committed by them.

Taking into consideration their repentance and admission of guilt, the court also takes into account the most active role [in VSKhSON] of the accused *Platonov, Ivanov, Ivoilov* and *Borodin* and deems that they should be subjected to punishment consisting of a lengthy deprivation of liberty.

Taking into consideration the actions, repentance and personality of each of the accused, the incomplete repentance of the accused *Veretenov*, the less active role of the accused *Sudarev, Ivlev, Zabak, Shuvalov* and *Konstantinov* in the crimes committed, the court considers that their punishment should be assessed in the form of deprivation of liberty for less lengthy terms. As far as Konstantinov is concerned, considering his degree of guilt, the condition of his health and that of his mother, the court deems it possible to select as punishment for him deprivation of liberty within the limits of the preliminary imprisonment already spent by him [awaiting trial].

On the basis of the above, and being instructed by Articles 71, 301-303 and 317 of the Code of Criminal Procedure of the RSFSR,[73] the court collegiate

SENTENCED

[All, except those given a term amounting to the time spent in prison awaiting trial, were sentenced to the strict-regime camps, without a subsequent period of exile. The terms:

Platonov—7 years
Ivanov, Ivoilov and Borodin—6 years
Konosov—4 years
Ustinovich—3 years 6 months
Miklashevich, Buzin, Nagornyi and
Baranov—3 years
Bochevarov and Veretenov—2 years 6 months
Sudarev and Ivlev—2 years
Zabak and Shuvalov—1 year
Konstantinov—10 months]

After the court passed its sentence, Zabak, Shuvalov and Konstantinov were set free, and the remaining fourteen rank-and-file were sent off to the Mordovian camps. Leonid Borodin was later to compose a ballad in which he attempted to capture the feelings of the VSKhSON members as they journeyed toward the camps:

> Coaches with bars
> Fly by.
> Crawl by.
> Where are they going?
> Why are they going?
> Whom are they carrying?
> Eyes bluer than snowdrops
> Look out with hate
> With love . . .

Whom are they carrying?
  —Rebels!
Where are they taking them?
  —To Mordovia![74]

CHAPTER VIII

Imprisonment

"THEY BROUGHT TWO fellows to us from another camp—
Leningraders," political prisoner Iurii Galanskov wrote to
his mother from the Mordovian camps in late March, 1969.
"They call themselves Social-Christians and maintain that
[Russian] Orthodoxy is the expression of the thought of the
Russian people and that Russia will save the world from
all corruption. That is what they think, and they believe
strongly in it. Only they speak about it in a more complex
and intelligent fashion. They're good boys. One of them is
a teacher who worked in a school. The other finished the
Eastern division of Leningrad University, completed his grad-
uate work there and was an instructor in the Eastern division.
His name is Slava Platonov, and his friend's is Lenia
Borodin . . ."[1]

In the same year of 1969, Aleksandr Petrov-Agatov,
finding himself under arrest in Lubianka Prison for the contents of his poems, by chance made the acquaintance of
Mikhail Sado's brother, Iurii, who had been arrested for currency violations. Discovering that his cellmate was a poet,
Iurii Sado asked to hear some of Petrov-Agatov's poems. The
bard willingly obliged.

'Magnificent!' he shouted [after hearing two].
'What a pity my brother did not know these verses!
They had a whole group. All young people who
had completed the university. From Leningrad.
Haven't you heard of them?'

'This is the first time', I admitted.

'O! How is it possible?' Iurii Iukhanovich exclaimed in sincere astonishment. 'I'll tell you about
them now. Would you like me to?'

'Of course...'[2]

Once he had learned some of the details of the revolutionary organization, Petrov-Agatov found his interest in-
tensely aroused. "I was shaken. In Russia, in the sixties—a
military-political organization! People having set themselves
the goal of restoring the monarchy and reviving true Orthodoxy. You will agree that in the twentieth century, in the
Soviet Union, among the youth, this was more than unusual.
I was now impatient to get to the camps and soon! If only
to make the acquaintance of these people."[3]

At the time the VSKhSON members were sentenced, an
estimated 2,000 of the Soviet Union's at least 10,000 political prisoners were held in a large concentration camp complex in Mordovia ASSR.[4] "The whole south-west corner of
Mordovia," one inmate reported, "is criss-crossed with barbed
wire and fences of a special kind of construction, strewn
with watch towers and lit up at night by the bright beams
of coupled searchlights."[5] Prisoners, such as the VSKhSON
participants, who had been sentenced under Articles 64-88
of the Criminal Code were confined to the following camp
zones: 3, 10, 17, 17a and 19. These zones were unusually
small, probably intentionally so in order to keep the political prisoners separated. In the Mordovian camp complex

there were four regimes in effect—"ordinary," "hard," "strict" and "special." All VSKhSON members, being sentenced under Articles 64-88, were automatically assigned to the "strict" category.[6]

Anatolii Marchenko, a dissident of extraordinary courage who was in the camps from 1960-1966, has written a guidebook to the Soviet camps and prisons entitled *My Testimony*.[7] It has received the endorsement of camp specialist Aleksandr Solzhenitsyn.[8] We shall not attempt to repeat Marchenko's appalling information but would merely refer readers with iron nerves to his study. The worst aspect of the camps, Marchenko and all other recent graduates unanimously agree, is the fact that the prisoners are deliberately kept in a state of semi-starvation. Performing heavy labor, they are fed $1\frac{1}{2}$ times less than what a normal man needs to accomplish light work. Consequently, they suffer unceasingly from gnawing hunger. Other infringements of basic morality are the frequent use of punishment cells, in which prisoners are kept in damp, unhealthy conditions on reduced rations, the requirement that convicts perform manual labor to the point of serious illness, the banning of all religious literature or activity, inadequate medical treatment, and the permitting of only rare visits by parents and relatives.[9]

Sixteen VSKhSON members arrived in the Mordovian camps in 1968. The following year Mikhail Sado was transferred, ahead of schedule, to Mordovia from Vladimir Prison. It will be recalled that many members of the organization had not distinguished themselves during the investigation and trial and that all but three of them (Ogurtsov, Sado, Veretenov) had "repented" of their revolutionary activity. Once in the camps, they seem to have recovered the courage of their convictions. We find them gathering together as a group to celebrate Russian Easter, and every February 2nd they would solemnly meet to commemorate the founding of the All-Russian Social-Christian Union for the Liberation of

the People.[10] That they had not abandoned their former views
is attested to by Petrov-Agatov:

> At the large table specially brought in from some-
> where for the occasion seven persons were seated.
> Besides Nagornyi and Ivoilov, here were Boris
> Anatol'evich Averichkin ... Mikhail Borisovich
> Konosov ... Georgii Nikolaevich Bochevarov ...,
> then Iurii Petrovich Baranov, an engineer of 33 to
> 35 with a tatoo on his right arm, phlegmatic with
> a long and well cared-for but grayish face. There
> was also a person whose last name I was not given
> [Veretenov?], who looked like Tsar Nicholas II,
> with near-sighted, tearful eyes. And finally Sudarev:
> short, always thinking of something with great con-
> centration and, as I later learned, dreaming of be-
> coming a writer ... They asked me to give my opin-
> ion of their organization, to share with them my
> prognoses for the future and to read the verses for
> which I had been arrested.
>
> I of course told them what I thought: 'The appear-
> ance of your organization in this country is an ex-
> traordinary event. Christianity, Orthodoxy, a con-
> stitutional monarchy—that, in my opinion, is the
> sole foundation on which Russia can stand and be
> great. What you arrived at, being young men living
> under conditions of pitch-black tendentiousness and
> spiritual castration, not only does you honor but
> testifies to the great spiritual and creative potential
> of each of you. However, I am convinced that by
> means of plots, rebellions and coups nothing can be
> changed in Soviet Russia. Therefore your whole af-
> fair was doomed from the start. But your *appear-
> ance*—this, I repeat, serves as a testimony that the

nation is alive and that Russia has not perished. I bow low to all of you'.

There was neither applause nor approving looks, but the ice had been broken . . .

'And how do you see the liberation of the country from Communism?' asked Ivoilov.

'The abyss must be suffered through to the end', I answered . . .

An argument began. Passions grew with every moment, and God knows how long it would have continued had I not made use of my privilege as a guest in polite company to read my poetry.

They liked my poems."

From Petrov-Agatov's colorful account it would appear that the VSKhSON membership's "repentance" had been tactical rather than heartfelt.

As has already been mentioned, the clandestine bi-monthly *Chronicle of Current Events* followed closely the fates of the VSKhSON participants in the Soviet camps and prisons. When the *Chronicle* was temporarily suppressed in late 1972, in its fifth year of publication, Aleksandr Solzhenitsyn felt impelled to deliver an obituary, "For several years the dedicated *Chronicle* quenched a universal and natural human thirst to know what is going on . . . Now without the *Chronicle* we won't get to know so quickly perhaps about future victims of the regime in our prisons and camps . . . Concealed from our gaze and our knowledge will be the further destinies of those who have already been sentenced: [there follow 11 names, including] . . . Ogurtsov . . . Viacheslav Platonov, Evgenii Vagin . . . and many, many others

known only to their families, fellow workers and neigh-
bors."[12] Understandably, most of the *Chronicle's* reportage
concerns those VSKhSON members with longer sentences:
Ogurtsov, Sado, Vagin, Averichkin, Platonov, Ivanov,
Borodin and Ivoilov. Of these, four—Sado, Platonov, Ivanov
and Borodin—seem to have made the most nuisance of themselves for the authorities.

At first, the *Chronicle* reports, all VSKhSON members
(except Ogurtsov and Sado, who were in Vladimir Prison)
were kept in the 11th *lagpunkt* [camp zone].[13] By early February, 1969, however, Platonov and Borodin had annoyed
their jailers sufficiently to be transferred to 17a, a zone
reserved for those who, in the eyes of the camp administration, particularly deserved to be isolated from their fellow
prisoners.[14] (Previous to this transfer, Platonov had been
placed in camp 11's BUR [barrack of intensified regime]
and he and Borodin had been sent to the investigative prison
in Saransk.[15]) At 17a the new arrivals joined forces with
such noted dissenters as Galanskov, Iulii Daniel', Aleksandr
Ginzburg and Valerii Ronkin to defend themselves and their
fellow prisoners against arbitrariness on the part of the administration. When, for example, Ronkin was deprived of a
visit from a relative because he had the audacity openly to
term himself a "political prisoner," Platonov joined Daniel',
Galanskov and others in a sharp protest to the authorities.[16]

In May, 1969, Aleksandr Ginzburg began a hunger strike
[*golodovka*] because the administration was refusing him
permission to see his wife Irina Zholkovskaia. Ginzburg had
been arrested six days before his *de facto* marriage to
Zholkovskaia had been due to be officially registered. While
Ginzburg fasted, his friends, including Platonov and Borodin,
wrote letters of appeal to the Attorney General of the
USSR. This failing, they wrote to the Supreme Court. On
June 2nd, Ronkin commenced a sympathy hunger strike; he
was joined by Galanskov on the 3rd and Borodin and
Platonov on the 5th.[17] On the day they began their strike,

both Platonov and Borodin sent letters to the Presidium of the Supreme Soviet explaining their actions. Platonov wrote:

> By this statement I inform the Presidium of the Supreme Soviet of the USSR that from June 5th, as a sign of solidarity with A. I. Ginzburg, who has already been fasting for twenty days, I am declaring a hunger strike. I think the reason for A. I. Ginzburg's fast is already known to the Presidium, as are his lawful demands that he be permitted to see his wife I. S. Zholkovskaia. I have exhausted all the means of assistance at my disposal (appeals to the Division for the Supervision of Places of Detention of the Procuracy of the USSR, to the Attorney General of the USSR and to the Supreme Soviet of the USSR) and am forced to resort to extreme means, i.e. to declare a hunger strike, since my conscience will not permit me to remain indifferent to the fate of A. I. Ginzburg. I should like to hope that the Presidium of the Supreme Soviet of the USSR will take most urgent measures to satisfy the lawful (i.e. in accord with legality) and just (in accord with conscience) demands of A. I. Ginzburg.
>
> 5 June 1969 *Platonov*[18]

Borodin's statement was shorter but similar in tone:

> I no longer have the strength to be conscious that a man next to me is suffering and to feel my inability somehow to help him. From June 5, 1969, I am refusing to take food as a sign of solidarity with A. I. Ginzburg.
>
> 5 June 1969 *Borodin*[19]

How the authorities finally halted the hunger strike is revealed in a letter by Ginzburg:

> By Monday the administration nonetheless finally figured out a way to make us stop. They took us all out for a common exercise period. It was a well-aimed blow. Perhaps Slava Platonov looked better than I. Our ulcer-sufferers Iurka [Galanskov] and Lenia [Borodin] were barely on their feet and constantly kept doubling over from the pain in their stomachs. Ben [Ronkin] was of a gray-green hue . . .
>
> The following morning I halted my hunger strike. The boys did so after me. And it's a pity. I could have held on.[20]

Borodin's feelings about the strike are expressed in a letter to his relatives:

> According to existing regulations, the administration of a camp is supposed immediately to isolate a person declaring a hunger strike; instead, they kept Alik [Ginzburg] five days in the zone and forced him to go out and work. It was unbearable to have to witness that. Imagine that next to you a person who is not eating is walking about and working. We, his closest friends (ten persons), began to shower various departments with appeals. Five days later Alik was at last removed to the isolator. Only on the 11th day did we learn that they had begun to feed him by artificial means. If someone had earlier told me that a man could not eat for 10 days and, at the same time, go out for exercise periods, go to the bath and even smoke and read literature in his speciality, I would not have

believed it. And Alik's build is even slighter than
mine, and I weigh 54 kg. . . . Time passed. Alik fasted. Our declarations flew to various departments,
and they kept silent. Seventeen days later two of
our number declared a hunger strike. On June 5th,
I refused to take food. I kept the hunger strike for
five days, i.e. until such time as Alik halted it. And
after 25 days he was in a condition no worse than
mine. They say he even looked better. There's a
case of matter determining consciousness for
you! . . . Irina [Zholkovskaia] is supposed to come
soon. And the husband will see his wife. But at
what a price! And who needs all this?[21]

In the same year of 1969, Borodin and Platonov, together
with Mikhail Sado who had arrived in Mordovia, joined
Galanskov, Ginzburg and two others in penning a "letter
of the seven" to a number of leading Soviet cultural figures,
such as Aleksandr Tvardovskii and Leonid Leonov, in which
they described conditions in the camps and asserted that the
camps represented a Stalinist practice still in force.[21] December, 1969, saw Borodin and Platonov joining Ginzburg and
another prisoner in a hunger strike protesting the transfer of
Iulii Daniel' and Valerii Ronkin from 17a to Vladimir Prison.
The four strikers were incarcerated in the BUR.[23]

By October, 1970, reports *Chronicle* No. 17, the authorities had had enough of Borodin, and he was shipped off,
along with Aleksandr Petrov-Agatov, to Vladimir Prison to
await the end of his sentence in early 1973. The same prison
tribunal which made this decision decided to send VSKhSON
member Nikolai Ivanov and Iurii Galanskov to the BUR for
two months. Both ended up in the hospital as a result of
this experience.[24]

Even within the grim confines of Vladimir Prison, we
find Borodin taking part in hunger strikes, despite a severe
ulcer. In December, 1970, he joined other prisoners, includ-

ing Ogurtsov and Petrov-Agatov, in a fast seeking to obtain better conditions for women prisoners, an improvement of medical conditions (doctors were in the habit of appearing 20 days after being summoned), permission for inmates to use their own books, the ceasing of the serving of rotten food etc. The hunger strike was timed to coincide with the Day of the Constitution and Day of the Rights of Man, both of which fall in December.[25] In September, 1971, Borodin utilized the weapon of a hunger strike to gain his removal from a cell in which he had been incarcerated together with a mentally ill prisoner named Tarasov.[26] December, 1971 witnessed Platonov and 29 other prisoners in camp 3-1 carrying out a four day hunger strike on the anniversary of the U.N. Declaration of Human Rights to protest conditions of imprisonment in Soviet penal institutions.[27] For this he was refused permission to receive parcels, go to the canteen or have visits from relatives; he was also given eight days in solitary confinement.[28] Nevertheless, he proceeded to affix his signature to an "Appeal of the Nine" to the International Red Cross, written later the same month, in which Soviet prison conditions were described. Some excerpts:

> In the camps every method is put into service with one objective—to break our wills and force us into submission. Our personalities are methodically destroyed and we are reduced to a state of physical exhaustion . . .

> The basic element in this 're-education' is a chronic food shortage. People are kept here for years on near-famine diets, in the fear of hunger . . . After a few years of this sort of diet, a man is so reduced that he becomes the prey of every type of disease. Not to mention the sick prisoners or those suffering from stomach ulcers . . .

We demand to be treated with decency—within the
law—as set out in the charter of Human Rights and
adopted and adhered to by all civilized men. We
ask for recognition of our status as political prisoners.[29]

In his "Prison Encounters," for which he was transferred
to Vladimir Prison in November, 1970, Petrov-Agatov adds
flesh to the spare *Chronicle* accounts of the activities of
VSKhSON members in the camps. He informs us, for example, that in 1969 three VSKhSON members—Vagin,
Platonov and Borodin—were sent off to Saransk for two
months of "prophylactic" chats.[30]

'It was a comedy', smiled Vagin. 'The local writers
and other Mordovian celebrities come and try to
change your mind, naturally at the instigation of
the KGB. Sometimes they even take you to a restaurant, or for a ride through the city or to the
stores. Look, they say, how beautiful is the life of
the Soviet people. There's bread, movies, you can
freely visit a restaurant. You can listen to jazz.
There's even cognac sometimes. What more do you
need?"[31]

Such crude efforts at "converting" the VSKhSON members of course failed. The authorities must have been especially dismayed when Platonov used one of his "prophylactic" discussions with Colonel Arbuzov, deputy head of
the Mordovian KGB, to request that he be taken to an Orthodox church to make his confession and receive the sacra-
ment.[32]

On one occasion, Petrov-Agatov reports, Borodin was
placed in the camp-prison for refusing to attend political
indoctrination sessions. The next day all VSKhSON members in the camp refused to go out to work. They were

supported in their demands by a group of neo-Marxists, headed by Sergei Khakhaev, and liberals, led by Nikolai Dragosh. The result of this protest was that Borodin was released from the prison, and the authorities, for a time, ceased pressuring unwilling prisoners to attend indoctrination.[33]

According to Petrov-Agatov, the influence of VSKhSON was particularly felt in camp 17, where Nikolai Ivanov and Georgii Bochevarov served as magnets for the youth who "came to them, listened to them and imitated them."[34] This could not but become known to the authorities. Once the head of the operations division, accompanied by his suite, came to Ivanov and asked, "What pretensions do you have to being in the [camp] administration?"

> Ivanov very conclusively and objectively elaborated everything: the poor nourishment, the rotten herring, the absence of wares in the store, the irregular delivery of newspapers, the poor working of the bath and the impossibility of fulfilling the work norm, since no-one had previously sewn mittens. To sew 60 pairs a man was beyond their strength . . .
>
> The lieutenant-colonel sniffed the herring which someone had shoved virtually into his mouth.
>
> 'Yes, the herring could be better', he said, and turning to Garkushev [a high-ranking subordinate] ordered: 'Forbid its being served'.
>
> 'Yes sir'.
>
> 'As far as your work is concerned . . . I'll give you two months' learning period. We won't ask for norms during that time. Newspapers, the bath, bread—you'll get it all'.

'Guarantees!' demanded Ivanov.

'You have to believe a man', smiled the lieutenant-colonel.

'A man, of course . . .', Nikolai Ivanovich answered
not becoming confused. 'But you are, forgive me,
a jailer'.

'Aren't you ashamed of yourself, Ivanov?'

'I'm not the head of the operations division', the
prisoner cut him off. And then not giving the
lieutenant-colonel time to come to himself: 'And
what about wares in the store?'

'We ourselves eat almost the same thing as you
have in the shop', unthinkingly let drop the head
of the operations division.

'It's very bad that in the 52nd year of the Soviet
regime you are fed so poorly . . .'

General laughter.

The lieutenant-colonel, having lost control of his
speech, shot out: 'Well, you know . . . When *you*
run things, we'll see if it will be better'.

'But in order for that to happen you and I will
have to change places', Nikolai Viktorovich summed
up.

The victory was complete.

The lieutenant-colonel and his suite quite literally
ran off.[35]

And so it went. Such moral victories were psychologically very necessary for the VSKhSON members, who were fighting to survive physically and spiritually under trying conditions. Their combativeness and firmly held convictions reportedly led a number of young neo-Marxists to come under their influence in the camps.[36] By their defiant and self-sacrificial behavior in detention, Platonov, Ivanov and Borodin would appear to have redeemed whatever laxity they exhibited during the investigation and trial.

In early July, 1972, the authorities, perhaps upset by the prodigious amount of information finding its way out of the Mordovian camps to Moscow and the West, decided to disperse the prisoners by shipping 500 of them, from zones 3, 17 and 19, off to the north-east, to Perm'. The strategy did not work. After an initial delay, information concerning the activities and tribulations of Perm' inmates began to flow to Moscow with the same regularity as such data had previously flowed from the Mordovian camps. Since being resurrected in 1974, the *Chronicle of Current Events* has attentively followed events in the Perm' camp complex, and a number of documents, some of them of considerable length, have reached Moscow from Perm'.[37] From such materials we learn that Sado and Platonov were transferred to Perm', where they continued their protests against unjust correctional practices. On one occasion, we find them uniting with 60 hunger-strikers in protests to the USSR Procuracy, the Procuracy of Perm' Province and the Soviet division of the Red Cross. On September 5, 1972, they participated in a memorial service for all those who had perished in the Soviet camps (prisoners of each major religion held their own service). A similar service was repeated in September, 1973, but we do not have the names of the participants.[38] In the same month of September, 1973, Sado and Platonov joined 14 other political prisoners in signing an open letter (Platonov's signature appears first on the document and Sado's fourth) in which, among other things, it is said:

"We greet the struggle of Academician A. D. Sakharov for civil rights and liberties in the USSR ... We believe that the work of democratizing the Soviet system, the work of Sakharov, Solzhenitsyn, Bukovskii and Grigorenko, will triumph."[39]

In March, 1974, Viacheslav Platonov, the last of the VSKhSON rank-and-file in captivity, was released from the Perm' camps.[40] February, 1975, saw the release of Vagin and Averichkin from Mordovia.[41] That leaves only Igor' Ogurtsov and Mikhail Sado in prison. Their plight will be the subject of the chapter which follows.

CHAPTER IX

Calvary

"I call upon you during your meeting
to devote attention to problems of humanity and the basic rights of man...
Assist the immediate liberation of such
shining and courageous individuals as
Bukovskii...Sado, Ogurtsov..."

(From an Appeal by Academician
Andrei Sakharov to L. I. Brezhnev
and Richard Nixon on the occasion
of their summer, 1974, summit
meeting)[1]

TOURISTS TO the Soviet Union are frequently taken to the
ancient city of Vladimir, which was founded at the beginning
of the 12th century by Prince Vladimir Monomakh, to see
its magnificent churches and the iconography of one of the
world's great artists, Andrei Rublev. These visitors most
definitely are *not* shown another monument of historical
significance: Vladimir Prison. There some one thousand
prisoners, less than half of whom are "politicals," languish
under conditions calculated to break the body and, more importantly, the will. Reveille at six A.M., toilet break, inspection, breakfast, lunch either preceded or followed by
an exercise period, supper, inspection, lights out at ten P.M.,
a bath every ten days. Such is the Vladimir regimen. A

149

cell for five persons measures five yards by three or three square yards per man. Political prisoners are housed in ill-lit cells of Soviet construction, appreciably worse than the pre-revolutionary ones in the same prison. The cells are perenially damp and cause one to shiver even in summer, while in winter "even wearing a reefer jacket it was impossible to get warm. Thrusting their hands into their jacket sleeves and with the collars well turned up, the cons would stamp about the cell and bang their feet together, while those who didn't have room to walk about would sit hunched up on the benches . . . their noses tucked into their jackets."[2]

For those on strict regime, meals consist of 450 grams of bread, several sprats and hot water for breakfast, a scoop of cabbage or other soup for lunch and several spoonfuls of porridge for dinner. Sugar, meat and all fats are forbidden. In the prison shop the convict is permitted once a month to buy two rubles worth of non-food products, such as tobacco, a toothbrush, pencils, etc.[3]

It is scarcely surprising that on such a diet (or even the slightly better normal regime fare), "Prisoners in jail soon begin to fall prey to stomach disorders—catarrh, colitis, ulcers. The sedentary life gives rise to hemorrhoids and heart disease. And all this together leads to nervous complaints."[4] Another Vladimir alumnus refers to the "torture of hunger" which never leaves a prisoner. The effect of Vladimir Prison, he writes, is that one "is almost unable to read, is quickly fatigued, becomes sleepy, or, in brief, manifests all the signs of physical and nervous exhaustion."[5] After two years in Vladimir, Anatolii Marchenko found that he "could hardly walk."[6]

One might think that the exercise period (half an hour a day for those on strict regime and an hour for those on normal) would be a pleasure for the prisoners. But the exercise yards, newly constructed to replace the spacious ones formerly used, are no larger than a cell for five; with their concrete floor and walls they inevitably serve to remind the prisoner of a cell with the roof off.[7] Over the long Russian winter, the exercise period is "just one more form of punishment and torture, especially for the old and sick." It makes it impossible for haggard and emaciated prisoners to get warm for the rest of the day.[8]

A final factor which ought not to be neglected is interpersonal relations between prisoners. By the malicious design of the authorities, a cell frequently contains a convict who is at least partially insane, such as the unbalanced Tarasov encountered by Borodin or the "screwy Sania" mentioned by Marchenko who was wont to urinate on his sleeping cell-mates.[9] The administration also enjoys a free hand to mix incompatibles together, e.g. a common criminal and a "sensitive" political prisoner. Considering all this, one can appreciate Marchenko's conclusion that, "Prisoners in a cell need great discipline and great moral strength to preserve themselves in such inhuman conditions, in order to preserve their human dignity and human relations with one another."[10]

Before his arrest Igor' Ogurtsov had been in superb physical condition, an "excellent sportsman, swimmer and fencer."[11] During his first years in Vladimir, as we have seen earlier, he devoted himself assiduously to reading and abstracting and studied four foreign languages: English, Italian, Spanish and French. He is reported to have filled up sixty notebooks with his notes and abstracts.[12] Eventually, however, Vladimir began to take its toll even on one so physically fit. As Vladimir Osipov put it in an appeal to Sean MacBride of Amnesty International, "Before his arrest Igor' Ogurtsov was an excellent sportsman . . ., now he is hypertonic, an invalid of the second group. Vladimir Prison brought him to the loss of his physical health."[13] A sense of how this occurred is conveyed by the anonymous but highly trustworthy *samizdat* account "Information about Igor' Viacheslavovich Ogurtsov," dated July 21, 1974:

He [Ogurtsov] spent the first period of his incarceration, seven years, in Vladimir Prison, a prison with a very difficult regimen. We know little about this regimen since prisoners are not permitted to write about it or discuss it at meetings [with relatives]. I can give two examples of this. Once a prisoner was put into his cell who tried to provoke a fight. Since this was on the eve of a visit, Ogurtsov, fearing he would be deprived of a meeting with his relatives, took up a defensive position and only by chance escaped a fatal kick to the groin. Nevertheless, he was forced to have recourse to medical assistance. When during the meeting he tried to tell his parents about this episode, such an alarm was raised that a lieutenant-colonel, major, senior lieutenant and several sergeants literally burst into the room. A second episode: from inadequate nourishment he began to contract avitaminosis and continuous furunculosis. In one of his letters he asked that he be sent in the next packet (one is allowed to send a prisoner two packets a year weighing not more than one kilogram each) 300-400 grams of garlic. The packet was returned with the inscription 'not permitted'. When his mother nonetheless placed three or four heads of garlic in the next packet, the packet was accepted, but the three heads of garlic were returned to her.

In Vladimir Prison he became ill with hypertension, as a result of which he is classified an invalid of the second group—avitaminosis. He became very weak and lost his hair but served his seven year sentence in full.[14]

Besides fruitlessly attempting to assist their son in his losing struggle with avitaminosis, Ogurtsov's parents twice asked lawyers to appeal his sentence on the grounds that he should not have been sentenced under Article 64 and that he had received an excessively severe sentence. Despite the lawyers' detailed argumentation, the appeals came to naught.

Some information is available concerning Ogurtsov's behavior during his seven years in Vladimir Prison. At least one of the VSKhSON leader's cell-mates, Anatolii Radygin, is now in the West, while other persons have been permitted to emigrate who succeeded in speaking with former Ogurtsov cell-mates before leaving the USSR.[15] Ogurtsov's cell-mates seem invariably to have been struck by his total calmness and self-assurance. When taken to an interrogation, he never hurried, always took his time. He was constantly neat in appearance and well-groomed. His uncompromising behavior frequently got him into trouble with the Vladimir authorities, as a result of which he would be deprived of meetings with his relatives and packages. We know that he participated in hunger strikes organized by the political prisoners.[16] And he reportedly suffered great pain from the disease he contracted in prison—hypertension.

Once, it is said, Ogurtsov's father came to visit him in Vladimir. The authorities ordered him to be shaved, even though his cell-mates had not been shaved for several days. Ogurtsov refused on the grounds that this would be a *"pokazukha"* [for show]. He said he would agree to be shaved only if the entire cell was. The authorities then backed down and accepted his condition, something which does not often happen in Vladimir. This incident is described as typical; Ogurtsov never thought only of himself but always took his cell-mates into consideration.

The VSKhSON leader spent considerable time debating the various individuals whom the authorities would malevolently assign to his cell. Surely it was not by accident that this Russian patriot frequently found himself together with Ukrainian and Lithuanian nationalists, Zionists and Russian liberals. The well-known Leningrad "hijacker," the Zionist Eduard Kuznetsov, has left a brief account of his association with Ogurtsov in a Vladimir cell. Terming Ogurtsov the " 'Führer' of the demo-Christians," he mentions that "once or twice we nearly quarreled to the point of blows, but we parted on good terms." When a girl of "exalted" temperament who was listening to Kuznetsov's narration asked, "Did your ideological differences really reach such sharpness?" he replied, "What ideological differences? Once we quarreled about tobacco and once about the latrine."[17] Kuznetsov's irony aside, one may suspect that "ideological differences" did indeed cause some sharp exchanges, but, as he says, he and Ogurtsov parted amicably.

One tradition Ogurtsov apparently maintained was always to address his cell-mates by their first-name and patronymic. In return, he insisted that he be addressed as "Igor' Viacheslavovich." This seems to have been a practice among the VSKhSON membership.[18] When one Ukrainian cellmate insisted on addressing Ogurtsov as "Igorek" [a nickname], he reportedly refused to respond. (Speaking impressionistically, the use of the first-name and patronymic lends an added dignity and formality to a human relationship; it is a sign of respect and is also "traditional," hearkening back to a more widespread pre-revolutionary usage.) Ogurtsov is also supposed to have used the "you" [*vy*] rather than the less formal "thou" [*ty*] form of address when communicating with cell-mates.[19] With this in mind, one can appreciate the humor in an event described by Anatolii Radygin:

> There exists a whole arsenal of devices [employed by the prison authorities] to suppress bursts of vanity and pride. During the initial interrogation, the questioner will, like an old friend, try imperceptibly to move into familiarity and use the winning and degrading 'thou' form of address ... A man who is afraid or who is attempting to gain the interrogator's 'sympathy' will not notice this change or will excuse it. A 'tough nut', on the other

hand, must show his teeth. When they brought I. Ogurtsov into Vladimir Prison, a KGB official, N. Obrubov, met him in almost friendly fashion, 'A-a-a, Igor', I know *thee!*' Ogurtsov immediately answered in tone, 'A-a-a, Kolia [a nickname], I know *thee* too'. Naturally, Obrubov immediately went over to the 'you' form of address required by the regulations. But he revenged himself skilfully and for a long time for this show of pride...[20]

It is reported that Ogurtsov's behavior at first irritated a number of cell-mates but that most eventually came to respect him and that many fell under his influence. One liberal dissident, who was a fierce opponent of VSKhSON's ideas, changed his opinion of Ogurtsov completely after meeting him in person in Vladimir. He stated that he found the VSKhSON leader an "exceptional" individual, not at all what he had expected.

On February 15, 1974, seven years elapsed since the date of Ogurtsov's arrest. He was accordingly released from Vladimir Prison and sent off to camp V.S. 389/35 in the village of Vsesviatskaia, Perm' Province. He arrived on March 1st. The authorities were no doubt somewhat jittery about transferring this iron-willed natural leader to a community of political prisoners, but they probably hoped that his physical debilitation would reduce his influence. Once Ogurtsov had arrived in Perm':

... he began to rest up physically and morally from his lengthy and difficult incarceration [in Vladimir]. For the first time in seven years he was able to breathe fresh air, observe a blue sky not covered by a barbed wire netting, see the sun, walk freely about an area significantly larger than that of a small cement prison exercise yard. After a week of

quarantine, he began to work on general projects . . ."[21]

Three weeks later, however, Ogurtsov was suddenly removed from the camp and transferred to the Perm' Municipal
Jail, where, on April 4th, he was placed in solitary confinement. In answer to queries, the head of the jail replied
that Ogurtsov had been transferred to Perm' for a "psychiatric examination." The local procurator added the information that this was being done on the recommendation of the
psychiatrist of Vladimir Prison, Rogov.[22]

Chronicle of Current Events No. 32 tells us something
more about this Dr. Rogov and his relationship to the
VSKhSON leader. In May, 1973, using an assumed name
and posing as a laryngologist, Rogov had examined Ogurtsov
in Vladimir Prison. Having finished, he then told Ogurtsov
that he had acquainted himself "with his case and [per-
sonal] correspondence" and had concluded that Ogurtsov
was suffering from "rheumatism of the brain [*revmatizm
mozga*]." The VSKhSON head immediately submitted a
written protest to Butova, the head of the prison medical
unit, who had been present at the examination. Soon Rogov
was named the psychoneurologist of Vladimir Prison. In
that capacity, he summoned Ogurtsov on February 8, 1974,
for an examination. The latter, however, refused to appear,
claiming that there was no reason for such an examination,
since he had made no complaints and the prison administration had passed no resolutions concerning him.[23] According
to the *Chronicle,* therefore, the authorities had carefully
prepared the ground for declaring Ogurtsov insane before
sending him off for a trial period to the Perm' camps.

It is certainly no secret that under Khrushchev and, especially, under Brezhnev psychiatry has been used in the Soviet
Union as a tool for political repression. Dissidents, nationalists and religious believers have been arrested, declared
"schizophrenics" and immured in special prison psychiatric

hospitals. A renunciation of one's "anti-Soviet" convictions and a promise to cease one's undesirable activity in the future earns one his or her freedom. Steadfastness in adhering to one's beliefs, on the other hand, can lead to long years of incarceration at close quarters with the genuinely insane. This happened in the well-known case of Major-General Petr Grigorenko. A convenient collection of documents relating to the misuse of psychiatry in the USSR, entitled *Abuse of Psychiatry for Political Repression in the Soviet Union*, was published by the U.S. Senate Committee on the Judiciary in 1972, and important new materials have recently appeared in the British journals *Survey* and *Index*.[24]

One can grasp without difficulty why Ogurtsov's parents became "extremely agitated" when they heard of their mentally alert son's forthcoming psychiatric examination. They immediately wrote the Committee on State Security [KGB] and Ministry of Internal Affairs asking that this unjustified examination be cancelled in order to avert a crime being committed: the internment of a mentally healthy person in a hospital for the insane.[25] The answers they received were evasive, avoiding discussion of the central issue. On May 17, 1974, Ogurtsov's father flew to Perm' in the hope of discovering the true reason behind the threatened examination. There he was refused permission to see his son on the grounds that they were planning to send him off to Moscow or perhaps Leningrad or Tashkent for examination. In private conversation with Ogurtsov's father, the head of the Perm' prison expressed the opinion that his son was mentally a perfectly healthy individual; he was at all times proper and polite in his behavior and never made any remarks or caused any difficulties for his jailers.[26]

On May 30th, Ogurtsov's father wrote to the Assistant Attorney General of the USSR to protest both the unlawful forthcoming psychiatric examination and the fact that, having served his sentence in full in Vladimir Prison, his son was once again, illegally, being held in a prison and deprived of meetings with his relatives. As before, an evasive answer was received. Throughout the month of May, Ogurtsov was held in prison awaiting an examination which did not take place. Then, on the 30th, he was suddenly taken off on transport to Mordovia. There on June 14th, "being psychically a perfectly healthy man," he was interned in the psychiatric ward of a hospital in the village of Barashevo, Ten'gushevskii District, Mordovian ASSR. In this hospital:

> he lives under conditions completely inadmissible for a healthy man, conditions which are unnatural and utmostly degrading for one's sense of human worth. He has been placed in a common ward with truly insane persons and is locked in with them for 22 hours a day (2 hours are permitted for exercise). He wears a striped jacket, the assigned uniform of the insane, and is taken out for exercise in only his underwear, accompanied by a male nurse. He is deprived of the possibility of even reading newspapers, let alone journals and books.[27]

Ogurtsov's parents had an opportunity to speak with the director of the hospital's psychiatric wing and were told that their son had been sent there for *observation*. Asked his opinion of Igor's mental health, he replied that he thought him to be psychically sound but refused to give any assurances that such would be the final verdict, citing "certain special orders relating to state criminals."[28] The doctor who had originally received Ogurtsov into the hospital's isolator was also of the opinion that he was of sound mind. Thus, a person perfectly healthy in his mind was put, without a preliminary examination, into close quarters with the genuinely insane. One can scarcely avoid agreeing with A's conclusion that, in so doing, the regime was seeking to "destroy his normal psyche" and thereby rid itself of a gifted opponent.[29]

Fortunately for Ogurtsov, dissident circles and the Western press learned of his plight and undertook to publicize it. A number of Western newspapers carried accounts of his ordeal under such headings as "Russia May Rule Dissident Insane."[30] One foreign correspondent, Julian Nundy of Reuters News Agency, was expelled from the Soviet Union for reporting on Ogurtsov and Orthodox priest Dimitrii Dudko. This expulsion prompted a statement in Nundy's support by Academician Andrei Sakharov, who reported, "I have been kept regularly informed on these two cases [i.e. of Ogurtsov and Fr. Dudko] and can only confirm the accuracy of Nundy's reports."[31] Vladimir Osipov sent a letter of appeal, dated May 25, 1974, to Sean MacBride of Amnesty International asking him and his organization to "come to the defense of one of the noblest and most courageous Soviet dissidents Igor' Ogurtsov."[32] As a result of such publicity, *Chronicle of Current Events* No. 33 was able to report that Ogurtsov had in September, 1974 (i.e. after three months of internment in a mental hospital) been returned to the Perm' camps.[33] Shortly thereafter, the same issue of the *Chronicle* informs us, he joined other prisoners in signing a protest to the International Red Cross. One of the abuses mentioned in the document is the incarceration of mentally healthy individuals in Soviet prison psychiatric hospitals.[34]

As the authorities had a problem deciding what to do with Ogurtsov when he arrived in the Perm' camps in 1974, so they had difficulties in resolving the fate of Mikhail Sado when he was transferred from Vladimir Prison to Mordovia in April, 1969. First he was placed in camp 11, then 17, then in a mixed zone, and finally assigned to work in the hospital of camp 3.[35] The administration seems to have decided that a job as furnace stoker for a hospital would minimize his influence on his fellow prisoners. He was, how-

ever, able to meet those placed in the hospital; with camp
conditions in mind, one can understand that this number was
not small.

"In general it's boring without the boys," Iurii Galanskov
wrote his mother from the hospital in late November, 1969.
"Only Mishka Sado visits me in the evening. I'd like to treat
him to coffee, but I don't have any..."[36] The following
month Sado wrote this card to Galanskov's sister:

> My dearest Elena!
>
> I greet you and your mamma with the New Year
> and the Nativity of Christ. I wish all of you good
> health and happiness in the coming year. May this
> year return your Iura to you and bring joy to
> your family.
>
> With regards to all of you,
M. Sado
28.12.69 Barashevo, Mordovia[37]

While in the hospital, Aleksandr Petrov-Agatov had a
chance to deepen his acquaintance with Sado, whom he had
previously met only briefly in one of the camp zones:

> Before I had time to enter the [surgical] ward...
> Mikhail Iukhanovich flew in. We embraced, kissed.
> They say that everything in a man begins with his
> eyes. If they shine, the man shines. If they are
> clouded, the man is a cloud. Mikhail Iukhanovich's
> eyes shone. Deep and dark, they preserved wisdom
> and grief in their lowest depths; the light of his
> soul and his love flows up to the surface. His face
> is lusterless, his lips thick (the sign of a broad na-
> ture) and his thick beard is like a black half-moon.

'I'll bring you some warm pajamas immediately, if you'll permit me . . .'

Tact and deep, non-superficial culture could be sensed in this man, in his every word and gesture.[38]

And in his "The Russia They Don't Know" Petrov-Agatov writes:

Sado speaks little. Like a full teakettle, he is silent most of the time. He treads the earth with a sure stride and open mien. He sees straight into the heart. And not so much with the eyes as with the heart. Yes, yes, he looks with the heart into the heart.

For a long time I tried to discover what his most outstanding trait was and why he was always surrounded by people. They used to surround him in Petersburg [Leningrad]; a varied, ill-matched lot . . . students and scholars, simple peasants and highly-educated intellectuals.

When Sado was jailed, a well-known specialist in Eastern Studies, a man with a world reputation, sought a way to send Mikhail Iukhanovich a friendly word.[39]

The account continues:

Now he is working as a stoker, and one can see him more often covered with coal and soot than with a clean face framed, as in an icon, by a beautiful black beard.

Nevertheless, there are still always people around

Sado. Ukrainians and Armenians, Jews and Latvians, and Estonians . . . Germans, and Russians of course . . .

'What is Sado's peculiar attraction?' I asked myself.

When people are cold, they look for a fire, a warm hearth. Mikhail Iukhanovich is like an eternally burning bonfire. People warm themselves near him. In his proximity the knots of contradiction are broken. Here enemies are reconciled and stretch out their hands to one another . . .

Recently Mikhail Iukhanovich was permitted a visit from his wife. God only knows how he managed to smuggle groceries out of that room since Soviet law forbids the bringing of food into the camp zone. For prisoners a taboo is placed on everything; all is forbidden.

Mikhail Iukhanovich smuggled it out. Sausage, oranges and red caviar, the last-named of which, in the words of the old-timer prisoner and artist Iurii Evgen'evich Ivanov, is sacrilege in a labor camp.

Sado smuggled it out—and gave it all away. And not only to his close friends; he still uses every convenient occasion to send these dainties to other [Mordovian] camps, to members of the [Social-Christian] union and simply to other prisoners, even those with whom he is unacquainted.

'Love covers all!' said the Lord.

'Love one another! Love one another!' St. Paul constantly repeated.

I think that such a love is precisely the basic, distinctive trait of Sado's personality.

This love both enligtened and continues to illumine him. From this love comes his knowledge; from it comes his constant, inextinguishable fire.[40]

In both the Mordovian and Perm' camps Sado entered wholeheartedly into the life of the political prisoners, participating in hunger strikes and signing various petitions and letters of protest. Shortly before meeting Petrov-Agatov in the camp hospital, for example, he joined Galanskov, Ginzburg, Borodin, the prisoner-artist Iurii Ivanov and others in a hunger strike provoked by the refusal of the administration to give Latvian convict Kalnyn'sh a package rightfully his.[41] Sado also seems to have run a kind of discussion group. "This evening I'll bring you some sweets," he tells Petrov-Agatov. "And I'll come for you. We'll be very glad to see you in the furnace room. This evening is my turn of duty. Iurii Timofeevich Galanskov and Vania Cherdyntsev—tried together with Dragosh—will be there. He is a sympathetic person. Like myself, he [Cherdyntsev] was recently transferred from Vladimir."[42] Shortly before his death Galanskov reportedly became a "Russian patriot."[43] One wonders if this was not due in part to Sado's influence. The Russian patriotism of an Assyrian might well have attracted the interest of a "democrat." As for Cherdyntsev, a former *zapadnik* [Westernizer], when he was eventually released from imprisonment, he joined the Russian nationalist journal *Veche*.[44]

Sado's paternal concern for the VSKhSON members in the camps emerges from Petrov-Agatov's account. He asked about all of them and wept when the poet opined that "many of their group [VSKhSON] were not ready for anything serious."[45] Sado's religious mysticism is also stressed by Petrov-Agatov:

> Nikolai Viktorovich Ivanov, an art instructor at Leningrad University... had a dream after the trial: Sado enters a church and orders all members of the organization:
>
> 'On your knees! On your knees all of you! Repent!'
>
> And all the members of the Union, who had somewhat compromised themselves during the investigation, kneel down and pray, pray...
>
> Why Sado?
>
> Why not Ogurtsov, who behaved irreproachably during the investigation and trial and was a model of courage and resolution? Why was it Sado that Ivanov dreamed of?
>
> Sado himself recently saw Christ in a dream, Christ descending from heaven.
>
> 'The Saviour! [he cried out in the dream] Look, the Saviour! On your knees all of you!'[46]

Presently interned in camp 36 of the Perm' complex (Ogurtsov is in camp 35), Sado has five difficult years to go before he will at last be reunited with his wife and two children.

CHAPTER X

Soviet Communism:
A Totalitarianism Worse
Than Fascism

> "The Communist attempt to build a
> new world and rear a new man has
> only resulted in the creation of an in-
> human world. Since it is the sickly
> offspring of materialistic capitalism,
> Communism has only succeeded in de-
> veloping and bringing to fruition all
> the harmful tendencies inherent in
> bourgeois economics, politics and ideol-
> ogy. This is the source of the striking
> similarity between Communism and
> Fascism."
>
> (VSKhSON Program, Introduction)

IT WAS INDEED FORTUNATE THAT the VSKhSON leadership
had the prescience to send a copy of their Program to the
West shortly before the revolutionary organization was uncovered by the KGB. Without this document, our knowledge
of the underground union's goals and theoretical views
would be severely and frustratingly limited. While the text
of the Program which we possess suffers from a few minor
gaps in the early sections due to faulty photocopying, it is

165

nevertheless fundamentally intact. Its principal author, according to all the information presently at our disposal, was Igor' Ogurtsov. He alone of the four VSKhSON leaders made a theoretical defense of the program at his trial.[1] When one considers that this document was written by a young intellectual only twenty-six years of age, one can hardly but be impressed by its depth of analysis and topical sweep.

Despite certain self-evident flaws, the VSKhSON program compares favorably with other programmatic texts of dissenters which emerged in Soviet Russia in the 1960s and 1970s, e.g. Academician Sakharov's 1968 "Memorandum,"[2] the 1969 program of the "Democrats of Russia, the Ukraine and Baltic,"[3] or Solzhenitsyn's 1973 *Letter to the Soviet Leaders*.[4] It succeeds in avoiding the principal error of Sakharov and the "Democrats"—a generally undiscriminating application of Western liberal solutions to indigenously Russian problems. And it is far more detailed and specific in both its negative critique and positive proposals than is Solzhenitsyn's *Letter*.

The Social-Christian Program appears to suffer in particular from two defects, one stylistic and the other theoretical. First, there is its language. As Albert Boiter has suggestively observed, a Soviet dissenter faces great difficulties in discovering "how to project anti-dogma in a programmatic way without engaging in counter-dogma" and "how to express democratic thought in a vocabulary where every positive political concept has been emptied of its original meaning . . ."[5] It cannot be claimed that the Program has been entirely successful in coping with these problems. In places, Soviet rhetoric seems simply to have been stood on its head, and one can weary of all-too-frequent apostrophes to "the people." Still, despite a certain woodenness of expression, the Program generally comes across as well-organized and can, in places, make compelling reading.

The Program's second most noticeable flaw is its uncritically positive opinion of the West and, in general, the whole non-Communist world. (The program of the "Democrats" suffers even more flagrantly from the same failing.) Granted, the West looked more stable and appealing in the early sixties than it does in the mid-seventies, but one is nonetheless tempted to smile when reading of the "growing prestige of the United Nations," of a "world-wide tendency toward the greater unification of mankind and toward mutual ties" or that "the historical development of society has been directed toward increasingly greater civil liberty and more advanced ethical relations between men . . ."[6] Of course it is Soviet blockage of information which is primarily responsible for the Social-Christians' misapprehensions. And VSKhSON's excessive optimism about the West, which it sees as "being transformed and freed of its negative traits,"[7] does contrast rather pleasantly with the uniformly bleak view of the West held by virtually all contemporary Russian nationalists.

Whatever flaws the Program possesses pale before its immense political significance. The document's negative section, upon which we shall be concentrating in this chapter, represents an unsparing and total rejection of Soviet totalitarianism: its philosophy, economics and ideology. As S. has indicated, the Program's originality lies in its "complete and uncompromising break with all known and possible variations of Communist and Social-Democratic ideas, schemes and illusions. [It] considers Bolshevism as a whole to be a tragic stage in the national development and terms all of its practical manifestations immoral, inhumane and anti-national."[8] That VSKhSON arrived at such a position in 1964, when Khrushchev was still in power and "revisionism" yet in the air, is quite remarkable. Solzhenitsyn and the group of liberal Russian nationalists gathered about him began to articulate similar views only in the 1970s. Also, while the Program's negative critique clearly owes much to other writers, in particular Milovan Djilas and Nikolai Berdiaev, it is not a derivative text. Its assimilation of Djilas' and

Berdiaev's thought has been a creative one. By combining the Dostoevskii-Berdiaev critique of materialism and economic determinism with Djilas' exposé of the emergence of the Soviet political bureaucracy as a new ruling class, VSKhSON has come up with a highly combustible solution, one which could induce *angst* within the regime even today.

What follows will represent an attempt to summarize the Program's "negative" message. First, let us deal with its treatment of the historical question of how the Bolsheviks came to power in Russia. As VSKhSON sees it, this was due to the Bolsheviks' exploitation of the legitimate social and political aspirations of the populace at the beginning of the twentieth century. During this period "Russia was in need of significant social transformation."[9] Unlike many contemporary Russian nationalists, the Social-Christians support the February Revolution of 1917: "The bloodless victory of the revolution of February, 1917, which resulted in the fall of the autocracy, was made possible by the unanimous opposition of the great majority of the people. For a short period of time—from the February Revolution to the Bolshevik coup in October—the Russian revolutionary movement succeeded in winning all those civil liberties and political rights which should have led to a broad economic transformation of a democratic nature, a transformation which had temporarily been held up by the First World War."[10] The Bolsheviks, however, succeeded in derailing Russia from her proper and necessary path of development. How they were able to accomplish this is explained thus: "The absence of a sizable and stable middle class, the tense situation resulting from the accumulated dissatisfaction of the masses, widespread disorganization caused by military failures and the political illiteracy of the populace—these were the conditions under which the small but well-organized Bolshevik Party seized power."[11] The result of this coup was "a totalitarian system which has thrown the people back to the age of serfdom."[12]

As VSKhSON sees it, Russia's grim experience since the

Bolshevik *putsch* has been no historical accident. Rather, the merciless inner logics of Marxism-Leninism, a teaching "inimical to mankind,"[13] have been working themselves out on the Soviet populace. On the philosophical level, the Program draws attention to two tenets of Marxist-Leninist teaching: its militant atheism and its determinism. The philosophical essence of Communism is declared to be "the denial of the existence of the Divine foundation of the world and the repudiation of non-material values and man's spiritual freedom."[14] "By renouncing God," the Program asserts in another place, "Communism deprived man of his individuality and rendered him an object and means."[15] Readers of Dostoevskii's writings will experience little difficulty in grasping the reasoning behind these statements. Like Dostoevskii and Berdiaev, VSKhSON holds that the unique worth of the individual is entirely predicated upon the existence of a personal God. If there exists no "true God," then "there is no room for Man."[16] Why? Because if one rejects God, one becomes hard pressed to explain why a transient "thinking reed" should be of more worth than, say, an animal or an insect. Man easily can become a "means" to a higher End. A state or society which has repudiated God and moral law is quite free to carry out social "experiments" costing scores of millions of lives. Following statistician Ivan Kurganov, Solzhenitsyn maintains that Soviet Russia lost sixty-six million in the various stages of the Terror.[17] Neo-Marxist dissenter Roy Medvedev feels that 25-26 million would be a more accurate figure.[18] Neither estimate includes the 20 million Russia lost during the Second World War. By anyone's calculation, the Soviet *homme revolté* has produced a holocaust of mind-boggling dimensions.

Besides being aggressively and "religiously" atheistic, Communism, in VSKhSON's view, is also deterministic and utterly hostile to the notion of human freedom. The individual, family and nation are all reduced to economic categories, a process which undermines their uniqueness and indeed their very justification for existence. All "non-material values" and higher ethical strivings are declared chimerical. Marxism-Leninism's determinism encourages its adherents to be bold and ruthless in pursuing their ends; after all, they are merely assisting the "necessary" unfolding of historical inevitability.

The Terror, thus, is a direct result of the underlying philosophical tenets of Marxism-Leninism.

VSKhSON's assessment of Marxist-Leninist economics, which it sees as a "direct outgrowth" of Marxist "philosophical dogma,"[19] is scarcely more positive. Communism, the Program maintains, represents "an abnormal economic formation" which is "deeply reactionary."[20] "Marxist-Leninist economics leads to discord in the whole economy, to unproductive expenditure of labor and to a squandering of the national wealth."[21] The essence of Marxist economics is its relentless striving toward complete socialization of the economy, i.e. toward "the expropriation of the people as a whole and their transformation into proletarians."[22] Here, too, VSKhSON sees an internal logic at work. Communist ideology requires its adherents to seek the total abolition of all private property and the binding, in *de facto* slavery, of all citizens to their place of work. "The material base of Communist slavery is formed as a result of attempts to coerce society into socialized Communist consumption . . . The sphere of individual free consumption must constantly be narrowed. Wages must be reduced to payment-in-kind, meals at one's place of work, etc. Life is planned according to an official budget with mandatory conscription of labor. This path leads to the destruction of the individual, the family and the nation."[23] Unfortunately for the Communists, attempts to bind the populace to communes (Russia in the twenties, China in the sixties) have led to economic collapse and "the fanatics have been immediately forced to retreat."[24] In his recently-published article "Socialism" Solzhenitsyn's close friend the mathematician Igor' Shafarevich has come to remarkably similar conclusions.[25]

The Soviet economic system, which VSKhSON, with no pretensions to originality, terms "state monopoly capitalism," is seen as an unmitigated disaster for the nation. Communism carries out industrialization "by more inhumane methods than ever before" and completes "the process of the proletarianization of the masses begun by capitalism."[26] Industrial workers find that "forced labor" has replaced the "relative freedom characteristic of capitalist labor-relations."[27] They discover that Communist trade unions have no independence whatever from the state and that the new Party owner-monopolists are "much stronger than the capitalists."[28] Likewise, the intelligentsia is subjected to "cruel and subtle exploitation."[29] Female labor is put to use with unprecedented severity. Besides inflicting great hardships on women, this leads to the deterioration of the home. (Western feminists should be aware that the Soviet woman is normally forced to work whether she wants to or not; frequently this is with pick and shovel.)

Along with their expropriation of the large landowners, the Communists also uproot the peasantry. Collective farm workers, shackled to the estates of the Communist bureaucracy, become its "rural laborers."[30] Serfdom, putatively abolished once and for all in 1861, has been fully restored by the Soviets (a point also frequently made by Solzhenitsyn).[31] VSKhSON does not deem it necessary to mention the commonly-known fact that the essence of this new serfdom lies in the collective farmers' not being given their internal passports and therefore being unable to leave the farms.

Both Soviet industrial and agricultural policy have, VSKhSON maintains, led to calamitous results. "Socialist planning" in industry results in basic capital being plowed into "unprofitable branches" of the economy.[32] The collective farms have brought about "chronic backwardness in agriculture."[33] No marked improvement in the standard of liv-

ing of the populace is foreseeable. In fact, the Program con-
tends, it is in the regime's interest to keep the people on the
verge of destitution. Otherwise, they might begin to dabble
in questions unrelated to material survival.

Like Milovan Djilas, VSKhSON believes that the Bolsheviks, after destroying the former privileged classes, replaced them with a far more predatory "new class"—the
ruling Communist Party elite. "The establishment of a one-
party totalitarian regime and the transformation of private
property into state property become the preconditions for the
engendering of an omnipotent class of exploiters."[34] Although
the Communists have liquidated the pre-revolutionary forms
of property, "a new form, created as a result of socialization"
has come into existence.[35] The national wealth has passed into
the hands of the ruling Party bureaucracy, a class "far more
powerful than all the ruling classes of previous social systems."[36] Dissident Soviet writers, such as Solzhenitsyn in *The
First Circle* and Andrei Siniavskii in *The Trial Begins,* have
depicted the life-style of this new ruling elite: its opulence,
snobbery, satedness. Unlike Milovan Djilas, VSKhSON does
not ponder the interesting question of the extent to which
the "new class" is aware of its actual status. The Program
does, however, assert that this class, which it sees as utterly
parasitic, instinctively fears the expropriated "class of have-
nots" who are "compressed into a faceless enserfed mass."[37]

As socialization is the linchpin of Marxist-Leninist economics, so dictatorship is the "gravitational center" of its
political theory.[38] The unrestricted rule of the Party elite
over the populace, moreover, represents a *totalitarian* dictatorship. And totalitarianism, in VSKhSON's view, is "the
greatest evil known to history."[39] The Program contains a
number of highly illuminating passages on the mechanics of
Soviet totalitarianism. The twin foundations of the entire
Soviet system are: coercion and deceit. While the regime
can, whenever necessary, resort to "brutal terror"[40] and "mass
repression"[41] and can marshall "a whole monstrous system

of oppression,"[41a] spearheaded by the secret police, it cannot rely solely on terror. "Terror alone is not enough to support the Communist system."[42] Equally as important are the "veil of illusions" and "careful masking" with which it continually confuses the populace and defuses discontent.[43] Thus, to take an example we have already cited in passing, workers are granted trade unions. Although these unions "have nothing in common with the free trade unions of capitalist countries" and are deprived of "even a shadow of independence," they nevertheless serve "to create an illusion among the workers that they have their own class organization."[44] Similarly, citizens are offered access to a sham judicial system, which actually "carries out its punitive functions automatically," but provides an illusion of legality.[45] Thus, while the Communist dictatorship "in its very essence represents lawlessness," it is able to pose as a bastion of due process.[46] Such intricate and skilfully employed deceit is as much a key to the regime's survival as is its use of coercion.

In describing the phenomenology of Soviet totalitarianism, the Program does not neglect such "common occurrences" as "informers, mutual shadowing, blackmail, provocation, slander, corruption, torture and concentration camps..."[46a] But it chooses to concentrate on the system's muddling and warping of the human spirit. It points, for example, to the "gigantic factory of disinformation, *ersatz*-culture and falsification of history" which floods the nation with untruth and hopelessly confuses the populace.[47] The ruling Communist elite "strives to enslave the mind of a people and lay waste its soul."[48] It "encroaches upon people's feelings and thoughts" and "transforms its world-view into official state creed..."[49] Communist education, to which the regime grants careful attention, "stands for the fabrication of a rootless, faceless mass man."[50] An assault is launched upon the national religion and popular tradition, so that the "false religion" of Marxism-Leninism can be erected on their ruins.[51] Culture is castrated by the regime's insistence on

"Party-mindedness" [*Partiinost'*]. *De facto,* "culture is replaced by propaganda."[52] The new rulers even lay their hands on natural science and "violate" it so that its findings will conform to the dictates of ideology (the reference is to such episodes as the well-known Lysenko affair).[53] It is this penetration of ideology and the lie into all corners of life which makes Communist totalitarianism so difficult to resist. "A harsh moral oppression ... corrupts men in an atmosphere of all-pervasive hypocrisy."[54]

A central point made by the VSKhSON Program is that Soviet totalitarianism is a more "all-embracing tyranny" than Fascism. Although both ideologies are the "sickly offspring of materialistic capitalism," Communism is worse.[55] "While a Communist dictatorship concentrates all three spheres of social life into the hands of the Party bureaucracy, a Fascist dictatorship seizes only a political and ideological monopoly. The absence of [Fascist] Party control over the main level— the economic one—weakens the effect of its political and ideological yoke."[56] The economic coercion resulting from the Communist state's being the sole employer in a country affords it a benefit not accruing to the Fascists. Furthermore, "the Fascist Party does not form a parasitic, all-powerful class of exploiters similar to the Communist bureaucracy."[57] It hardly needs to be stated that the Social-Christians are no admirers of Fascism. The point of their comparison of Communism and Fascism is to stress that even a repugnant Fascist totalitarianism lags behind the Communist variety in the extent of its repression.

Another important point made by the Program is that Soviet totalitarianism represents a danger not just for the citizens of the USSR but for all peoples of the world. The promotion of "world revolution" is seen as inherent and vital to Communism.[58] The ruling political bureaucracy *has* to be aggressive in its external policy; the moment it ceases to be such, it will wither and disappear. Also, non-Communist nations serve as an undesirable alternative example

for the peoples of Communist countries. The fewer such nations, the better. For these reasons the Russian Revolution
has been "a painful historical lesson for the whole world."⁵⁹

What was VSKhSON's attitude toward Khrushchev's
"reforms" and de-Stalinization? The Program exhibits an
extreme skepticism concerning Communism's ability to re-
form or improve itself. "This system is such by nature that
it cannot improve without at the same time undermining its
foundations. Any improvement in it would result in the
ruling class losing its unlawfully gained right to rule
monopolistically in economics, politics and ideology. Freedom in any one of these spheres would inevitably lead to
full freedom and the liquidation of the totalitarian system.
Therefore this class will never voluntarily yield anything
without a struggle."⁶⁰ Communism, in short, cannot improve
without ceasing to be Communism. The system will not
"evolve" in a more acceptable direction but must, in a condition of decay, swiftly and as bloodlessly as possible be
overthrown by force. The struggle between "dogmatists"
and "revisionists" in the Soviet Union (and in the Sino-
Soviet dispute) simply demonstrates that Communism's
"much-vaunted unity is visibly crumbling."⁶¹ Revisionism is
a "negative and half-way movement" incapable of producing a program.⁶² The dogmatic wing of the Party is stronger
but suffers from its lack of "a broad social base."⁶³ In alter-
nating between repression and concession, dogmatism and
revisionism, the Communist regime will ineluctably approach
its ruin.

But how, specifically, does VSKhSON see Russia's liberation taking place? Primarily through *a recovery of its
sight.* "Revolution," the Program asserts, "first occurs in
the mind. A liberation from illusions is taking place; Party
propaganda and agitation have lost all influence."⁶⁴ As we
have seen, VSKhSON believes that totalitarianism needs to
deceive as much to coerce. Force alone cannot guarantee the
new class its continued power. "The true nature of this

class is becoming increasingly apparent to all . . . Its only aim is to hold on to its possessions and power at all cost."[65] Increasingly "isolated and alone," increasingly recognized for what it is by a resentful populace, the ruling bureaucratic elite must adopt the psychology of "occupying forces."[66] It senses itself that its doom is sealed.

A remarkably similar assessment of the regime's future prospects was penned in 1968 by the Russian Orthodox *samizdat* writer Boris Talantov. In his important essay "Soviet Society 1965-1968" he articulates a powerful critique of the system (like VSKhSON, he seems to have been influenced by Djilas' *The New Class*). At the conclusion of his essay Talantov asks, "What is the strength and weakness of the Communist Party of the Soviet Union?" He answers that its strength is in its "all-embracing, unlimited and uncontrolled power which permits it to keep the masses in submission and quickly to suppress any protest."[67] Its weakness, on the other hand:

is in the fact that the official ideology is no longer accepted by the broad popular masses and holds on solely by means of powerful, organized constraint (economic and administrative). No-one is any longer attracted by the idea of a Communist paradise, about which they speak as follows, 'The Communists deceive us with an earthly paradise, which they promise us in the future when we won't be alive, and *they* strive to build a paradise for themselves in the present. . . .' The popular masses see in the leaders of the CPSU, despite the fact that they profess to speak in the name of the people, only the leaders of the ruling class, which more and more is becoming an anti-popular force.[68]

To return to the VSKhSON Program, it is of the opinion that at the zenith of its power Communism is virtually invincible and "successfully suppresses any unrest."[69] Decaying Communism is another matter. The wave of anti-Communist demonstrations in Eastern Europe in the 1950s showed the extent of decay within the Soviet empire. Especially significant was the Hungarian Revolution:

> The first successful people's revolution broke out in 1956 in Hungary. The elementally inflamed resentment of the populace destroyed a tyrannical system within a few days. The stage sets were removed and reality revealed. All social strata of the populace were united. A real national front consisting of all fighters for freedom was formed ... Only a few agents of the secret political police defended the Party oligarchy ... The Communist Party fell apart ... The Hungarian Revolution of 1956 has enormous world-wide significance. It marked the initial awakening of the people from Communist hypnosis ... It became the prelude to the liberation of all peoples enslaved by Communism.[70]

VSKhSON of course overstates the parallels between the Hungarian and Soviet situations. Communism was imposed on Hungary after World War II by occupying Soviet troops, while in Russia it represents an indigenously imposed creed. Moreover, as S. has pointed out in his criticism of VSKhSON, Communism has sunk deeper roots into the popular psyche than the Program seems to perceive.[71] Russia's liberation from "illusion" must necessarily be a more difficult and protracted process than was the case in Hungary. Another factor is national temperament. Russians tend to be an extraordinarily passive people, whom it is most difficult to stir to action. Once galvanized, however, they represent a formidable power, as Hitler and Napoleon discovered. Yet, despite such cavils, we think that VSKhSON's central point is well taken. All indications point to the fact that the

Soviet populace no longer believes in the ruling ideology, and this *is* extremely important. As the Program astutely points out, we now have to do in the Soviet Union with a "despotism" rather than a totalitarianism.[72] And a despotism may be cast off far more easily than a totalitarianism.

Do events since 1964 tend to substantiate VSKhSON's predictions? The Program clearly anticipates the ephemeral nature of the Khrushchev reforms and would see the Brezhnev-Kosygin period as a "dogmatist" stage in the regime's degeneration. Recent Communist successes in South-East Asia and the West, on the other hand, would probably have surprised the Program's drafters. As has been pointed out, the Program's strength is in its analysis of the Soviet Union, not in its relatively uninformed comments on the non-Communist world. Still, one suspects that the VSKhSON leaders would argue that the USSR's recent external successes only marginally improve the regime's position at home. In fact Moscow's bankrolling of various foreign "liberation movements" is a sensitive issue, one which the Soviet rulers have no desire to publicize to a populace which might feel the money could have been better spent elsewhere. Coercion will not be able to hold a society which has regained its sight in check for ever. "World-wide collapse," the Program prophesies, "will ensue for this class [i.e. the Communist bureaucracy] precisely at the moment when it will feel that it has become all-powerful on earth and in heaven."[73]

CHAPTER XI

VSKhSON's Alternative Vision: The Third Way

> "Both capitalism and its sickly off-
> spring, Communism, can be overcome
> only through a Christianization of the
> entire life of society...Christianity
> opposes both egoistical individualism
> and personality-less collectivism."
>
> (Program, VI)

THE DRAFTERS OF the VSKhSON Program were well aware that no critique of the Soviet system, however devastating and incisive, would be sufficient to win the allegience of the populace. A "positive" alternative to Marxism-Leninism was called for, one taking into consideration the peculiarities of Russia's historical development and the national psychology. What they produced was a vision of boldness and considerable originality.

In reading the Program's "positive" section, one should keep in mind that its suggestions are *tentative* ones: "While promoting a Social-Christian program as the basis for the future organization of social relations in the country, the Union for the Liberation of the People is not hostile to programs which are different but close in spirit. The final choice

179

[concerning Russia's future] must be made only after the overthrow of the Communist dictatorship and the destruction of the statist system, under conditions of freedom and peace."[1] A liberated Russia will make the final choice concerning the desired shape of her government and society.

Though, like its "negative" section, the Program's "positive" part should in no sense be dismissed as derivative, it does show the influence of certain writings. Most significant of all would appear to be Berdiaev's 1924 programmatic work *The New Middle Ages.* While VSKhSON has modified certain of the philosopher's suggestions and passed over others, the book conceptually underpins much of the Program. Filtered through Berdiaev, an amalgam of ideas traceable back to the 19th century Slavophiles and Populists may be discerned in the "positive" section. Other writers, such as economist Wilhelm Röpke and Russian émigré publicist and religious writer G. P. Fedotov, may also have influenced the thought of the VSKhSON leaders.[2]

Another major influence are the demands and aspirations of the Russian people, as VSKhSON interprets them, at the time of the February, 1917 Revolution:

> The peasantry ... was striving for free use of the land on the basis of individual labor ... The workers were demanding the right to partake of the profits of industry and ... democratic control over production ... The intelligentsia ... were demanding a curtailment of the absolute power of the monarchy, the introduction of a constitutional system, judicial guarantees and civil liberties.[3]

Apparently VSKhSON felt that the populace basically desired the same improvements in the early 1960s as it did in 1917. A more contemporary influence are the aims and ideals, as VSKhSON views them, of the Hungarian Revolution of 1956:

> The common will of the populace rejected both the
> Communist path and capitalism ... The basic slo-
> gans of the revolution were: freedom of labor,
> a government of law, civil liberties and a renais-
> sance of national religio-cultural tradition. These
> are the main features of the program of the anti-
> Communist peoples' liberation revolution.[4]

Although of less volume in terms of pages than the
"negative" section of the Program, VSKhSON's "positive"
proposals are perhaps deserving of greater attention, as they
represent an attempt at liberal Russian nationalist theoretical
pathbreaking. It is also noteworthy that a number of these
proposals mesh with those advanced by Solzhenitsyn in his
programmatic *Letter to the Soviet Leaders.*

The Social-Christian positive program offers a sweeping
substitute for the philosophy, economics and politics of
Marxism-Leninism. On the philosophical level, it stresses the
inestimable worth of the individual human being (*lichnost'*—
literally, "person").[5] "The Christian religion attributes the
highest and most absolute value to the human personality..."[6] As opposed to the flinty anti-humanism of Communism, which sees the individual as an economic category,
"object" or "means," VSKhSON advocates a Christian *personalism* seeking to achieve "brotherly relations between
men."[7] This personalism, VSKhSON believes, represents the
only sure defense against a recrudescence of the Stalin Terror, which was largely due to the nation's enthrallment to
an ideology uninterested in the individual.

Before entering upon a discussion of VSKhSON's economic proposals, we should examine certain attitudes expressed in Berdiaev's *The New Middle Ages* which undoubtedly influenced the organization's views. Although
VSKhSON does not seem to share Berdiaev's strictures
against the West and even sees the West as gradually giving birth to "a free society where there will be no poverty

and all will have rights,"[8] the philosopher's criticism of classical capitalism and the economics of Western democracies appears to play a role in the Program's deciding what structures should be avoided. Berdiaev's critique of the West emphasizes two points in particular: (1) its inherent moral and aesthetic unattractiveness, (2) its special unsuitability as a model for Russia. Concerning the first point, he asks, "Is there much that is ontologically real in stock markets, banks, paper money, in monstrous factories which produce unnecessary goods or instruments for extermination, in external luxury, in the speeches of parliamentarians and lawyers, in newspaper articles...?...The whole capitalist system of economics is the child of devouring and annhilating lustful desire [*pokhot'*]. It could arise only in a society which had once and for all repudiated any Christian ascetism, had turned away from heaven and given itself over exclusively to terrestrial satisfactions."[9] To the secularized triviality and minimalism of the Western democracies Berdiaev prefers the medieval theocracies with their spiritual strivings. Not that he wants to return to the Middle Ages *tout court*. The medieval theocracies erred gravely in seeking to infringe upon "the freedom of the human spirit" and tried to effect the "Kingdom of God" by force. A synthesis of modern liberal respect for the individual and medieval spirit-centeredness is what must be brought about.

Berdiaev's second point—the particular unsuitability of Western democracy and economics for the Russian people— is expressed thus, "The Russian people is incapable of creating a middling humanistic kingdom...It is an apocalyptic people by the structure of its spirit; it is directed toward the end of history, toward a realization of the Kingdom of God."[10] Berdiaev is here simply elaborating upon the Dostoevskii *dictum* that the Russian people is an inherently maximalistic people of a "religious" cast of mind. For such a people, the West, with its calculation and "sensible" materialism can have little appeal.

The aim of VSKhSON's economic program is to enable the populace, through "personalization," to regain control of the economy, which has been alienated from it by the ruling bureaucracy. It seeks to achieve the opposite of Communist socialization, i.e. it desires the "universal differentiation" of property and national wealth among the populace.[11] In drafting their proposals, the VSKhSON leaders attempted to avoid two dangers: excessive state interference in the economy, and monopoly. "Christian Socialism" may be something of a misnomer for the economics being propounded in the Program. The term may well derive from a certain lack of clarity in Berdiaev's nomenclature. In *The New Middle Ages* the philosopher writes, "I am prepared to admit myself a Christian Socialist. But this is a very imperfect use of words. Christian socialism is not real socialism, and real socialists cannot abide it. Socialism, in the strict sense of the word, should be a term reserved for that current which, by external material-coercive means, wants to resolve the fate of human society. Such is not Christian Socialism. It only recognizes the injustice of the individualistic capitalist system."[12] The touchstone of Berdiaev's Christian Socialism is manifestly his antipathy to classical capitalism and not any commitment to collectivism. While VSKhSON advocates that the state should maintain control over transport, oil, mining, etc.—which would render it "socialist" for some—it also champions a widespread de-nationalization and de-collectivization, which might render it "capitalist" for others. Actually, like one of their mentors, Wilhelm Röpke, the drafters of the Program are trying to "grope over and above capitalism and collectivism" and promote an organic building up of society, which Röpke, disclaiming any originality, chooses to call "The Third Way" or "Economic Humanism."[13]

In kernel, VSKhSON's economic program is this:

Freedom of labor is only possible under a new,

personalized form of property which would bind labor and the means of production into one and place them at the disposal of the individual ... The Social-Christian system creates conditions under which each worker is provided the means of production with the help of special institutions. To accomplish this, a mixed economy must be created. And the widest possible personalization of capital and land must be carried out so that the national wealth will be accurately distributed among the populace and personalized property will be put to the service of social goals. The transfer of the means of production into the hands of the workers— something which preserves inviolate the fundamental condition of civilization: division of labor— leads to high productivity, unleashes popular initiative and liquidates proletarianization. Self-governing, personalized collectives, organized into national corporations, will become the decisive force in the economic life of the country. The obligatory result of such an economic order will be a balance between productivity and consumption and the distribution of the greater part of the national income in the interests of the majority. Only a Social-Christian economics can insure a decent standard of living for all, liberate labor and remove the material obstacles on the road to man's spiritual development.[14]

Let us now look at some of the ramifications of this economic program. First, ownership. VSKhSON's principal aim here is to expropriate the expropriators, i.e. to return the "collective class property of the Communist bureaucracy" to the populace as a whole.[15] In both agriculture and industry this policy, if applied, would have enormous repercussions. In agriculture it would of course administer the *coup de grâce* to the Soviet collective farms. The lands of "Great Russia" [*Velikaia Rossiia*] are, the Program proclaims, to be available to all desiring to work them. "They will have the right to farm them, either individually or in free union with other landholders. And they will have the right freely to dispose of the products of their labor."[16] While private agriculture will again become a possibility, VSKhSON seems to hope that the co-operative principle ("in free union with other landholders") will predominate. The Program advocates the granting of credit to farmers to assist them in obtaining farm machinery and in raising the level of agricultural production. It also stipulates that there should be no limit set for the number of cattle or poultry raised on a given farm. Behind VSKhSON's land policy there lies an obvious desire to resurrect the nation's agricultural greatness and make Russia once again the major grain exporter she was before 1917.

In one sphere the Program's land proposals strike one as a curious holdover from collectivist theory. The Program states, "The land must belong to the entire people as national property not subject to sale or any other form of alienation. Citizens, communes and the state may use it only on the basis of limited holding."[17] While it is not difficult to understand VSKhSON's desire to establish "maximum norms of ownership" and a "progressive tax" on land-holding,[18] one would think that an organization of personalists would want citizens to *own* the lands they work, something which would seem to satisfy a primordial human need too long ignored by the Soviets. But, while the Program would permit "the transfer of the basic land allotment through inheritence within the family,"[19] it does not fully restore land to the masses. As might be expected, VSKhSON reserves to the state alone the right to exploit the nation's mineral resources, forests and waters.

In industry and trade "freedom of labor" is guaranteed by the right of all workers to obtain credit enabling them to acquire the means of production.[20] All industrial workers also have the right to own land. As opposed to the Soviet system, where industries are owned by the "state," i.e. *de facto* by the ruling bureaucracy, the Program affirms that industrial enterprises and service industries "must be owned and directed by collectives which work or finance them."[21] Only small businesses may be owned by individuals, and the state may own enterprises only when private or collective ownership is unable to bring to life an enterprise vitally needed by the nation.[22] Collective ownership, however, is to be the norm. This is because VSKhSON wishes structurally to foster and encourage brotherhood and cooperation and to "embody" Christianity's ethical principles in economic practice.[23] Not only will most enterprises be owned by "free collectives" but profit-sharing will also be required. "The collective of each independent enterprise forms a single shareholding company (association)."[24] A normative share of the profits must be established for each worker, engineer, scientist and technician; these shares will be gradated in accordance with professional qualifications, thereby leaving a modest wage hierarchy.

In its economic program, VSKhSON seeks to find a middle ground between collectivism and *laissez-faire* capitalism. The state administers energy, mining, military industry, public transport and keeps a watchful eye out for monopolies and other dangers to a "free market."[25] "To coordinate the entire economy, all individual companies must be organized, without any harm being done to their autonomous rights, into single corporations according to the branch of industry to which they belong. Through these corporations the state will be able to perform its social functions: to thwart the formation of monopolies, to safeguard honesty of competition, to regulate taxation, to even out the distribution of goods among the populace and to offer financial help to needy enterprises."[26] The highest body of management will be the Corporation Chamber, on which both individual corporations and the state will be represented. As for banking, it "should not be a government monopoly" but should also "not be in the hands of private individuals."[27]

As VSKhSON sees it, the state should keep its hands off the economy to the maximal extent possible and let free cooperatives manage it. By encouraging profit-sharing, the Program seeks to invest employees with a real and vital interest in their place of employment and to foster brotherhood among workers. The underlying idea behind VSKhSON's economics finds expression in Berdiaev's *The New Middle Ages,* "The principle of competition will have to be replaced by the principle of cooperation. The principle of private property in its eternal foundation will be preserved, but it will be limited and spiritualized. The monstrous private wealths of recent history will not exist. There will also not be equality, but there will be no hungry and none perishing from need."[28]

Whatever Western readers think of VSKhSON's economic views, they should be aware that such ideas have great currency in contemporary Soviet Russia. Virtually all Soviet dissenters are united in considering the collective farms a disaster. Indeed, many within the regime may secretly agree. Were it not for the regime's fear that a retreat here would trigger off demands for a retreat in all spheres, Russia would long ago have de-collectivized her agriculture. Worker management of enterprises and profit-sharing are also schemes enjoying considerable support.[29]

Let us now move on to a discussion of VSKhSON's view of the state. The Program seeks a clear delimitation of the state's powers and prerogatives, a necessary step, of course, for effecting de-totalitarianization. "The Social-Christian view of the state does not confuse it with society. The state has certain specific and irreplaceable functions, which serve the common good and cannot be passed on to anyone else. The strength of the state should always correspond to those tasks which it is called upon to perform.

On the other hand, only in exceptional cases may the state be permitted to interfere in those broad areas which are the domain of social forces and individuals ... The real rights of citizens, both spiritual and material, are guaranteed when there exists a separation of the spheres of activity of the state and of private individuals. The political sphere, considerably limited, should primarily belong to the state."[30]

The Program, which in no sense pretends to be a constitution and attempts only to sketch in the broad contours of a post-Communist Russian state, stipulates that the government should be divided into four branches: legislative, executive, supervisory [*bliustitel'naia*] and judicial. While this separation of powers does provide for certain "checks" and "balances," the specific mechanics of their operation is not spelled out in detail.

The nation's highest legislative body is to be the Popular Assembly [*Narodnoe Sobranie*]. It is to be elected from "village and urban communes on the basis of proportional representation" and from "industrial and commercial corporations, associations of the free professions and from the organizations of political movements."[31] One has to do, thus, with a syndicalist structure. VSKhSON is strongly opposed to the Western concept of political parties' providing candidates for a nation's legislative assembly. Political parties are seen as too removed from the real interests of workers' cooperatives; their effect is only to bog a nation down in worthless and debilitating rhetoric. (Solzhenitsyn, incidentally, shares VSKhSON's strictures against political parties.[32]) As the Program puts it:

> The Social-Christian doctrine of state sees as positively evil any system in which power becomes a prize for competing parties or is monopolized by one party. In general, the organization of state power along party lines is unacceptable from the point of view of Social-Christianity. Society should

be able to participate directly in the life of the country through local self-government and the representation of peasant communes and national corporations (the latter being large unions of those engaged in physical and mental labor) on the highest legislative body of the country. Political currents and movements may be permitted to be formed without hindrance (without, however, taking on the character of parties) in order to allow open expression of opinion and to exert a beneficial influence on everyday decision-making.[33]

Syndicalism and a desire for decentralized government have long been popular in Russia. The Kronstadt sailors, who rebelled against the Bolsheviks in 1921 and were thereupon savagely suppressed, proclaimed "All power to the Soviets but not the parties" and wanted direct mass democracy through free soviets.[34] In *The New Middle Ages* Berdiaev forecasts that "the future will belong to a syndicalist type of society, but not of course in the sense of revolutionary syndicalism" and advocates "business-like professional parliaments" composed of representatives from corporations. These should, he feels, replace the "degenerate talking-shops" of the Western democracies.[35] G. P. Fedotov, feeling that "political parties ... are too distant from the productive process,"[36] also favors syndicalism, though he speculates about the possibility of a second legislative body which would be based on the territorial principle.[37] Solzhenitsyn, who has clearly been influenced by Berdiaev and considers Fedotov one of his "preferred readings,"[38] appears to be sympathetic to syndicalism. "Don't imagine that a republic automatically means bread and circuses for all," warns a character in *August 1914*, "What would happen? A hundred ambitious lawyers would assemble—and who talks more hot air than lawyers do?—and shout each other down. The people will never be able to govern themselves in any case."[39] Incidentally, it should be pointed out that both Berdiaev and Fedotov believe that under a syndicalist system of government the state will have to be strong, in order to umpire the competing desires of corporations.[40]

The executive, as VSKhSON sees it, should consist of a Head of State and a Cabinet of Ministers. Although the term is not used in the Program, VSKhSON evidently envisages a constitutional or "limited" monarch, one who, it seems, would have considerably more power than, say, Elizabeth II of England but less than Russia's last tsar. It should be clearly understood that the Program is *not* counselling a return to pre-1905 Russia. In this area, as in so many others, it seems to be following views expressed by Berdiaev in *The New Middle Ages:*

> The popular masses may themselves desire a monarch ... But, if monarchies are still possible, they will of course be of a new type ... For a long time I have been thinking, and I expressed this thought as early as 1918-1919, that we, especially Russia, are moving toward an original type which one could call a 'soviet monarchy' or syndicalist monarchy, a monarchy of a new social coloration ... The monarchies of the New Middle Ages will not be formalistic-legitimist monarchies. In them the principle of social realism will predominate over the principle of juridical formalism. Not estates will surround the monarchy, but social and cultural professions in a hierarchical structure.[41]

A revitalized monarchy, enjoying the respect and support of the populace and ruling the country in conjunction with syndicalist unions and corporations—this would seem to be VSKhSON's vision.

The Head of State, whom the Program terms "the representative of national unity,"[42] is to be elected by the government's supervisory body, the Supreme Council [*Verkhovnyi Sobor*], and confirmed by popular vote.[43] Probably VSKhSON had the election of Mikhail Romanov, the 17th century founder of Russia's last dynasty, by a Land Assembly [*Zemskii Sobor*] in mind as a historical model. In any case, popular assent to the monarch's election is an important element in the Program's view of his legitimacy. According to the Program, the Head of State will have the right to appoint and remove government administrators and will serve as commander in chief of the armed forces. He appoints a Prime-Minister and, on the latter's recommendation, a Cabinet. The government is then responsible both to the monarch and the Popular Assembly.[44] Above all, the monarch is intended to represent a *moral* force. He is elected by the nation's moral watchdog, the Supreme Council, and is prohibited from belonging to any political movement. The Program, unfortunately, does not answer a number of tantalizing questions, such as: Will the monarchy be hereditary? (Apparently not.) What will the powers of the monarch be vis-à-vis the Popular Assembly and vice versa? How much control will he have over the Prime-Minister and Cabinet? (It would seem that he can dismiss them at will.)

The Program provides for the emergence of a legal opposition to the government. "Specific conditions must be stipulated to insure the unhindered emergence of a lawful opposition in the Popular Assembly. This opposition would be able legally to criticize the government."[45] It should be remembered, however, that this opposition cannot take on the form of a political party. And, since the powers of the legislature vis-à-vis the executive are not spelled out by the Program, it is impossible to judge to what degree an opposition in the Popular Assembly could actually alter or reverse government policies.

The Supreme Council is intended as a major check against the "misuse of political power."[46] Possessing no "administrative functions or legislative initiative," it has the right to veto any law or government action "which does not accord with the basic principles of Social-Christian order."[47] One-third of this body is to come from the upper ranks of the Russian Orthodox Church hierarchy and two-thirds from outstanding representatives of the populace, elected for life. VSKhSON seems to have felt a need to institutionalize Julien Benda's well-known concept of *les clercs* as a counterweight to the power of the state.[48] Wilhelm Röpke, who explicitly approves Benda's idea, has expressed it thus: "There must always be standing above the government and independent from it a class of intelligent and reliable men who courageously represent those supra-national forces against the lurking tyranny of society . . . Since they represent what is highest and best, we must seek them first from amongst the representatives of religion . . ."[49] Because of Russia's sad experience with "socialist legality" and the "Stalin constitution," VSKhSON must feel that *moral* safeguards to abuse of power are at least as important as juridical ones.

The Program, however, does not neglect legal safeguards. The courts are accorded a vital role in resolving "points of contention" between the government and a corporation, the government and an individual, a corporation and an individual or between corporations.[50] The independence of the judiciary from the other branches of government, the Program asserts, "must be *de facto* established as a guarantee of the rights and liberties of citizens and society."[51] Judges are not to be removed from their posts except for reasons stipulated by law, and they may not simultaneously belong to any other profession. The Program also insists that they must possess "moral authority." The courts are to be for the use of all citizens. All are "equal before the law" and have the right to use the courts in defense of their constitutional rights.

In its proposals which concern the cultural and scientific spheres, VSKhSON seeks, first of all, to release these domains from the claws of the state. Like economics, they are seen as a sphere which should not be politicized through state interference.[52] While the government is obligated to support cultural and scientific activity, it may not tamper with such work, "The people's cultural development and the activity of cultural and scientific institutions must be independent of any compulsory control by administrative organs of the state."[53] No official methodology may be prescribed, and "free experimentation and competition between different points of view" must be guaranteed.[54]

In the areas of health, education and welfare, the state will retain an important role and be responsible for maintaining standards. Its grip, however, will be significantly loosened here also. Thus, while guaranteeing a secondary school education and system of public health for all, the state will not impede those opting for a private alternative. Universities will be granted autonomy. As for society's underprivileged, VSKhSON's "personalistic" philosophy will insure them a decent life, "All handicapped have the right to state social security benefits sufficient to insure them a dignified form of existence."[55] And in the sphere of housing the Program proclaims, "The state must rapidly provide individual housing for the entire population through offering credit and taking other necessary measures."[56]

Censorship is to be abolished and the "means of information"—radio, television, newspapers, publishing, etc.—are to be removed from the monopolistic control of the state. At the same time, the Program warns that, "Freedom of communication, however, presupposes full responsibility,"[57] i.e. those who use the media will be legally and morally accountable for what they say.

In the sphere of religion, the Russian Orthodox Church is to assume a role of great importance but is not to be "reestablished" in the strict sense of the word. VSKhSON implicitly accepts that the Church's submission to the state since Peter the Great has been an unhealthy phenomenon. "Since the full independence of the Church from the state can be achieved only on condition that the Church is not materially dependent on the state, the Church must receive sufficient support for its needs from common national funds."[58] All known religions will have the right to preach and to perform their rites freely.

In contrast with many contemporary Russian nationalists, VSKhSON is unabashedly universalistic in outlook. Here too its views coincide with those of Berdiaev, who writes, "Of all peoples in the world the Russian people is the most pan-human and universal in its spirit. This belongs to the structure of its national spirit. The calling of the Russian people must be the task of world union, the formation of a single Christian spiritual cosmos."[59] Berdiaev admits to being influenced in this sphere by Vladimir Solov'ev, the 19th century philosopher. While the universalism of the VSKhSON Program is an admirable quality, it does in places seem to be quite superficial, perhaps reflecting the superficiality of Solov'ev in this area (a point made by S.).[60] The Program's statement, for example, that, "Universal Christianity, which is in process of uniting, is laying the religio-cultural foundations for supra-national unity,"[61] betrays a superficial ecumenism, one, moreover, uncognizant of the marked decline of the influence of the Western confessions.

Perhaps the most glaring omission in the Program is its virtual ignoring of foreign policy and the sensitive nationalities question in the USSR. It is possible that VSKhSON decided to pass over these questions because of their potential divisiveness. The Program's references to the "peoples of Great Russia"[62] would lead one to think that its drafters saw Great Russia as a multi-national entity, something like Great Britain. One clear intimation of the Program is that the fall of Soviet Russia would be likely to lead to the collapse of the East European Communist regimes as well, "Those foreign countries in which Soviet forces are temporarily stationed can be offered help to initiate their own national self-determination on the basis of Social-Christianity."[63]

Fortunately, Bernard Karavatskii has given us a brief glimpse of the views of the VSKhSON leaders in these two important areas passed over in silence by the Program:

> The VSKhSON Program does not provide any information concerning the external politics of the new Russia. From conversations which I conducted with the leaders of the organization, it emerged that they intended to preserve the [Russian] state in its existing boundaries but, in practice, to offer all republics full autonomy, including independence in conducting their foreign affairs, i.e. the new state would exist as a federation of independent countries. The basic changes which would occur in Russia would lead to a shifting of the inflammatory point of the planet to China, which would remain, with its aggressive politics, the sole hotbed of a possible world war. A mutual assistance pact [*dogovor*] with Europe and America would be one of the first acts of its foreign policy. The normalization of relations with the U.S.A. and Europe would lead to the emergence of a belt of neutral countries, which would include Poland, Czechoslovakia, Hungary, Rumania, Bulgaria, Yugoslavia and Greece. These countries, once having become neutral, would bloom forth in the course of a few years, since they would have designated the enormous sums of money presently spent on armaments for the needs of the populace. Under these new political conditions, there would arise the preconditions for a world government, which would come into existence on the foundations of the already existing U.N. but would have significantly expanded powers. The new government of Russia would

not intend to offer any assistance to countries proceeding along the course of so-called 'Communism' but would instead direct all existing funds toward improving the material well-being of the peoples of Russia, since the giving of assistance to other countries is unethical when one's own people is lacking. It is self-understood that the politics of the present ruling Communists have brought the countries of Eastern Europe to full economic dependence on the USSR and that this dependence could in the future cause many misunderstandings. But the leaders of VSKhSON were convinced that these misunderstandings could be eliminated if Russia were to repudiate the politics of 'big brother' and consider all countries equal partners in negotiations.[64]

While, it must be stressed, these views do not represent "official" VSKhSON policy, they do provide a helpful insight into the organization's intentions. Although they may not be sufficiently "liberal" to satisfy some "democrats" in the Soviet Union, they are remarkably tolerant views if one remembers that they stem from a Russian "patriotic" organization. On many points they dovetail with those recently articulated by Solzhenitsyn.[65] Reading Karavatskii's summary, one can understand why non-Russians, such as Sado and Bochevarov, felt themselves able to participate in the organization and why several East Europeans assisted it in its work.[65a]

On the transfer of power from the Soviet Communists to their successors, the Program is quite clear: "Following the overthrow of the Communist dictatorship, state power must pass into the hands of a provisional popular-revolutionary government, which will immediately carry out all urgent radical reforms, work out a constitution securing [social] transformation and present it to a national referendum.

After this, normal state order must ensue. The provisional government must root itself in the local representative bodies which will be formed by the workers, peasants, intelligentsia, student youth and military."[66] The ultimate decision concerning Russia's future, thus, rests with the entire populace. VSKhSON's views remain merely suggestions. After the Communists are overthrown, the next priority, VSKhSON believes, must be to dismantle the entire apparatus of totalitarian control. Thus, the Communist Party, "which has lost all moral right to existence,"[67] should be abolished. Nürnberg-type trials should be held only for those *directly* responsible for "crimes against the populace and humanity."[68] The secret police, Communist state apparatus and Communist judiciary should be disbanded. After this is accomplished, Russian émigrés should be invited home and a statute for Distinguished Citizenship established "in the first instance for strugglers for national liberation."[69]

To conclude, despite a few questionable proposals, the VSKhSON Program should be recognized as a remarkable document, potentially capable of attracting broad support within the contemporary Soviet Union. It is certainly a misfortune for the regime that a copy of it succeeded in reaching the West. Were the Program put into effect, Russia would be able to breathe once again. The individual citizen would be free to select his profession, write and publish what he wants, move freely about the country and travel abroad. He would be eligible for public office and could even, without hindrance, attend meetings and demonstrations and form unions, associations and societies.[70] In his family life, he would be free from the long arm of the state, could bring his children up in the religion of his choice and send them to private schools, if he so desired. "The rights of the family," the Program maintains, "may not be infringed upon."[71] While the society brought into existence would undoubtedly displease some Western libertarians (one suspects that pornography, for example, would be prohibited), it would inevitably represent a marked improvement over the Soviet system. VSKhSON's society would be more "authoritarian" than the Western democracies but that may very well be what the populace *wants*. The great similarity of VSKhSON's views to those of Solzhenitsyn and his friends is also significant.

One feels safe in predicting that in the coming decade we will witness new variants of VSKhSON's "program" emerging in Soviet Russia.

CHAPTER XII

VSKhSON Encounters Veche

By February, 1975, the entire membership of the revolutionary union—with the exception of Ogurtsov and Sado—had served their sentences and returned to society. Only one of them, Sudarev, seems to have received permission to live in Leningrad. He found work as a translator of technical literature at a construction plant.[1] Several members appear to have been given menial jobs as added "retribution" for their crimes against the state. Thus, Veretenov, an economist by training, was assigned work as a loader in the city of Nevel', Pskov Province. Bochevarov, formerly an engineer, became a furniture polisher in a factory in Luga, Leningrad Province, while Konosov, previously a correspondence student and gas fitter, could only find employment as a loader at the Shushara State Farm near Leningrad.[2] (Vladimir Osipov thinks that those with an education in the humanities were victimized after their release,[3] but degree of participation in VSKhSON rather than education seems to have been the regime's criterion in assigning unattractive work.) Other VSKhSON members found more congenial employment. Miklashevich became a chief engineer in a factory making reinforced concrete materials. Ivlev found work as an engineer in a home construction bureau, and Ustinovich took up employment at the Luga Television Studio.[4] Since Osipov's January, 1972, report—on which the above information is based—several union members have been allowed to change their place of residence. Bochevarov, for example, now lives in Leningrad.[5] One former VSKhSON participant, Iurii Petrovich Baranov, died unexpectedly on February 21, 1970, only eleven days after being released from prison. He is buried in the city of Chekhovo. The death of this young (age 31) electrical engineer was probably due, at least in part, to the grueling conditions of his three years of confinement.[6]

In 1973 three of the revolutionary organization's more zealous participants—Ivanov, Borodin and Ivoilov—completed their terms. Ivanov settled in the village of Brykovy Gory, Vladimir Province.[7] Borodin, on the other hand, seems to have been in constant motion. First we find him living in Siberia,[8] then in Obninsk, a scientific community south of Moscow,[9] then in Kaluga Province.[10] The former high school principal is now classified as a "worker."[11] About Ivoilov's whereabouts and activities subsequent to his release, nothing is known.[12]

The *Chronicle of Current Events* reports that in March, 1974, Viacheslav Platonov was released from the camps and permitted to take up residence in the city of Tartu, Estonia.[13] It also states that on February 15, 1975, Evgenii Vagin and Boris Averichkin completed their sentences and returned to the outside world.[14] Where they took up residence is not mentioned.

When VSKhSON members who still had an appetite for reforming society emerged from the camps, they must surely have felt that history was moving in their direction. To discover why this should have been so, one must engage in some historical backtracking. As has previously been stated, Khrushchev's program of de-Stalinization and, in general, the events surrounding the 20th and 22nd Party Congresses had far-reaching repercussions in Soviet society. Indirectly, they paved the way for the emergence of a powerful neo-Slavophilism, i.e. a religious-based Russian nationalism.[15] For if the early years of the Khrushchev "thaw" had proved encouraging to neo-Marxist reformers and the proponents of various "socialisms with a human face," the failure of the regime to put Stalinism to rest had put a number of intellectuals on their guard. Once Khrushchev had been sacked, the Brezhnev-Kosygin "collective leadership" confirmed fears by undertaking a cautious but nonetheless real "re-Stalinization." Communism, it appeared, would not permit itself to be reformed. By the late fifties some intellectuals, such as Solzhenitsyn, were already moving toward various forms of Russian nationalism. As we have seen, by as early as 1962 Ogurtsov had lost all hope in the possibility of Soviet society improving itself and had begun to plan a revolutionary coup which would usher in a Social-Christian order.

By revealing at least some of the atrocities perpetrated by Stalin and by ordering the tyrant's remains removed from the Lenin mausoleum in Red Square, Khrushchev compromised Marxism-Leninism in the eyes of a great many Soviet citizens. An ideological vacuum was created which Khrushchev's hesitant and confused "revisionism" was unable to fill. Thus, Khrushchev unwittingly cleared the path for an ascendant neo-Slavophilism.

He paved the way in another sense as well. But, in order to understand this, some background is necessary. By the late 1930s it appeared that all religion had been extirpated from the face of the Russian earth. Only four bishops and a few hundred parishes remained of what had once been the mighty Russian Orthodox Church. The Nazi invasion of Russia in 1941, however, radically altered the Church's position. The massive onslaught of a superbly equipped and disciplined antagonist required that Stalin do everything to encourage and nothing to offend the populace. He therefore ordered a halt to anti-religious activities and, jettisoning the hapless slogans of "Soviet patriotism," appealed directly to *Russian* love of country. Bishops were released from the camps, parishes opened and the names of Russian generals of the tsarist past made respectable once again. In doing all this, Stalin was unquestionably tactically correct, as even his severest critics will grant.

Eyewitnesses testify to a remarkable explosion of religious feeling among the Soviet populace during the war. When the Germans permitted a carefully-controlled opening of churches on occupied territory, they were astonished to witness hundreds of Orthodox believers standing and kneeling outside completely jammed churches in the snow while two-hour services went on inside. Mass baptisms frequently occurred in which priests would scramble up to the rafters of a church and sprinkle the sanctified water on the masses below.[16]

After the war, ideological unanimity was reimposed by the regime with a vengeance, and the stifling period usually known as the *Zhdanovshchina* set in, which lasted until Stalin's death in 1953. The Russian Church, however, was, somewhat paradoxically, permitted to continue to enjoy a measure of the fruits of wartime *détente*. To be sure, her activities were strictly limited and controlled; some believers were arrested, anti-religious literature continued to be printed at state expense and the Church forbidden to reply, etc. But, despite such annoying restrictions, her influence continued to expand. In fact, it could be argued that by the late 1950s resurgent religious sentiment among the populace was already too strong to be suppressed.[17]

In 1959 Khrushchev launched a fierce assault upon "religious survivals," calculated to halt the inroads which religion had been making in the country since the Second World War. This campaign, which Solzhenitsyn has aptly termed a "late-blooming and frenzied atheism,"[18] continued unabated until 1964, when it began to be slowed down by Khrushchev's successors (for tactical rather than humani-

tarian reasons). In the period 1959-1964, some 10,000 Orthodox churches were forcibly closed and many, including a
great number of architectural treasures, razed. The fate of
the village church in Korshik, Kirov Province typifies the
"flavor" of the campaign. In March, 1963, a brigade of
workers headed by the chairman of the local Party District
Executive Committee arrived in the village:

> First they drank all the church wine. Then, having
> fortified themselves on wine, they began to tear
> out the icons, smash the highly-ornate carved icon-
> ostases with axes and to break up with hammers
> the expensive censers and other church utensils.
> All the icons, the iconostases from both sections
> of the church, the church banners, and all the old
> service books were burned.[19]

Clergy and laity who protested the onslaught were automatically subjected to administrative sanctions and the most
intrepid imprisoned or, on several occasions, murdered. The
forcible closure of churches, often carried out with maximum
effrontery to the sensibilities of believers, served to convince
many not only that the regime's *détente* with religion was
at an end but that it had only been tactical all along. Furthermore, the wanton destruction of many churches representing
national architectural treasures—not to speak of the burning
of icons and pulping of ancient church books—appalled
many intellectuals and served to push some in the direction of neo-Slavophilism. As we have seen, VSKhSON was
keenly interested in the Khrushchev persecution, which it
presumably saw as added confirmation of its belief that
Communism represents a "false religion" which will brook
no competitors, and used the letter of protest of two Moscow
priests, Frs. Eshliman and Iakunin, in its recruitment work.

The two factors we have been examining—the gradual
evolution during the late 1950s and early 1960s of a num-

ber of intellectuals away from Marxism toward Russian
nationalist views and the revulsion of the populace at the
brutal anti-religious campaign of 1959-1964 with its attendant razing of architectural monuments—fused dramat-
ically in the mid-sixties. In 1964, the same year that
VSKhSON was founded, a group of Moscow students
established the "Homeland" [*Rodina*] society after making
a pilgrimage to the ancient Russian towns of Zagorsk,
Suzdal' and Vladimir. By the end of the following year, the
organization had 500 members, mostly students of literature, physics and architecture.[20] The society's visits to reposi-
tories of medieval architecture appeared to show that they
were seeking a link to the past. The year 1964 also saw the
appearance of Andrei Tarkovskii's celebrated and controver-
sial film "Andrei Rublev," about Russia's greatest icon
painter, who is considered a saint by the Orthodox Church.[21]
In 1965 an "All-Russian Society for the Preservation of
Historical Monuments" was founded with the aim of halt-
ing the destruction of national monuments, particularly old
churches, and of restoring and keeping them in good repair.
A year after its official inauguration, this purely voluntary
society numbered three million; by 1972 its ranks had swollen
to seven million.[22] A similar organization, the "All-Russian
Society for the Preservation of Nature," dedicated to protecting the Russian environment, is reported to have recruited
19 million members by 1971.[23] As the remarkable growth of
such voluntary societies indicates, there is *mass* support for
Russian patriotic sentiments in the USSR. The Russian
Church represents an even broader base. Utilizing necessarily fragmentary data, such as officially-published burial
and baptismal statistics, one *émigré* specialist recently calculated that 115 million Soviet citizens remain at least
passively attached to Orthodoxy.[24] Solzhenitsyn appeared to
support such an estimate when he observed in mid-1974,
"In Riazan' Province, which I had a chance to observe more
than any other, up to 70% of the newborn are baptized,

notwithstanding all interdictions and persecutions, and at the cemeteries crosses are more and more crowding out the Soviet columns with their star and photograph."[25]

During the period 1967-1970, neo-Slavophilism seems to have been tolerated by the regime and apparently even tacitly encouraged by elements within it. To take one startling example, the journal *Molodaia gvardiia* [*Young Guard*]—no less than the organ of the Central Committee of the Komsomol—was *de facto* taken over by a group of neo-Slavophiles who proceeded to publish a series of extraordinary articles and poems having little in common with Marxism-Leninism. Anti-industrialism, anti-proletarian internationalism, and a lightly masked attachment to Russian Orthodoxy—such were just three of this Komsomol journal's heresies.[26]

The same years of 1967-1970 also witnessed a burgeoning of neo-Slavophile themes in *belles-lettres*. Vladimir Soloukhin's remarkable "Black Boards" (English title: *Searching for Icons in Russia*) may be taken as representative.[27] This period also saw a substantial growth in native tourism to Russia's historic sites; in 1971 fifty million Soviet citizens did the rounds, precisely double the number in 1964.[28] In addition, huge printings of up to 75,000 copies served to feed a growing interest in such subjects as Russian architecture and iconography.[29]

By late 1970 the regime had become concerned at this trend. In November, at a session of the Secretariat of the Central Committee of the Communist Party, the editor of *Molodaia gvardiia* was sacked from his post and the journal placed in "safe" hands.[30] This crackdown was only the first step in a wide-ranging assault on "russophilism" and *rusoznavstvo* [the desire for an excessive knowledge about Russia]. Nationalists were advised that an interest in old churches could be invidious and that the 19th century Slavophiles (Khomiakov, Ivan Kireevskii, etc.) had been reactionaries.[31]

The campaign proved incapable of stemming the rising tide of Russian nationalism. Two months after the firing of Nikonov, the *Molodaia gvardiia* editor, an important new *samizdat* publication made its appearance: *Veche,* named after the medieval Russian popular assembly. Its editor, Osipov, several of whose writings we have already treated at length, had been an adherent of Yugoslav socialism when sentenced in 1961 to the camps for a seven year term. When he emerged in October, 1968, his views had altered. In his words, "Not without reason is a concentration camp officially called a corrective labor colony. They come in atheists and go out Christians. They have been corrected..." And he continues, "The camp made me a man believing in God, in Russia and in the legacy of my forefathers."[32]

Veche sought to provide a forum for the debate over Slavophilism which had arisen, within strictly controlled limits, in the official press (i.e., in such publications as *Molodaia gvardiia* and *Voprosy literatury* [*Questions of Literature*]). Many of the journal's concerns, such as its desire to halt the razing of ancient churches, had already been aired in the official press. But, being a *samizdat* publication, *Veche* was able to tread ground prohibited to official journals. The straightforward commitment of the majority of *Veche's* contributors to Russian Orthodoxy and the journal's heated debate over Solzhenitsyn's *August 1914*—at a time when the writer could only be villified in the official press—showed the extent to which it could go beyond the cautious and often Aesopian circumlocutions of neo-Slavophile writings in Soviet publications. At its best, *Veche* unquestionably served a valuable purpose—it sought to preserve Russia's art, architecture, history, literature, philosophy and religious thought from nihilistic oblivion and to point up their contemporary significance and relevance. At its worst, the journal foundered in chauvinistic suspicion of the West and racist animosity toward Soviet Asiatics and Jews. Of one thing there can be little doubt, *Veche's* interests meshed with those of a not inconsiderable reading public. As Osipov put it to a Western correspondent, "We sought out readers after publishing the first number [of *Veche*] ... Now readers seek out the journal themselves."[33]

It is not overly difficult to grasp the appeal which *Veche* would have exerted for former Social-Christian revolutionaries. At least two of them—Georgii Bochevarov and Leonid Borodin—and probably a third, Nikolai Ivanov, became *Veche* "correspondents" after emerging from imprisonment. Borodin contributed an article under his own name to *Veche*, No. 8. And, in a related field of activity, Borodin and Ivanov signed a number of open letters and appeals originating for the most part from *Veche* circles. In December, 1973, for example, Borodin joined six other former political prisoners, including Osipov, in greeting Solzhenitsyn on the occasion of his 55th birthday. Since the novelist was decidedly a *persona non grata* for the regime at this time and was shortly to be expelled from the country, the open letter was an act of courage. It reads:

Dear Aleksandr Isaevich!

We, former political prisoners, greet you warmly on the occasion of your 55th birthday. In your person we acknowledge not only the most significant Russian writer of the 20th century but also one of the most courageous battlers against injustice and falsehood. The exploit of your life is like a candle shining in a dark world ...

We hope that your latest statements in defense of the prisoners of conscience Ogurtsov, Bukovskii, Platonov and hundreds of others and your wrathful accusations of indifferent public opinion abroad will finally force it to heed the voices coming from Russia.

We wish you good health and long years for the
benefit of the country.[34]

At the end of 1973, Nikolai Ivanov joined six former
political prisoners, including the well-known Orthodox dissenter Anatolii Levitin-Krasnov, in addressing the European
Conference on Questions of Security and Cooperation. The
letter, which is permeated by a strong religious tone, seeks
to draw attention to the severe malnutrition suffered by those
in Soviet camps and prisons and to show the frightening
human costs of a system of forced labor. It also discusses at
length how prisoners are prevented from carrying out religious practices.[35]

Veche's dissemination was viewed with growing irrita-
tion and apprehension by the Soviet authorities. Osipov was
repeatedly stopped on the street, searched, warned and
variously harassed.[36] He was urged to cease his visits to
Moscow. One issue of *Veche* (No. 7) was seized at the
typist's and a reconstructed copy reached the West with some
delay.[37] The KGB also seems to have done its best to sow
suspicion and dissension in the *Veche* ranks, not overly difficult considering the "decentralized" structure of the journal's network of contributors and the fact that many were
personally unacquainted. Sometime in late 1973 or early
1974 elements within the regime appear to have made an
attempt to co-opt at least some of *Veche's* participants.[38] According to Melik Agurskii, a Jewish activist who was closely
acquainted with a number of Russian nationalists before recently emigrating to Israel, this effort failed because the
Veche contributors found the neo-pagan national socialism
being proposed by their preferred "partners" out of keeping
with their Christian convictions.[39] In early March, 1974, matters came to a head, and *Veche* split into two factions, one
pro-Osipov and the other anti. The pro-Osipovites suspected
their opponents of cooperation with the KGB, while the
anti group accused their adversaries of moral turpitude.[40]

My own intuition (and that of L. Sergeeva of *Posev*) is that the majority of the accusations of both sides were unjust and that KGB disinformation and meddling were primarily responsible for the schism.[41] In any case, in March, Osipov announced that he was suspending publication of *Veche* with issue No. 9.[42] His opponents vowed that *Veche* would carry on and succeeded in publishing No. 10.[43] Then, in July, they too were forced to halt their activities.[44]

Once the KGB decided to sweep down upon the network of *Veche* editors, it found itself once again acutely interested in former VSKhSON squad leader Georgii Bochevarov. As the No. 32 (July 17, 1974) *Chronicle of Current Events* reports:

On April 1 [1974] the Leningrad KGB conducted searches at the homes of *Veche* contributors G. N. Bochevarov and P. M. Goriachev, and also at V. E. Konkin's ... As the tenth issue of *Veche* informs us in its chronicle section, all numbers of *Veche* were seized, as were Goriachev's typewriter and a 'Memorial to the Victims of Stalin's Cult of the Personality', compiled by Bochevarov. The 'memorial' [*pamiatnik*] is a list of the names of 1500 top Party and state activists and of persons in science, literature and art who perished as a result of Stalinist arbitrariness or who committed suicide. The name of each of the deceased is accompanied by short biographical details and a photograph. Literary appendices to the 'memorial', compiled by Goriachev, were also seized.

The following day all three were summoned to the Leningrad KGB for interrogation. The interrogations mainly concerned the journal *Veche*. To one of those being questioned the investigator declared that to them (i.e. evidently to the KGB) there arrive hundreds of letters demanding that Stalin be rehabilitated.[45]

Bochevarov, thus, owns the somewhat dubious honor of being the first VSKhSON member to undergo interrogation and have his flat searched *after* his release from prison. The reader with a long memory may recall the name of V. E. Konkin as well. While not formally a member of the underground union, Konkin helped its leaders during the period of crisis initiated by Aleksandr Gidoni's informer's report (see Chapter VI).

In June, 1974, it became known that the KGB of the city of Vladimir was conducting a case in connection with the journal *Veche*.[46] (The case's number was thirty-eight.) The reason the investigation of *Veche* was assigned to the Vladimir secret police was that Osipov and a number of other important contributors to the publication (including, probably, Nikolai Ivanov) lived in Vladimir Province. An example of the KGB's activities is provided by *Chronicle* No. 32:

> [Moscow mathematician Iurii] Gastev was interrogated at the Vladimir KGB by senior interrogator Major P. I. Pleshkov, heading up 'investigative case No. 38'. The investigator was interested in whether Gastev was acquainted or 'maintained ties' with V. N. Osipov, G. N. Bochevarov, P. M. Goriachev and V. E. Konkin . . . Gastev declared that he had no relationship either to the publication or dissemination of *Veche* and that he did not consider *Veche* or the papers seized from him to be criminal in content. To the question where had he received the papers from, he declined to answer.[47]

During the same month of July, Bochevarov, Konkin and other *Veche*-ites were summoned for interrogation.[48] It was this relentless KGB persecution and intimidation which brought about the final demise of *Veche* that month. From the *Chronicle's* account, it would appear that Bochevarov's role in editing the journal had not been a small one.

Veche had been suppressed. Or had it? The September 6, 1974, *Le Monde* reported the appearance of a new *samizdat* publication entitled *Zemlia* [*The Land*]. Its editor: a certain Vladimir Osipov "qui a déjà eu des difficultés avec le K.G.B." According to *Le Monde*, the new journal was consecrated to "the resurrection of national morality and culture among the Russians." Subsequently, the first issue of *Zemlia*, which contains 170 pages and is dated August 1, 1974, arrived in the West. Its most noteworthy contributions concern the persecution of the Russian Orthodox Church—in particular the tribulations of intrepid Orthodox priest Fr. Dimitrii Dudko—and the spoilation of Moscow's architecture.[49] Although the KGB did not refrain from making its acute displeasure at the contents of this new journal known, Osipov and his young assistant, concentration camp graduate Viacheslav Rodionov, forged ahead and on November 25th released *Zemlia* No. 2. Like the first number, No. 2 contained a contribution by Solzhenitsyn's friend, the liberal nationalist Igor' Shafarevich, and materials by Fr. Dudko.[50] Three days later Osipov was arrested, but his deputy editor, Rodionov, ringingly declared that he and the journal would not be intimidated:

The editor of the journal *Zemlia* is arrested. I, his assistant, am threatened with no less harsh repression. They openly declare (Investigator Pleshkov) that people were correctly sentenced in the Beriia era and that they will likewise sentence us. But just as openly I, the assistant editor of a Russian national journal, declare that the task of an uncensored press will not be stopped in Russia. Problems of national unity, culture, conscience and faith have already matured and can no longer be stopped by any repressions.[51]

To those threatening him Rodionov firmly asserts, "The journal will continue to come out." And he concludes with the liturgical refrain, "God is with us! [*S nami Bog!*]"

On the day following Osipov's arrest, sixteen dissenters signed a protest against the regime's action. Two signatories—Borodin and Ivanov—were former VSKhSON members. Three others—Shafarevich, Agurskii and Vadim Borisov—had contributed to *From under the Rubble,* a liberal nationalist collection assembled by Solzhenitsyn before his expulsion from the Soviet Union. On December 28th, Osipov's wife, Valentina Mashkova, lodged a protest of her own, "On November 28, 1974, my husband Vladimir Osipov, who for a long period of time was the editor of the Russian Christian journal *Veche,* was arrested by the organs of the KGB. I, his wife—who in the past have spent eleven years in the political camps for participation in the democratic movement and who gave birth to my first child in an investigative prison and am now seven months pregnant—I am being subjected to shameless provocations from the KGB in connection with my husband's arrest."[53] Besides physical intimidation, the KGB's chief threat against Mashkova was that they would take her child away from her once it was born.

Not long after the appearance of the first issue of *Zemlia,* the authorities must have been dismayed to learn of the publication of a *second* Russian patriotic *samizdat* journal: *Moskovskii sbornik* [*Moscow Miscellaney*], whose compiler was former VSKhSON member and *Veche* contributor Leonid Borodin. In his opening compiler's statement—written as much, it would seem, for the security organs as for his readership—Borodin stresses that the sole purpose of his publication is to communicate *samizdat* writings on religious and national themes. The journal is neither

"ideological" nor "political" in intent and pursues no organizational aims; nor is it geared at a mass reader. It has
no permanent editorial board or circle of authors and intends
to publish only materials already circulating in *samizdat*. The
journal is to appear on a bi-monthly or quarterly basis.[54]

Roughly speaking, *Moskovskii sbornik* represents a "cen-
trist" neo-Slavophile publication while *Zemlia* is of a "liberal" neo-Slavophile tendency.[55] One should, however, be
cautious in seeking to discern vast differences between the
two journals. Both share considerably more views and as-
sumptions than they differ upon. Each, for example, is
acutely interested in the fate of the Russian Church, and
both gave detailed coverage to the Fr. Dudko "affair." Each
manifests a deep admiration for Solzhenitsyn and a venera-
tion for the memory of Iurii Galanskov. Finally, each opens
its pages to non-Slavophiles and shows respect for members
of the other camp.[56] The major difference between the journals seems to be in their attitude toward the liberal, Western-
ized "democratic movement." *Zemlia's* attitude is essentially
one of tolerance, while *Moskovskii sbornik* is quite sharply
polemical. It is noteworthy that Anatolii Levitin-Krasnov,
politically a *zapadnik* though he is Orthodox by religion, is
a contributor to *Zemlia* and the object of a heated attack in
Moskovskii sbornik.[57]

Having now completed a necessarily sketchy survey of
contemporary neo-Slavophilism, we should like to focus in
upon the evolution of the thought of two VSKhSON members since the time of their arrest in 1967. The first of this
pair is Evgenii Vagin, formerly director of VSKhSON's
"ideological division." Our information on him comes from
Iurii Handler, who spent two years together with Vagin in
a concentration camp brigade and had numerous discussions
with him.[58]

After his arrest, Vagin consciously sought to become independent of Ogurtsov's intellectual influence. In the camps
he discovered his interest in politics to be waning while his

interest in religion increased. He studied the Old and New Testaments and Russian religious thought of the 14th-16th centuries (i.e., the period anteceding Russia's "westernization" and witnessing the greatest flourishing of Russian iconography). His chief interest became religious and philosophical thought, and his preferred thinkers were Dostoevskii, Berdiaev and Konstantin Leont'ev. He also liked Fedorov and Nikolai Gogol's *Selected Passages from Correspondence with Friends.*[59]

Politically, Vagin became more of a monarchist than he had previously been. He believes that it is necessary for lawful "authority" [*vlast'*] to return to Russia. Deep down, he feels, even the present leaders of the Soviet Union realize that they are "pretenders" [*samozvantsy*] and have no legititimate claim to power. Since the last lawful authority in Russia was the Romanov dynasty, Vagin advocates its restoration. He also holds that a monarchy should be hereditary. Vagin admires the present British monarchy but feels that the sovereign should have more power than Elizabeth II enjoys. Most importantly, the monarch should have *moral* authority. In Russia, Vagin stresses, there is a great desire to find and respect authority. And this, he insists, is not equivalent to marking an "idol" of authority. Like Solzhenitsyn, he believes that freedom can exist under an authoritarian system,[60] but he is decidedly opposed to any return to the pre-1905 form of monarchy and feels that the mistakes of that system have to be corrected. In his views on monarchy, then, Vagin would appear to differ from the VSKhSON Program both in his desire to restore the Romanov dynasty and in his favoring of hereditary succession.

Vagin believes in one, indivisible Russia and is categorically against breaking up the union of Russia, Belorussia and the Ukraine. The Russian state, he maintains, is *by nature* a multi-national state, which in the course of its history drew other nations into it. These nations were attracted to Russian culture and accepted it with their whole heart.

Iurii Handler thinks that Vagin—and other VSKhSON members as well—might be willing to grant self-determination to the Baltic states, the Asiatic populace of the USSR and the western area [*Lvovshchina*] of the Ukraine. In general, the only grounds that Vagin might accept for separation from Russia would be religious ones. The Western Ukrainians might have a case because they were formerly under Poland and adhere to the Uniate [Catholic] faith. On the other hand, since Georgians are Orthodox by religion, they have no right to separate. (In the case of both Georgia and the Ukraine, Vagin feels it should be remembered that both asked at one time to join the Russian state.) A great nation, he insists, like parents has responsibilities for its children. To say that, for example, the Kalmyks should comprise a separate state is, he feels, ridiculous. If Russia is divided up into pieces, it will mean the end of Russian civilization.

It is difficult to decide to what extent, if any, Vagin's views on the nationalities question diverge from those held by the VSKhSON leaders during the period 1964-1967. As has already been noted, the Program passes over this entire issue in frustrating silence, leaving us no choice other than to rely on Karavatskii's brief summary of the leaders' views (which we discussed in Chapter XI). If Vagin espouses granting autonomy to the nationalities comprising the Soviet populace, then his scheme is less "repressive" than it might otherwise seem. His views, in any case, remain less "liberal" on the nationalities question than those of Solzhenitsyn and his friends, who feel that no nation should be kept in the Russian Federation by force.[61]

According to Handler, Vagin, "like all VSKhSON members," emphatically believes that, "The Soviet regime is not Russian." [*Sovetskaia vlast' ne russkaia*]. Rather, he sees it as a new foreign "Tatar yoke" imposed on the Russian people.

In his economic views, Vagin supports cooperative ven-

tures because, as he sees it, the average Russian is less individualistic than Western man and has a real "striving for
brotherhood" [*stremlenie k bratstvu*]. In this area, then, he
remains in accord with VSKhSON Program.

Finally, while a Russian patriot, Vagin entertains no hostile feelings toward the West. In this regard, he continues
the "universalistic" thrust of the Program.

Such is a short summary of Vagin's views based on my
interview with Iurii Handler. While Vagin's ideas may
elicit scorn and even repugnance on the part of some Western readers, they should not be dismissed out of hand
simply for being "un-Western." Monarchism, for example,
while a political absurdity in the United States, maintains
its attraction for more than a few peoples of the globe.
Certainly, Vagin's ideas lack sophistication and in the places
where they diverge from the Program generally strike one
as weaker and less convincing. (When I asked Handler if
Ogurtsov's influence was not to make most VSKhSON members more liberal than they would otherwise be, he readily
agreed.) But Vagin's views are important, if only because
they are shared by many Soviet intellectuals seeking an alternative to Marxism-Leninism while rejecting Western
models.

The second member of the revolutionary union whose
views we shall examine is Leonid Borodin. Our exposition
of his thought will be based on his article "*Vestnik R.S.Kh.D.*
and the Russian Intelligentsia," which appeared in the eighth
issue of *Veche* and his shorter piece "*Merci,* or Hair Standing on End" which was published in the first number of
Moskovskii sbornik. The first-named—the more significant
of the two—is an extended (40 pages) polemic against three
samizdat articles published under pseudonyms in the No. 97
(1970) issue of the Paris-based *Messenger of the Russian
Student Christian Movement.*[62] All three pieces are by neo-
Westernizers [*neo-zapadniki*] living in the USSR. They served
to raise the ire of neo-Slavophiles of all persuasions as no

other recent texts have been able to do. In addition to Borodin, they have been attacked by "Radugin," "Ibragimov," Gennadii Shimanov (twice), Solzhenitsyn and Osipov.[63]

While the recent revival of the great 19th century debate between Slavophiles and Westernizers is far too vast a topic to be covered here, a few words of background may be beneficial. The great majority of neo-Slavophiles are of Great Russian or Eastern Slavic descent, while most—but not all—influential neo-Westernizers are of Jewish or part-Jewish origin. These Jews, it should be stressed, are those who consider themselves in some sense to be Russian and have little interest in Zionism or in settling in Israel. Frequently they are baptized members of the Orthodox Church; some are Roman Catholics. It is against the ideas of these *zapadniki,* many of whom have recently emigrated to Europe or America, that most neo-Slavophile polemics are directed.[64]

In his *Veche* article Borodin contests the tenet of the *Vestnik* authors that the Russian people is primarily responsible for the Stalin holocaust and world-wide Communist expansion. The very term "Russian Marxism," Borodin insists, is "an absurdity."[65] Only in its "negative maximalism" may Bolshevism be considered an indigenously Russian phenomenon.[66] The component elements of Communist revolutionary psychology can be found in *The Communist Manifesto,* whose authors were not Russian. As for Lenin, he was more concerned with world revolution than the fate of Russia. The Bolshevik Revolution represents a denial of "the whole complex of positive ideas" informing Russian history.[67] The revolution occurred as a result of the "denationalization" of Russians. To identify Bolshevism with the Russian people *per se* is, therefore, manifestly a simplification. Were, Borodin asks, the foreign troops and Jews who fought with the Bolsheviks during the Civil War battling for the "Russian Idea"?

Concerning the *Vestnik* authors' charge that the Russian people has "shocked the whole world by its Satanic hatred for God," Borodin points to Western phenomena such as the "Renaissance, which began the crisis of World Christianity," the "guillotines of the French Revolution," the first two Internationals and Fascism.[68] The truth, he maintains, is that "Russia, like the whole world, has slowly and unswervingly fallen away from God."[69] Borodin prefers misdirected Russian maximalism to Western minimalism and indifference, the "possessed physiognomy of a Russian People's Will revolutionary shooting at the tsar" to the "pious physiognomy of an Italian Catholic, who votes for the Communists, or an English Communist who celebrates Christmas."[70] In the innate maximalism of the Russian people lies the pledge of the nation's renewal.

As for the *zapadniki,* time is against them. Today's "educated stratum" is evolving through nationalist thought.[71] (Borodin admits that there exists the danger of a Russian variant of national socialism, which he terms "a phenomenon truly incompatible with the Russian idea,"[72] but feels it unlikely to prevail.) The Westernizers are historically doomed:

> In this milieu there are many courageous and highly respectable people, but there are not and cannot be in it persons of a national and creative bent because, firstly, there predominates in it the sense of a clan, or order or sect (and, most often, simply of a *salon*). Second, and let no-one accuse me of Judophobia, a significant part ... belongs to the Jewish intelligentsia which, in its foundations, was and has remained internationalist in spirit. At present, it has become disillusioned with the Russian socialist variant, for which it tends to blame the 'vileness of the Russian soul'. In this milieu there predominates the conviction that Russians spoiled Marx. This milieu has many ideals: British democracy, Swiss federalism, American economism, Eastern European conformism, but all these ideas

are paralyzed by a fear of Russia and a pathological hatred for everything which, for convenience
and self-justification, they call 'nationalism'.[73]

The influence of the *zapadniki* must inevitably wane,
Borodin feels, not only because so many of their number
have emigrated abroad but, more importantly, because of
"Russia's national intolerance for half-truth."[74] Borodin un-
derlines that he is not an advocate of Russian "superiority"
but simply of Russian "particularity," i.e. he believes that
the nation should follow its own path. Quoting Berdiaev,
he declares, "I am not a nationalist but a Russian patriot."[75]

The *Vestnik* No. 97 authors had advocated that believers
in Russia should form "secret Christian brotherhoods."
Borodin, a former member of an underground union, treats
the suggestion with some irony. "Besides the fact that the
Church does not recognize secret societies," he writes,[76] "how
can one conceive of a secret Christian brotherhood in Soviet
conditions? Underground?" But this, he stresses, leads to an
unhealthy "standing askew" [*krivostoianie*] since one must
continue hypocritically to function in society. He also wonders why the *Vestnik* authors intend no political aims for
their secret brotherhoods. A secret organization, he points
out, "cannot but be political" in the Soviet context.[77]

In his *Moskovskii sbornik* piece, which is directed against
zapadnik Anatolii Levitin's bulky *samizdat* work "Earth
Standing on End" [*Zemlia dybom*], Borodin sharply contests his opponent's "program" for the transformation of
Russia. (The "merci" in the title of Borodin's essay refers
to a work by the writer Karmazinov, an insipid Westernizer
universally acknowledged to be a caricature of Turgenev, in
Dostoevskii's *The Devils*.)[78] Borodin roasts Levitin for his (in
truth) intemperate and condescending attack on Solzhenitsyn's *Letter to the Soviet Leaders* and for his bizarre attempt to combine Orthodox Christianity with an admiration
for Lenin, Chernyshevskii, the French Revolution and the

Renaissance. "Who is this Krasnov-Levitin," he queries, "who interprets the Gospel . . . And whence has he the right to pat Solzhenitsyn on the shoulder? Is there even one reader of *samizdat* who would put Krasnov-Levitin not only next to Solzhenitsyn but even sideways to him?"[79] Borodin concludes that Levitin is a hopeless "dilettante" who has only succeeded in making a mockery of himself.[80]

Having briefly summarized the contents of Borodin's two articles, we are now entitled to a few criticisms. While Borodin would seem to be justified in certain points in his controversy with the *zapadniki*—the *Vestnik* authors do have an excessively bleak opinion of the capabilities of the Russian people and Levitin's positive suggestions do, on occasion, come across as confused and unrealistic—he all too frequently betrays a narrowness and lack of intellectual subtlety of his own. He simply lacks the keenness of a Berdiaev or Solzhenitsyn. Moreover, his ponderous irony, so reminiscent of Soviet journalese, and his lack of charity toward his opponents are counter-productive. Most importantly, Borodin, despite his protestations to the contrary, does strike one as an insufficiently discerning student of Russian history. In Borodin's polemics with the *Vestnik* authors, one cannot help suspecting that the truth is half-way between the warring sides. Personally, I am quite attracted to Solzhenitsyn's view, expressed in the collection *From under the Rubble*, that both those who refuse to admit that their nation has committed any wrongdoing (toward which Borodin has a *tendency*)[81] and those who take a cold, detached delight in flailing their native land, as if they too did not participate in her guilt (the temptation of the *Vestnik* authors), are equally in error.[82] And surely Solzhenitsyn's call that nations should seek to discover and then atone for their own historical sins, rather than indulging in shrill recriminations against other peoples, makes more edifying reading than Borodin's blanket attacks on a "bourgeois-Philistine" West about which he knows relatively little.[83]

As the instances of Vagin and Borodin demonstrate, former VSKhSON members have now become droplets in a rising tide of Russian neo-Slavophilism. While neither of them would seem to possess the intellectual machinery of Igor' Ogurtsov—probably the sole seminal thinker in the revolutionary union—both have a contribution to make to the debate among contemporary neo-Slavophiles which could be deciding the future shape of Russia's society and government. VSKhSON has encountered *Veche*. Their meeting may yet bear unexpected fruit.

Conclusion

In December, 1825, a group of young guard officers, influenced by the ideas of the French Revolution and the Enlightenment, with which they had become acquainted during the war against Napoleon, rose up against the new tsar of Russia, Nicholas I. Their inept rebellion was easily suppressed, and five of the organization's leaders were subsequently executed. Another 120 received prison sentences. While their revolution turned out to be a hapless venture, however, the Decembrists [*Dekabristy*], as they have come to be known, are generally credited with beginning the ferment of ideas which eventually resulted in the Bolshevik coup of 1917. For this reason they have been called "the fathers and first martyrs of the Russian revolution."[1]

Approximately 140 years later, another group of young revolutionary idealists unconsciously set out to undo what the Decembrists had initiated. (Formed in February, 1964, and arrested in February, 1967, the Social-Christians could be termed "Februarists" [*fevralisty*].) While VSKhSON, like the Decembrists, did not constitute a serious military threat to the existing order, the *ideas* it propagated—and continues to propagate—represented a formidable danger indeed. From our vantage point, Russian neo-Slavophilism already seems to be the major ideological challenge to the continued hegemony of Marxism-Leninism in the USSR.

When in 1969 dissenter Andrei Amal'rik wrote his perceptive and provocative *samizdat* essay *Will the Soviet Union*

223

Survive Until 1984?, he discerned three major ideological viewpoints on which opposition had begun to "crystallize" in post-Stalinist Russia. These were "genuine Marxism-Leninism," which held that the regime had perverted Marxism-Leninism for its own purposes, "liberal ideology," which envisaged a transition to Western-style democracy while maintaining public or state ownership of the means of production, and "Christian ideology."[2] The last-named was identified with VSKhSON, an ideology, according to Amal'rik, which held that "the life of society must return to Christian moral principles, which are interpreted in a somewhat Slavophile spirit, with a claim for a special role for Russia."[3] Amal'rik insisted that "Christian ideology" should be considered a "political doctrine" and felt it should be distinguished from "neo-Slavophilism"—typified by the *Rodina* clubs—a current he found distastefully tinged with chauvinism.[4]

While most Western observers took note of Amal'rik's keen analysis of ideological crystallizations in the Soviet Union, some, such as Jacob Dreyer, refused to take VSKhSON seriously, dismissing it as "marginal or alien in relation to the mainstream of the Soviet dissent movement."[5] Others, such as the Italian journalist Pietro Sormani, drew a different conclusion. In his view, while VSKhSON is "the least known [Soviet oppositional ideology] in the West," it is "possibly this group which has the largest following among certain sections of the Soviet intelligentsia particularly sensitive to nationalistic appeal, and which is therefore the most dangerous to the regime."[6]

Five years after the appearance in print of Amal'rik's book, it has become quite clear that neither the "democratic movement" nor neo-Marxism exerts much attraction for the populace. Concerning "liberal ideology's" Western solutions to Russian problems, confirmed *zapadnik* Anatolii Levitin has recently admitted, "The main tragedy of the democratic movement was that it has, up to the present time, been in isolation from the broad popular masses of Russia."[7] As for "genuine Marxism-Leninism," its handful of adherents, led by the voluble Roy Medvedev, are almost desperately trying to combat neo-Slavophilism's evident appeal to the populace. An indication of the degree of their disquiet is the *samizdat* neo-Marxist journal *Twentieth Century* [*Dvadtsatyi vek*] which they recently launched. The publication's first issue contains an attack on Solzhenitsyn's *Letter to the Soviet Leaders,* a polemic against Vladimir Maksimov's "bloodthirsty Christianity," and an examination of "contemporary Christianity."[8] Medvedev has also felt compelled to provide *samizdat* "antidotes" for each of the first two volumes of *The Gulag Archipelago* and the *Letter to the Soviet Leaders.*[9] And in a recent interview published in the London *Observer* he shrilly warned, "If Solzhenitsyn, with his religious ideas, were to become Head of Government, that would be dreadful."[10] As Medvedev and other *zapadniki*—whether of the Marxist, socialist or liberal variety—are beginning to realize but fear to admit, the 19th century shoe is now on the other foot, and a revived Slavophilism is carrying the ideological field against a Westernism irretrievably compromised by the experience of the past sixty years.

To be sure, the powerful contemporary movements of minority nationalities (Ukrainians, Lithuanians, Armenians, etc.) are a factor that the regime can ignore only to its peril.[11] But it is unquestionably Russian neo-Slavophilism, which potentially enjoys the support of Great Russians, Belorussians and some Ukrainians—not to mention the perhaps not so few Mikhail Sados among the other Soviet nationalities—that has the potential clout to sweep aside a discredited but still lethal Marxism-Leninism. Neo-Slavophilism's rootedness in the Orthodox Church, which, despite its supine official leadership, remains an extraordinarily "popular" ecclesiastical body, is a crucial factor, as are its vociferous championing of such broadly-supported causes as the preservation of national monuments and the protection of the Russian environment against the ravages of industrialism. It is startling but true that many Russians today have the psychology of an oppressed minority. They see and profoundly resent: their country in thrall to an alien, "non-Russian" ideology—Marxism-Leninism, and their religion, culture, language, historical monuments and the Russian land itself under assault from a brutal and cynical nihilism.[12] Many believe that the moral decay directly resulting from the Marxist "Tatar yoke" has spread to such an extent that the Russian people itself is on the brink of spiritual extinction.[13]

In the context of contemporary neo-Slavophilism, VSKhSON remains significant for three reasons. First, its "positive" program is the best-thought-out alternative to the present Soviet system yet formulated by neo-Slavophile circles, while its "negative" critique of the regime comes perhaps only second to Solzhenitsyn's *oeuvre* in devastating impact. Thus, VSKhSON remains primarily alive in its ideas. Second, the organization's advocacy of a maximally bloodless revolutionary coup continues to be one plausible nationalist solution to Russia's dilemma. Recent émigrés from the Soviet Union have told me that VSKhSON's views on revolution represent a live option for a number of individuals in the USSR. The "moral revolution" being promoted by Solzhenitsyn and his friends is another solution,[14] while a passive waiting about for the regime to disintegrate is a third possibility.[15] Finally, VSKhSON retains its importance because of the truly heroic behavior of its leader and chief ideologue, Igor' Ogurtsov, who continues to bear his union's banner aloft through the prisons, camps and prison psychiatric hospitals of the Soviet Union. If he survives his imprisonment—he may well not—he could yet play an important role in Russia's political future. In Karavatskii's words, "[Ogurtsov] has not yet manifested himself in social life, and I am certain that when the time comes for him to lead the people after him, he will begin to shine on the horizon of the world as a star of the first magnitude."[16]

The regime has nothing to combat neo-Slavophilism with except coercion, disinformation and repression. Having lost the good faith of the populace, it is ultimately doomed despite its seemingly impressive armed forces, secret police and political successes abroad. As S. points out, with VSKhSON we have the "beginning of a real, positive overcoming of [the Bolshevik] idea of the nation," and it is inevitable that other Russian nationalist organizations should appear in the years to come.[17] And Karavatskii confidently asserts, "The falsifiers of Russia's history did not succeed in striking out of the memory of the people the fact of VSKhSON's existence, and I am certain that the main ideas of this organization will be realized in the Russia of the future."[18] Future historians sitting down to pen accounts of the regime's demise may well choose to pause for some pages on the role of a revolutionary union which contained only twenty-eight members and another thirty candidates for membership—the All-Russian Social-Christian Union for the Liberation of the People.

VSKhSON: Biographical Data and Other Materials

VSKhSON: The Leaders*

1. OGURTSOV, Igor' Viacheslavovich. Born August 22, 1937, in what is now the city of Volgograd. Russian nationality. Father a naval officer and Party member; mother a pianist. Finished the Eastern Faculty of LGU in 1966. A *semitologist* by training. Worked as a translator and reader at a Leningrad institute for shipbuilding. Unmarried. Non-Party. The "head" of VSKhSON.

2. SADO, Mikhail Iukhanovich. Born in 1934 in Leningrad. Assyrian nationality. Father a bootblack. Finished the Eastern Faculty of LGU and did graduate work there. A *semitologist* by training. May have taught at LGU. Married with two children. Non-Party. VSKhSON's "director of personnel, responsible for security."

3. VAGIN, Evgenii Aleksandrovich. Born in 1938 in Pskov. Russian nationality. Father a teacher in Pskov and Party

---

*All information concerns VSKhSON members *at the time of their arrest* and has been taken from items listed in the notes or from private conversations with recent émigrés from the Soviet Union.

member; mother completed a pedagogical institute. Finished the Philological Faculty of LGU and completed his graduate work there. Worked on a dissertation on Dostoevskii. A *literary critic* by profession. Employed as an editor by the Pushkin House publishing firm in Leningrad. Married with one child. Non-Party. Director of VSKhSON's "ideological division."

4. AVERICHKIN, Boris Anatol'evich. Born in 1938 in Leningrad. Russian nationality. Parents' occupation unknown. Grandfather reportedly a Soviet admiral. A fifth-year student in the Faculty of Jurisprudence at LGU. A *law student* by profession. Unmarried. Non-Party. Served as VSKhSON's "keeper of the archives."

VSKhSON: The Rank-and-File*

1. PLATONOV, Viacheslav Mikhailovich. Born January 14, 1941, in Leningrad. Russian nationality. Father a worker. Finished the Eastern Faculty of LGU in 1963 and his graduate work in 1966. Completed but did not have time to defend a dissertation entitled "Ethiopian Historiography: Chronicles of the 14th-15th Centuries." An *Ethiopologist* by training. Taught in the Department of African Studies at LGU. Unmarried. Non-Party. A member of VSKhSON's "ideological division."

2. IVANOV, Nikolai Viktorovich. Born August 11, 1937, in Leningrad. Russian nationality. Father a Party member. Finished the History Faculty of LGU in 1961 and completed his graduate work there in 1964. An *art historian* by training. Taught in the LGU Department of Art History. Unmarried. Non-Party. A member of VSKhSON's "ideological division."

3. USTINOVICH, Sergei Sergeevich. Born March 11, 1938,

---

*Our order of listing the VSKhSON rank-and-file follows that of the *"Prigovor."*

in Kalinin Province. Russian nationality. Finished the
Eastern Faculty of LGU in 1966. Worked as an *engineer*
in a Leningrad project-construction bureau. Married.
Non-Party.

4. BOCHEVAROV, Georgii Nikolaevich. Born October 2,
1935, in the city of Kuibyshev. Russian nationality but
at least partly of Bulgarian extraction. Father a Party
member. Finished the Eastern Faculty of LGU in 1965.
Employed as a senior *engineer* in a central construction
bureau. Unmarried. Non-Party. Commander of a
VSKhSON "squad."

5. KONOSOV, Mikhail Borisovich. Born April 19, 1937, in
Leningrad Province. Russian nationality. Parents Party
members. A correspondence student at the Gor'kii Institute of Literature in Moscow. Unfinished higher education. Worked as a *fitter* at the Leningrad Gas Company. Married with one child. Non-Party. Commander
of a VSKhSON "squad."

6. MIKLASHEVICH, Aleksandr Andreevich. Born October 2,
1935, in Leningrad. Russian nationality. Finished the
Leningrad Agricultural Institute in 1960. Employed as a
senior *engineer* at the Central Scientific Research Institute of Fuel Apparatuses. Married. Non-Party.

7. BUZIN, Iurii Sergeevich. Born August 7, 1936, in Leningrad. Russian nationality. Finished the Leningrad Agricultural Institute in 1959. Employed as a senior *engineer*
at the Central Scientific Research Institute of Fuel Apparatuses. Married with one child. Non-Party.

8. NAGORNYI, Valerii Fedorovich. Born June 9, 1943, in
Vologda Province. Russian nationality. Finished the
Leningrad Institute of Exact Mechanics and Optics in
1966. Worked there as an *engineer*. Married with one
child. Non-Party.

9. ZABAK, Ol'gert Petrovich. Born December 20, 1941, in
the city of Biisk, Altai Region. Russian nationality. Unfinished secondary education. Worked as a *technician* at

the Leningrad Institute of Exact Mechanics and Optics. Married. Non-Party.

10. BARANOV, Iurii Petrovich. Born October 26, 1938, in Komi ASSR. Russian nationality. Parents Party members. Finished the Leningrad Institute of Film Engineers in 1963. Employed as an *electrical engineer* in the clinic of hospital surgery, First Leningrad Medical Institute. Unmarried. Non-Party.

11. SHUVALOV, Oleg Nikolaevich. Born November 5, 1938, in Leningrad. Russian nationality. Unfinished higher education. Worked as a *mechanic* in the Leningrad Institute of Exact Mechanics and Optics. Unmarried. Non-Party.

12. BORODIN, Leonid Ivanovich. Born April 14, 1938, in the city of Irkutsk. Russian nationality. Both parents teachers. Finished the D. Banzarov Pedagogical Institute in 1962. Employed as the *director of a high school* in Luga District, Leningrad Province. Married with one child. Non-Party.

13. IVOILOV, Vladimir Fedorovich. Born June 24, 1938, in Kemerov Province. Russian nationality. Finished the Economics Faculty of LGU in 1966. Worked as a *teaching assistant* in the Department of Political Economy at Tomsk Polytechnical Institute. Married with one child. Non-Party. Commander of a VSKhSON "squad."

14. SUDAREV, Anatolii Ivanovich. Born November 6, 1939, in Leningrad. Russian nationality. Finished the Philological Faculty of LGU in 1967. Employed as a *high school English teacher* in Leningrad Province. Unmarried. Non-Party.

15. IVLEV, Anatolii Georgievich. Born January 27, 1937, in Leningrad Province. Russian nationality. Finished the Chemistry Faculty of LGU in 1959. Worked as a senior *engineer* at a scientific research institute for petrochemical processes in Leningrad. Married with one child. Non-Party.

16. VERETENOV, Vladimir Fedorovich. Born September 2,

1936, in what is now Pskov Province. Russian nationality. Finished the Economics Faculty of LGU in 1966. Former teaching assistant in political economy at the Tomsk Polytechnical Institute. At the moment of his arrest employed as a *junior scientific employee* at a peat firm in Leningrad Province. Unmarried. Non-Party.

17. KONSTANTINOV, Stanislav Vladimirovich. Born September 13, 1943, in Vologda Province. Russian nationality. Unfinished higher education. Worked as the *director of the Valaam village library* in Karelian ASSR. Unmarried. Non-Party.

VSKhSON Rank-and-File Not Sentenced

1. FAKHRUTDINOV, Il'ias. Instructor at LGU. Of Tatar origin.
2. GONCHAROV, Vladimir P.
3. IOVAISHA. A Lithuanian.
4. KLOCHKOV, I. S.
5. KOZICHEV, V. M.
6. PETROV, Vladimir Fedorovich. Employee at the Leningrad State Institute of Optics.
7. SHESTAKOV, V. A. Student at the Leningrad Theatrical Institute.

VSKhSON Candidates*

1. ABRAMOV, E. P. History student (probably at LGU).
2. ALEKHIN, S. N. Inhabitant of Krasnodar.

---

*This list has been compiled from the names of VSKhSON candidates supplied by the *"Prigovor"* and Osipov (*"Berdiaevskii kruzhok..."*). Many of the names also appear in the *"Zakliuchenie sledstviia."* Osipov states there were thirty candidates for entrance into VSKhSON; we have the names of twenty-three.

3. ALEKHIN, E. N. Inhabitant of Krasnodar.
4. ANDREEV. History student at LGU.
5. ANTIPIN, V. N.
6. ANUFRIEV, Iu. E. A teacher in Tomsk.
7. BALAIAN, D. G. LGU student and translator. An Armenian.
8. CHIRKOV, A. A.
9. EKIMOV, M. K. A student.
10. EL'KIN, G. B. Economist at a Leningrad construction firm.
11. FREDERIKS, D. V. Grandson of court minister of Tsar Nicholas II.
12. GONOBLEV, L. N. Graduate of LGU Faculty of Chemistry.
13. KALININ, V. R. LGU student.
14. KRAGIN, V. A.
15. KULAKOV, S. N. Son of a Vice-Admiral of Leningrad.
16. LISIN. Graduate student.
17. ORLOV-CHISTOV, A. N. Resident of Moscow.
18. OSIPOVICH, A. I. Superintendent of a museum in Solovki.
19. PAEVSKII. LGU graduate student.
20. RAGINIAN, R. V. LGU student. An Armenian.
21. SPAILE, A. K.
22. STATEEV, N. V. A fitter in Tomsk.
23. VIROLAINEN, Iu. I. LGU student.

VSKhSON Recruitment*

1. *February 2, 1964*	Ogurtsov, Sado, Vagin and Averichkin found organization
2. *October, 1964*	Ustinovich recruited
3. *November 9, 1964*	Miklashevich
4. *November 19, 1964*	Platonov

---

*These dates are taken from the *"Prigovor,"* *"Zakliuchenie sledstviia"* and Osipov.

5.	*December, 1964*	Bochevarov
6.	*January 15, 1965*	Ivlev
7.	*February 15, 1965*	Sudarev
8.	*May 8, 1965*	Konosov
9.	*May 9, 1965*	Klochkov
10.	*May 16, 1965*	Buzin
11.	*May 18, 1965*	Konstantinov
12.	*October 18, 1965*	Borodin
13.	*October 18, 1965*	Ivoilov
14.	*1965*	Fakhrutdinov*
15.	*End, 1965*	Kozichev
16.	*End, 1965*	Goncharov
17.	*March 4, 1966*	Baranov
18.	*March 12, 1966*	Veretenov
19.	*May, 1966*	Nagornyi
20.	*May, 1966*	Iovaisha
21.	*June, 1966*	Ivanov
22.	*September 29, 1966*	Zabak
23.	*November, 1966*	Petrov
24.	*December 14, 1966*	Shuvalov
25.	*December 29, 1966*	Shestakov

Year of Birth

1934 Sado
1935 Bochevarov, Miklashevich
1936 Buzin, Veretenov
1937 Ivanov, Ivlev, Konosov, Ogurtsov
1938 Averichkin, Baranov, Borodin, Ivoilov, Shuvalov, Ustinovich, Vagin
1939 Sudarev
1940
1941 Platonov, Zabak

---

*According to Osipov, Fakhrutdinov was a member of VSKhSON for several months in 1965 and then voluntarily left the organization.

1942
1943   Nagornyi, Konstantinov

Education

1. *Graduate work (completed)*   Ivanov (1964), Platonov
                                    (1966), Vagin
2. *Graduate work (uncompleted)*   Sado
3. *Undergraduate work at LGU*
   (completed)
   a. Chemistry Faculty   Ivlev (1959)
   b. Eastern Faculty   Bochevarov (1965)
                                    Ogurtsov (1966)
                                    Platonov (1963)
                                    Sado
                                    Ustinovich (1966)
   c. Economics Faculty   Ivoilov (1966)
                                    Veretenov (1966)
   d. History Faculty   Ivanov (1961)
   e. Philological Faculty   Sudarev (1967), Vagin
4. *Undergraduate work at LGU*   Averichkin arrested as
   (uncompleted)   5th year senior in Facul-
                                    ty of Jurisprudence.

5. *Completed higher education*
   a. D. Banzarov Pedagogical   Borodin (1962)
      Institute
   b. Leningrad Agricultural   Buzin (1959)
      Institute   Miklashevich (1960)
   c. Leningrad Institute of   Nagornyi (1966)
      Exact Mechanics and
      Optics
   d Leningrad Institute of   Baranov (1963)
      Film Engineers
6. *Uncompleted higher education* Konosov, Konstantinov,
   (institution unspecified)   Shuvalov

7. *Uncompleted secondary education*   Zabak (9 years of schooling)

Profession

1. Teaching Assistant at institution of higher learning — Ivanov, Ivoilov, Platonov, Sado (?)
2. Literary Critic — Vagin
3. High School Principal — Borodin
4. High School English Teacher — Sudarev
5. Librarian — Konstantinov
6. Economist — Veretenov
7. Law Student — Averichkin
8. Technical Specialist, Translator and Reader — Ogurtsov
9. Engineer — Baranov, Bochevarov, Buzin, Ivlev, Miklashevich, Nagornyi. Ustinovich
10. Technician — Zabak
11. Mechanic — Shuvalov
12. Fitter — Konosov

Marital Status

1. *Unmarried* — Averichkin, Baranov, Bochevarov, Ivanov, Konstantinov, Ogurtsov, Platonov, Shuvalov, Sudarev, Veretenov
2. *Married* — Miklashevich, Ustinovich, Zabak
3. *Married with children* — Borodin, Buzin, Ivlev, Ivoilov, Konosov, Nagornyi, Sado, Vagin

VSKhSON: A Chronology*

1. February 2, 1964	VSKhSON founded by *Ogurtsov, Sado, Vagin* and *Averichkin*.
2. October, 1964	First rank-and-file member recruited.
3. November-December, 1964	Three new members recruited for a total of eight by the end of 1964.
4. January-December, 1965	Ten members recruited for a total of eighteen by the end of 1965.
5. December, 1965	A "squad" [*boevaia gruppa*] formed consisting of *Ivoilov* ("commander"), *Sudarev* ("ideologist and counter-intelligence"), *Ivlev* and *Kozichev*.
6. End, 1965	A "squad" formed consisting of *Konosov* ("commander"), *Miklashevich* ("counter-intelligence") and *Buzin*.
7. 1965	*Borodin, Ustinovich* and *Kozichev* acquire and conceal 41.5 kilograms of type, then transfer it to *Averichkin* for VSKhSON's planned underground press.
8. February-July, 1966	*A. F. Gidoni,* an object of recruitment efforts by *Ivoilov* and others, informs the KGB but fails, for lack of material evidence, to sink the organization. Summoned to the KGB for

---

*All dates taken from materials referred to in Chapter I, especially the *"Zakliuchenie sledstviia," "Prigovor"* and Osipov's *"Berdiaevskii kruzhok ...".*

"prophylactic chats," *Ivoilov, Borodin, Sudarev, Ustinovich* and *Veretenov* employ believable "alibis" [*legendy*]. The incident induces VSKhSON to speed up its activities.

9. April, 1966 — *Konosov* named commander of a "section" [*otdelenie*] and organizer of a "platoon" [*vzvod*]. He is told to increase his unit to eighteen. Warns subordinates they may have to go underground.

10. May, 1966 — *Konosov* orders unit to prepare hiding places [*tainiki*] for weapons. Plans also laid for automobile transport of arms.

11. May, 1966 — A "squad" formed consisting of *Bochevarov* ("commander"), *Platonov, Konstantinov* and *Klochkov.*

12. May-December, 1966 — Four new members assigned to *Konosov's* unit, including the future betrayer, *Petrov. Nagornyi* assumes post of *Konosov's* depputy.

13. Summer-December, 1966 — Actions taken in preparation for a thrust in Leningrad on the occasion of the fiftieth anniversary of the Soviet regime in the Fall of 1967. A building is studied as an object of armed seizure, plans are laid for the acquisition, concealment and transport of weapons, etc.

14. October, 1966 — Printer's ink and paper acquired and conspiratorially delivered to

	Vagin by *Nagornyi, Baranov* and *Zabak*. Materials intended for VSKhSON's printing press.
15. November, 1966	An "ideological division" [*ideologicheskii otdel*] founded consisting of *Vagin* ("director"), *Platonov* and *Ivanov*. Unit to coordinate all ideological work and publish "battle bulletins."
16. December, 1966	*Ogurtsov* and *Konosov* play war games on the theme "a platoon on the attack in the conditions of a large city."
17. Late, 1966-Early, 1967	*Ivoilov* moves to the city of Tomsk, Siberia. Prepares the ground for a VSKhSON branch there. Together with *Veretenov*, prepares two candidates for recruitment.
18. January 12 & 14, 1967	Two important meetings of the "ideological division."
19. January, 1967	*Konosov* writes a "project for a leaflet to the workers" to be used during the planned Fall activities.
20. January, 1967	*Borodin* journeys to Irkutsk, where he contacts *Goncharov,* and to Tomsk, where he sees *Ivoilov* and *Veretenov* and gives them materials necessary for the induction of new members.
21. February 4, 1967	VSKhSON member *Petrov* betrays the organization to the KGB.
22. February 7, 1967	Arrest of *Zabak, Konosov* and *Nagornyi*.

23.	February 8, 1967	Arrest of *Shuvalov*.
24.	February 10, 1967	Arrest of *Baranov*.
25.	February 15, 1967	Arrest of *Ogurtsov, Sado, Vagin, Averichkin* and *Miklashevich*.
26.	February 17, 1967	Arrest of *Platonov, Ivanov, Usti- novich, Bochevarov* and *Sudarev*.
27.	February 18, 1967	Arrest of *Borodin* and *Ivlev*.
28.	March 1, 1967	Arrest of *Konstantinov*.
29.	March 9, 1967	Arrest of *Ivoilov*.
30.	June 2, 1967	Arrest of *Buzin* and *Veretenov*.
31.	Late November-Early December, 1967	Four VSKhSON leaders tried *in camera* (in violation of Soviet law). Trial lasts about ten days.
32.	March 14-April 5, 1968	Trial of the VSKhSON rank-and-file. Seventeen receive sentences.

The VSKhSON Program

The Social-Christian Union
For the Liberation of the People

(The People's Revolutionary Charter)
VSKhSON

INTRODUCTION

The world-wide social crisis which has marked the entire history of capitalism and socialism and has brought tragedy to many peoples in the 20th century now threatens to turn into a world nuclear war resulting in the destruction of civilization.

Although there has never been such material abundance as in the contemporary world and although scientific discoveries have given men unprecedented power over nature, neither science nor material wealth has increased man's freedom or brought about permanent prosperity and a firm faith in the future.

The power over nature, which has been gained through science, has become dangerous for mankind in today's spiritually darkened world.

Insane policies directed toward the conquest of world dominion consume the fruits of the heavy labor of millions of men, entangle the world in webs of espionage, spawn paranoid suspiciousness and lead to the suppression of civil liberties. The division of the world into two opposing military camps, irreconcilable ideological antagonism, the arms race—all these are ominous symptoms of an approaching catastrophe which can only be averted through radical and swift change in the whole world situation.

The reason for this dangerous tension lies much deeper than in the economic and political spheres. The world needs spiritual rebirth. Only a renewed human spirit will discover new political goals and direct politics toward the benefit of mankind; only it will show the way to freedom and the satisfaction of the material needs of all peoples.

The social catastrophe which befell Russia as a result of the Communist Revolution represented a painful historical lesson for the whole world. In the half-century of its existence, the Communist system has proved to be the exact opposite of the ideals toward which humanity strives. The Communist attempt to build a new world and rear a new man has only resulted in the creation of an inhuman world. Since it is the sickly offspring of materialistic capitalism, Communism has only succeeded in developing and bringing to fruition all the harmful tendencies inherent in bourgeois economics, politics and ideology. This is the source of the striking similarity between Communism and Fascism. The integral parts of Marxist-Leninist teaching were borrowed from Western bourgeois theories. The only thing new in Marxist-Leninist "science" is its program of socialization, i.e. the seizure of the means of production belonging to the people by the class of the Party bureaucracy and this class's leadership in establishing a dictatorship over the people.

Superficial bourgeois materialism developed [in Soviet Russia] into a fanatical atheism which, in turn, has become the basis for a frightening anti-humanism and the negation of the worth of the human personality. By renouncing God, Communism deprived man of his individuality and rendered him an object and means. It not only deprived man of control over the economy but of his will, mind and heart as well. In this atmosphere of principled anti-humanism the cult of the false-saviors of humanity developed naturally and assumed pathological proportions.

Communism has completed the process of the proletarianization of the masses begun by capitalism. Forced labor has replaced the relative freedom characteristic of capitalist labor-relations.

In its internal and foreign policies, as well as in its economics, Communism has been unable to find goals other than those which the old capitalist world had previously pursued. It has only displayed a greater sense of purpose and used more indiscriminate means. The industrialization of the Communist countries was accomplished by more inhumane methods than ever before. Communist governments pursue an imperialistic policy aimed at establishing a Communist dictatorship over the whole world with unprecedented determination and on a large scale. By its very nature Communism has been unable to avoid the contradictions of capitalism; rather, it has intensified them to the very limit and become a worse and unbearable evil.

The modern world is in constant flux. The old classical capitalism is being transformed and freed of its most negative traits. Anti-trust laws regulate the economy. Many branches of the economy have been nationalized. Free labor unions are succeeding in their struggle for better working conditions and higher wages. The standard of living of Western Europe is very high and rising fast. The process of proletarianization has been checked, and the have-not classes are being replaced by a massive middle class which controls the means of production.

The social doctrine of the [Roman] Catholic Church and its appeals to nations and Christian Democratic parties seek to point out the need to change once and for all a situation in which workers do not participate in owning the means of production. The [Roman] Catholic Church has also proclaimed the existence of universal and eternal moral laws which, if followed, can save both the individual and society from the impasse which has developed. The non-Communist world is emerging from the social crisis by evolutionary means.

At the same time the Communist world is decaying. Many peoples have learned through difficult experience that Communism brings with it poverty and oppression, falsehood and moral degeneration. This system is such by nature that it cannot improve without at the same time undermining its foundations. Any improvement in it would result in the ruling class losing its unlawfully gained right to rule monopolistically in economics, politics and ideology. Freedom in any of these spheres would inevitably lead to full freedom and the liquidation of the totalitarian system. Therefore this class will never voluntarily yield anything without a struggle. The liberation of the peoples from the Communist yoke can only be achieved by armed struggle.

A popular revolution aimed at the overthrow of the dictatorship of the Communist bureaucracy and the establishment of a just social system bears an international character, both as concerns its tasks and its results.

To achieve complete victory, the people must have an underground liberation army which would overthrow the dictatorship and destroy the oligarchy's security forces. A people's liberation army must be organized under the leadership of a political nucleus which could provide the popular struggle with a purposeful character and develop a revolutionary strategy and tactics. Finally, the whole people must be united to insure a speedy and bloodless victory and the inspired creation of a just society through brotherly co-operation.

The world is approaching oneness. The efforts to create a common market both in the West and East show the need for close economic cooperation on a world-wide scale and prepare the necessary conditions for it.

The growing prestige of the United Nations bears witness to the possibility and need for political cooperation by all countries in the interests of their peoples. The U.N. exists despite the extreme difficulties which must be surmounted if the present division of the world into two hostile camps is not to destroy the organization and render all its endeavors fruitless.

Universal Christianity, which is in process of uniting, is laying the religio-cultural foundations for supra-national unity. Tomorrow's world will be founded on Christian ideals. Social-Christianity affirms the freedom of the individual, the sacredness of the family, brotherly relations among men and the unity of all nations. Social-Christianity stands for a personalized economics, politics and culture based on the lawful rights and interests of the individual.

SECTION I

Marxism-Leninism: The Totalitarian Ideology of the Communist Bureaucracy

To the extent which the Russian revolutionary movement of the 19th-20th centuries expressed popular interests, it was directly opposed to the ideational essence, methods and goals of Marxism-Leninism, which emerged as a deeply anti-moral, anti-humanist and anti-national current. All our great revolutionaries of the spirit, from Herzen to Dostoevskii and

Tolstoi, pointed out the terrible dangers concealed in Marxism.

The philosophical essence of Marxism-Leninism is the denial of the existence of a Divine foundation of the world and the repudiation of non-material values and man's spiritual freedom. Since experimental science does not and cannot confirm these [Marxist] tenets, they rest on an arbitrary and dogmatic foundation and represent, in the final analysis, a metaphysical materialism, the most hopeless and false of philosophical teachings. This represents a cult of the senselessness of existence and of absolute death.

The essence of Marxism-Leninism as an economic science is a direct outgrowth of its philosophical dogma. It boils down to a belief in a pre-ordained economic development, which is independent of the will and consciousness of man. This economic development supposedly represents the ruling factor and even the entire content of political, cultural and ethical life. The negative tendency of the former capitalist economics toward an excessive concentration of capital is seen by Marxist science as being inevitable and, moreover, desirable. Progress is deemed possible only through the absolute completion of this concentration in the Communist system of a state economy. Under this system the entire people must once and for all be expropriated and turned into a state proletariat.

The essence of Marxism-Leninism as a political doctrine is its assertion that the dictatorship of the bureaucracy represents the highest form of social relations in the industrial era and the highest type of economic organization. It also is manifested in its demand for a totalitarian system which permits any Party clique, under cover of socialist demagogy, to oppress the people by means of the people themselves.

The doctrine of dictatorship is the gravitational center of Marxism-Leninism. It represents the guiding principle toward the seizure of political power during a moment of national crisis and leads to a boundless extension of this power to all aspects of life and to its being constantly strengthened with the assistance of inhuman methods.

The Marxist-Leninist thesis of the antagonism of class interests in an organic economic system and of the necessity of armed class conflict leads to a civil war, which is suicidal for a nation, and to the dictatorship of the Communist oligarchy. For the first time in history the primary function of the state becomes the exercising of constant constraint over the populace. At the same time, the interests of the new ruling class become truly irreconcilable with the interests of the oppressed people.

The Marxist-Leninist thesis concerning the mission of the proletariat allows [the Party] at first to use a section of the working class as an organizing force for a political *coup d'état,* which results in even greater enslavement for the workers.

The Marxist-Leninist demand that the national economy be socialized by force leads to economic tyranny, to the absolute, slavish dependence of the people on their rulers, to a sharp reduction of production and a lowering of the quality of goods produced and to an impoverished level of existence for the workers.

The Marxist concept of the equality of men and women leads to women being forced to work in industry, which weakens the family and deprives children of a normal family life.

The Marxist-Leninist thesis concerning the unity of the Party, which has monopolized state power, inevitably leads to a cult of the Party leader, who is transformed into a despot.

The Marxist-Leninist principle of the "Party-mindedness" of science and art results in a degeneration of the social sciences, in a braking of all areas of learning, in the destruction of national tradition. Reality is falsified, and culture is replaced by propaganda.

The Marxist-Leninist demand for ideological unity and

the total Communist education of the populace gives rise to an extremely harsh moral oppression of the whole of society. It corrupts men in an atmosphere of all-pervasive hypocrisy.

The Marxist-Leninist theory of truth actually represents voluntarism and pragmatism under scientific guise.

The Marxist-Leninist thesis concerning the inevitability of a world-wide Communist revolution and the need to promote and support it by all-possible means has brought the peoples [of the world] to the brink of atomic war.

In the process of the development of the Communist revolution this doctrine has been somewhat modified in accordance with historical circumstances.

Actually Marxism, Leninism, Stalinism and Maoism are all links in the same chain. The whole teaching represents a logical whole and cannot be revised in part. It can only be rejected *in toto* after its underlying presuppositions have been recognized as false.

This teaching, which has brought the new ruling class—the Communist bureaucracy—to boundless power, is inimical to mankind. Objectively, it serves only this class in its work of dispossessing, deceiving and suppressing the peoples.

SECTION II

The Tasks of the Russian Revolutionary Movement of the Twentieth Century and the General Policy of the Communist Oligarchy

By the beginning of the 20th century Russia was in need of significant social transformation. The Russian revolutionary movement, begun by the populists, gradually grew to include all social classes with their varied demands. As in the case of any social revolution, the central problem was the agrarian one.

The peasantry, which comprised more than 80% of the

country's population, was striving for free use of the land on the basis of individual labor.

The workers were demanding the right to partake of the profits of industry. And they demanded democratic control over production.

The intelligentsia, the business and merchant strata and a part of the landowners were demanding a curtailment of the absolute power of the monarchy, the introduction of a constitutional system, judicial guarantees and civil liberties.

The bloodless victory of the revolution of February, 1917, which resulted in the fall of the autocracy, was made possible by the unanimous opposition of the great majority of the people. For a short period of time—from the February Revolution to the Bolshevik coup in October—the Russian revolutionary movement succeeded in winning all those civil liberties and political rights which should have led to a broad economic transformation of a democratic nature, a transformation which had been temporarily held up by the First World War.

Taking advantage of the country's difficult situation in the tense war-time atmosphere, the Bolshevik underground succeeded in corrupting the army by means of demagogic agitation. The Bolsheviks provoked civil war by playing upon the social and national antagonisms within the people. During this war they tried feverishly to create a totalitarian system, which has thrown the people back to the age of serfdom. As a result of the Communist coup, a great popular revolution . . . [GAP IN TEXT][1] . . . the rights won by the people were destroyed. The tsarist autocracy was replaced . . . [GAP] . . . of the peasantry, in the working class, in the ranks of the intelligentsia and in the Party itself.

While expropriating the large landowners, the Communist bureaucracy also expropriated the peasantry, turning

---

[1]*Translator's Note:* Here and subsequently "GAP" refers to indecipherable passages in the photocopy of the "Program" sent to the West by the VSKhSON leaders.

it into a village proletariat organized into communes.

The working class, enserfed on state enterprises which had become the collective property of the bureaucracy, became even poorer and more deprived of rights. The workers not only failed to receive the means of production as their property but were even deprived of their former possibility of uniting into free trade unions and openly struggling for higher wages and the betterment ... [GAP] ... in industry and trade was ... [GAP] ... a stratum not using hired ... [GAP] ... small merchants, etc.

Communist socialization of the economy means the expropriation of the people as a whole and their transformation into proletarians.

At the same time as the proletarianization of the vast majority of the populace was occurring, conditions were created which were favorable for the emergence of a new class of exploiters far more powerful than all the ruling classes of previous social systems and distinguished from them by its absolutely parasitic nature.

This class surpassed former ruling classes because of its militaristic organization and its widespread use of demagogy and terror.

It surpassed them because it gained monopolistic control over the entire national economy and thereby became the owner of the labor force.

It surpassed them because it created a historically unprecedented totalitarian system in order lawlessly to exploit and oppress the peoples.

It surpassed them because it organized a system of spiritual coercion which forced a man to think in accordance with the canons of the approved world-view. This totalitarian class of the Communist bureaucracy trampled both the individual and society under foot. The direction of the economy, which once belonged to the whole nation, is in its hands. It has usurped all the privileges and power of ownership, which it uses exclusively for self-interested aims, disregarding all the laws of morality.

The whole history of Communist rule represents an uninterrupted war, at times open and at times concealed, between the dictatorship of the bureaucrats and the people. Already in the period immediately following the conclusion of the civil war, the Party's authority was on the wane and its popularity catastrophically diminished even among the proletarian masses. The Party leadership did not trust the rank-and-file, while they did not trust the leadership. By 1921 many of the more aware workers had left the Party. The working class demanded that control of the economy be given to an all-Russian conference of producers and that the dictatorship over the people be abolished. In the struggle against their new masters the proletariat used the tried method of the strike. Peasant uprisings broke out in the Ukraine, the Don region, Siberia and many other areas. The sailors of Kronstadt mutinied. The popular anti-Communist revolution began under the slogan, "Power to the soviets, not to the parties!" But the Communists, using the advantages which their complete power gave the Party, gained control of the soviets by means of behind-the-scenes machinations and turned them into a screen for the dictatorship. The slogan "Soviets without Communism!" therefore meant: "Down with the dictatorship! Power to the people!" A situation was created which threatened to liquidate the new masters as a class. But the Communist dictators answered the demands of the working class, which they supposedly represented, with brutal terror. The old revolutionary workers' cadres were suppressed: some were shot, others filled up the concentration camps. The labor unions were continually being infiltrated by agents of the secret police; workers were executed for participating in strikes.

Since, however, the Communist class was not yet sufficiently strong, it was forced in 1921 to retreat and introduce the NEP, thereby temporarily abandoning the formation of agricultural communes. To revitalize the country and increase the productivity of labor, which had fallen to an unprecedented low level, private enterprise was temporarily permitted in industry and trade.

Having exploited this interlude, the Communist class, which had grown in numbers and strengthened its position, then began a new offensive in which it consistently pushed through its general policy with the aid of flexible tactics which frequently disoriented the populace. In 1929 this class began the forced collectivization of the peasantry. The Agricultural Decree, which had been ratified by the Second All-Russian Congress of Soviets, was once and for all trampled under foot. The Communist government suppressed the uncoordinated resistance of the peasants with the help of punitive detachments of the secret police. And it exiled millions of expropriated persons. Peasants interned in the concentration camps were used as unpaid labor on large government construction projects.

While engaged in surmounting the difficulties of collectivization, the Party leadership decided to organize a great famine in the 'thirties in order to break peasant opposition once and for all. Armed detachments were sent into the villages to requisition by force not only so-called surplus goods but also the basic supplies necessary for the peasants' survival. The frightful results of this measure—ten million persons died of starvation—have been carefully concealed from the rest of the world by the Iron Curtain. A second goal was simultaneously pursued: to force millions of peasants off the land so they might be used as a supplementary labor force for socialist industrialization ... [GAP] ... the population of dying villages filled the cities to overflowing ... [GAP] ... the world Communist revolution. At the 14th Party conference a directive was issued to link national economic development to the task of world-wide Communist expansion. Thus, the second promise with which the Bolshevik regime had veiled itself—the demagogic proclamation of peace to the peoples of the world—was openly deemed inoperative.

The Marxist Revolution, which has been carried out for decades by means of the sword and the lie, elicited opposition even in the Party itself. This resistance was expressed on the ideological level in theories which revised the theses of Marxism-Leninism. On the practical level it resulted in factional struggles within the Party. However, the class of Party bureaucrats, who had already transformed the country into a concentration camp, found little difficulty in dealing with their erstwhile comrades, and by 1937 many thousands of independently-thinking members of the Party had become victims of the Communist system. Periodic purges of the Party were carried out with the aim of removing from the ranks of the Communist class and its servants those elements which had ceased to approve the general policy of that class. The concept of class struggle was retained even after the destruction of the old privileged classes. Hence the new ruling class, while protecting itself with the help of the entire machinery of state, is able to disguise its struggle against the people by using a concept which originally had a totally different meaning. Purges within the Party were also justified as measures against the class enemy. During the same period, on the eve of the Second World War, the class of the Party bureaucracy exterminated tens of thousands of Red Army officers, which in effect represented a continuation of the use of terror against the people for the purpose of maintaining the Communist dictatorship.

The Second World War slowed down the internal struggle between the Communist bureaucracy and the people. The war was by nature a national struggle and was viewed only as such by the people. The Party leadership feared to use Communist slogans to summon the populace to battle and therefore permitted a limited revival of national tradition. It also manifested a more tolerant attitude toward the [Russian Orthodox] Church. Only after the war was there any attempt to attribute an ideological character to the war. Incidentally, even Fascism, a variant form of the totalitarian system, does not represent as all-encompassing a tyranny as Communism. While a Communist dictatorship concentrates all three spheres of social life into the hands of the Party bureaucracy, a Fascist dictatorship seizes only a political and ideological monopoly. The absence of Party control over the main lever— the economic one—weakens the effect of its political and ideological yoke. It should also be noted that Fascist dictatorships do not arise of themselves but are elicited as a reaction to the threat of Communism. As a rule, they are viable only as long as a Communist threat remains real. But the basic difference between Fascism and Communism is the fact that the Fascist Party does not form a parasitic, all-powerful class of exploiters similar to the Communist bureaucracy. In the struggle with Germany the people defended their homeland, not the Communist class and its terrible system. By starting a war for world dominion and carrying out a policy of extermination against subjected peoples, Germany aroused a powerful union of nations against herself and was destroyed as an aggressor-state.

The Communist oligarchy took advantage of the victorious outcome of the war and imposed Communist regimes on a number of countries. It continues to maintain these regimes by force of arms. By suppressing the national liberty and social rights of peoples by force, the Communist government [of the U.S.S.R.] provokes a hatred toward Russia which could become a burdensome legacy for our country.

Hopes for better conditions of life after the war were not fulfilled. To prevent any possible actions on the part of the people, the Party oligarchy resorted to a tried method: mass repression. The total number of imprisoned at the end of the 'forties amounted to about 20 million. As in the 'thirties, a blow was struck against the military. Communist propaganda attempts to justify repression and the low standard of living, which shows no improvement despite immense efforts on the part of the populace, by frightening people with the imaginary threat of imperialism. Conscious of the fact that its position will be insecure as long as non-Communist countries exist and provide an alternative example, the Communist bureaucracy continues its general policy of world revolution, although any such adventure is doomed from the start. Aggressiveness is inherent in the very nature of this class; its existence is inextricably linked to Communist revolutionary expansion. Communism will lose its strength and be easily destroyed as soon as this expansionism abates. Since hopes for a Communist revolution are dimming not only in Europe and the USA but also in Asia and Africa, and since at the same time the situation in Communist countries is becoming more and more threatening, individual elements in international Communism are already openly declaring the need for an atomic war as a last resort.

SECTION III

The Communist System

The ideological sources of the regime of the Communist dictatorship are the Marxist doctrine of socialization of the economy and the Leninist teaching that the Party represents the leading and guiding force in a Communist society. The establishment of a one-party totalitarian regime and the transformation of private property into government property become the preconditions for the engendering of an omnipotent class of exploiters. Since virtually everything belongs to the state and since a Communist state is nothing but the monopolistic power of the Party, the bureaucratic nucleus of the Party, once it has established its dictatorship, becomes the manager and the owner of the socialized national property.

The earlier form of property is liquidated, but a new

form, created as a result of socialization, opens up new potentials for exploiting all groups of the populace to an unprecedented degree. It also furnishes the new owner-monopolists means for repressing the dispossessed people which were previously completely unusable.

In the place of the former classes and their mutual inter-relationships, two new classes are formed, which have their own particular inter-relations. On the one hand there is the class of omnipotent monopolists, and on the other, a class of have-nots which includes everyone else. The latter are compressed into a faceless enserfed mass. This oppressed class is distinguished from former deprived classes (1) by its radical separation from any property which would assure it freedom of labor; within the framework of the Communist system it will never in the future be able to acquire such property; (2) by the fact that it has no rights and no opportunity for showing initiative in life; (3) by its encompassing social groups which had formerly been independent classes and social strata.

The proletariat did not come to control the means of production as a result of the Communist revolution. Their new masters, who are much stronger than the capitalist employers, have merely increased the exploitation by putting the workers in a position whence they cannot legally struggle for improvement of their lot.

In order to be allowed to till an insignificantly small personal plot, the peasantry, which comprises half the country's population, is forced to work off a Soviet *barshchina* [corvée] on government estates. The process of proletarianization, which is now nearing completion, should transform today's collective farmers into rural laborers of the Communist bureaucracy, which masks itself as the state.

Along with the workers and peasantry, the intelligentsia has been subjected to a cruel and subtle exploitation. This intellectual proletariat is forced to work under the strictest control of the Party oligarchy.

Finally, female labor is nowhere in the world exploited as widely as in Communist countries.

Having concentrated the entire national economy into their hands, the Communist proprietors show themselves to be poor managers. Rapaciousness and extravagance, inevitable under such a system, cause serious loss of resources, which the populace must bear, as well as huge losses due to unproductive waste of labor. The worst damage to the national economy is administered by so-called socialist planning. The dogma of "management" represents a special kind of planning, impossible under other social circumstances. Here basic capital is invested in unprofitable branches of the economy which play a decisive role in preserving and strengthening the power of the bureaucrats. Despite all the partial reforms which it is forced to adopt, the Communist class will not, as long as it holds power, reject this form of planning *in toto,* even though it is disadvantageous to the economy. Such planning is only possible at a time when the populace is in need of the most basic commodities. A raising of the standard of living plays no part in the plans of the ruling bureaucracy; in order to preserve the Communist system it is necessary to hold society on the verge of destitution.

Fenced off from the whole world, the Communist caste has created the isolated economic system which the oligarchy needs in order to preserve its possessions and power. This economy, however, represents a heavy burden for the people.

A chronic backwardness in agriculture is the lot of all countries where the Marxist system rules. The experience of countries with an advanced agriculture has shown that a free, small-scale economy most effectively assures food for the populace and raw material for industry. Collectivization, which has cost so many ruined lives, has over the course of decades produced economically harmful results which cannot be rectified within the present system.

Marxist-Leninist economics leads to discord in the whole economy, to unproductive expenditure of labor and to a squandering of the national wealth. And it assists the Communist class to preserve its limitless rule over the peoples.

This economic tyranny is created and supported by a particular political regime which for the time being suppresses the people's striving for economic, political and spiritual liberation. If from an economic standpoint the Communist system is a variety of state monopoly capitalism, from a political standpoint it represents an extreme totalitarianism in the process of degenerating into despotism.

The sole political organization—the Communist Party—monopolizes all power and removes the people from any participation in managing social affairs. The omnipotent masters, rulers and high-priests of Communism—the Party oligarchy—are situated at the very center of the system, whence "levers" and "gears" branch out to enmesh all of society. There does not exist a single social cell where this power is not felt and is not in fact all-powerful. The Party itself is not an independently existing and functioning organism. It is employed as only one of the major weapons of the Party clique which is grouped around the General Secretary-dictator, who confers all the prerogatives of power and even establishes the norms of "Communist morality."

The militaristic principle of the Party's organization precludes any democratism or real activity in its ranks. The whole history of the Party proves graphically that it is not capable of resisting the will of its leadership and that it is most often a passive tool in the hands of the oligarchy.

The system of "gears" and "levers" is not limited to the Party. All other organizations are set up under her control: the state apparatus, the trade unions, the judiciary, the armed forces, so-called social organizations, youth and cultural-educational organizations, etc.

State organs, from the local level to the Supreme Soviet, are indirectly Party-controlled and in no way represent the populace. This is especially true under the system of "elections" now practiced which is exclusively for show.

The Party-state trade unions are deprived of even a shadow of independence and serve as just one more tool for oppressing the laborers. They have nothing in common with the free trade unions of capitalist countries where these workers' organizations really do defend the interests of their members, openly struggle for better conditions and achieve victories. The task of Soviet trade unions is to educate workers in a Communist spirit and to organize, with the assistance of an agency of strikebreakers, "socialist competition," which is actually a subtle method of exploitation. The unions serve to create an illusion among the workers that they have their own class organization.

In the Communist state there are no guarantees of life, liberty or the worth of the citizenry. Class rights are entirely subjugated to the interests of the ruling bureaucracy. The judicial apparatus carries out its punitive functions automatically, convicting not only active anti-Communist strugglers but also those who seem insufficiently dedicated to the regime. If needed, any form of pressure can be exerted on the court. Under such conditions the constitution becomes a fiction and the scanty rights it proclaims, cynical mockery.

This whole monstrous system of oppression is permeated by the secret political police who have unlimited possibilities at their disposal. Both the Party itself and the state are under the control of the state security organs. The methods of the secret police serve as a mirror of the Communist regime. Hundreds of thousands of persons on all rungs of the social ladder are recruited by them as informers and secret agents. Mutual shadowing, blackmail, provocation, slander, corruption, torture, concentration camps, the planned annhilation of the flower of the nation—all these are common occurrences in the life of the Communist world.

But terror alone is not enough to support the Communist system. Along with its monopoly of property and power, the Party bureaucracy has also appropriated ideological monopoly. A totalitarian organization necessarily presupposes a dictatorship over thought. The individual is subjected to coercion even in the most intimate, treasured spheres of existence. The Communist oligarchy encroaches upon people's feelings and thoughts. It transforms its worldview into an official state creed, a falling away from which can result in the "apostate's" ruin.

Marxism-Leninism is hostile to religion, not because it is an atheistic teaching but because it is itself a false religion. This teaching rejects and proclaims as harmful all which does not correspond to its dogma; it violates science, mutilates tradition and prescribes its "morality" to humanity. This banal world-view imitates religious rites, introduces its own icons, church calendar, etc. But just as there is no true God in this false religion, so is there no room in it for Man. This rabid deviation and narrow sectarianism never was and never will be the world-view of the peoples.

The implanting of a false religion is a necessary condition for Communist rule. Such a grafting cannot, however, be accomplished until national tradition—the living soul of a people—is uprooted. A bitter struggle is therefore carried out against tradition and the historical religious consciousness of a people. This represents an attempt at psychologically suppressing a nation. In the place of true religion an idolatrous cult of the despot, of the "Leninist Central Committee," of the Party is instilled. Political power becomes a fetish. In the sphere of spiritual awareness peoples are forcibly thrown back to the pre-Christian era. The same thing occurs in the legal sphere. Ideological overseers take possession of the cultural heritage of a nation and adapt it in mutilated form to "Communist education." All the conditions are created for mass social hypnosis. An Iron Curtain isolates the population of the Communist camp from the life of the surrounding world. In an atmosphere of total spying on one's people every attempt at living communication within a Communist country is suppressed. All that is sincere, distinctive, gifted and noble in a people is forced to live in voiceless opposition. Not for one day does the gigantic factory of disinformation, *ersatz*-culture and falsification of history cease its work. There is no lie which would not be employed if it were deemed advantageous. An entire Communist dictionary has been created in which all concepts have been distorted. Through such an "education," to which it ascribes great importance, the Party oligarchy strives to enslave the mind of a people and lay waste its soul.

At a time when labor productivity in Russia is significantly lower than in capitalist countries, when a huge number of industrial enterprises are unprofitable, when a shortage of essential goods is sharply felt, when agricultural production is consistently falling, so that the country cannot meet its own bread needs, when laborers are exploited ever more shamelessly and when freedom of conscience is crudely violated—at such a time the Party leadership has announced in the new program of the CPSU that socialism has been fully constructed and that the next step, the construction of Communism, has begun. Such in brief are the results of a half-century's construction of socialism, for which the people have paid with human sacrifices unnumbered and with a general lowering of their moral and cultural level.

In the program of the Communist Party the next stage is defined as mainly one of constructing the material-technical base of Communism. As in the case of Marxist socialism, Communism cannot arise naturally as the result of the free development of the national economy, a progressive evolution of the political system and the independent cultural activity of the people. The decisive role in the construction of Communism belongs to the state, which represents an embodiment of the dictatorship of the class of the Communist bureaucracy. This class organizes the construction of the material-technical base of Communism and increases the coercive functions of its state in order to mobilize the masses and force them to do slave labor. This is also done in order to liquidate by gradual measures—and now already formally—the cooperative holdings of the collective farms and all other property which this class has not yet taken possession of; to achieve, in the spirit of forced labor discipline, rigid control over the balance of labor and consumption among the proletarianized masses; to preserve the "Communist" property belonging to this class; to expand its rights and privileges; to suppress the peoples' liberation struggle. The general strengthening of the Party state and the increasing of the power of the bureaucratic class signify the loss of even a semblance of personal independence on the part of the citizenry.

The material base of Communist slavery is formed as a result of attempts to coerce society into socialized Communist consumption. The commune projects worked out in the USSR at the end of the 'twenties and *de facto* created in China in the 'sixties may be taken as an example of such a structure. The sphere of individual free consumption must constantly be narrowed. Wages must be reduced to payment-in-kind, meals at one's place of work, etc. Life is planned according to an official budget with mandatory conscription of labor. This path leads to the destruction of the individual, the family and the nation.

The family, which is founded on a stable marriage and consists of parents and children whose mutual rights stand higher than any official prescription or law, represents the preserver of human individuality and the basic natural unit of society without which a social structure cannot exist. No measures of deceit, which have been developed by Communist agitators to the point of virtuosity, can hide the fact that Communism leads precisely to the destruction of the individual, the family and the nation. Marxist-Leninist ideologists, who are striving to liquidate the home and who declare their class monopoly over child care and education, plan the creation of an all-embracing network of pre-school institutions and boarding schools which would allow the mother to be fully enserfed at her place of work. The family is no longer seen as an organic unit, which is reinforced by ties free from the dictates of Party supervisors. Even the essence of love becomes unspeakably perverted and debased. Communist education is completely subjugated to the class aims of the Party bureaucracy; it stands for the fabricating of a rootless, faceless mass man.

The fact that Communism has posed such goals for itself and that fanatics strive, no matter what, to realize them, points to Communism's pretensions to become a new religion for humanity. No economic, political or philosophical system sets itself the task of transforming all human relationships and answering all questions.

The internal war against the people, which is a result of a new deepening of the Communist revolution, is achieving its maximal intensity at the present stage. All the power of the Communist class is being mobilized for a last decisive struggle. A delirious utopia seems close to being fully effected. But, despite the fact that history has brought this experiment to an almost maximally hideous form, the final goals of the Communist class remain unobtainable. World-wide collapse will ensue for this class precisely at the moment when it will feel that it has become all-powerful on earth and in heaven.

Section IV

The Historical Foredoom of Communism

The essence of Communism is so reactionary and amoral that its ideologists cannot reveal it in undisguised form. A veil of illusions is thrown over social reality. Careful masking is a characteristic trait of Marxist-Leninist ideology and an important means of Communist control.

Before seizing power the Communists employ common

socialist ideals in their propaganda and conceal their true aims. In order to facilitate the struggle for power they preach the creation of a single popular front and demand the broadest democratic liberties. After they have seized power, however, their tactics change radically. A totalitarian dictatorship is established, and the allied revolutionary parties are either destroyed or deprived of any real influence. Once the discrepancy between their promises and reality is revealed, the Communists organize an enforced "unanimity of thought."

The undisguised essence of Communism is that the Party, which seizes power under pretense of liberating men from exploitation, creates a class of omnipotent exploiters. The limitless power of the Communist oligarchy and a Party-state economy do not signify socialism. The "construction of socialism" organized by this bureaucratic class has proved to be nothing other than industrialization carried out by the most criminal manner in the interests of this class. Any other path toward constructing industry would not only not have called for bloody sacrifices but would have taken a considerably shorter time. Several highly important reasons have slowed down "socialist" industrialization and continue to do so. First, there was the civil war which brought industry to a state of collapse and disorganization. Second, there is the degradation of agriculture, which should have become the basic foundation of industrialization by providing raw material for industry, food supplies and additional funds from the sale of agricultural produce on the world market. Third, there is the use of the unproductive slave labor of millions of men uninterested in their work and the prohibition of all free labor outside the framework of the state economy. Fourth, there is mismanagement on a giant scale, which is inevitable under Communism, and the maintenance of an entire army of bureaucrats of all ranks. Fifth, there is artificial planning which results in irreplaceable losses for the national economy. Sixth, there is the loss of incalculable funds which the Communist bureaucracy squanders on the illusive goal of world dominion; this occurs in the form of aid to other countries in the interests of propaganda, to create a world-wide armed camp and to support Communist parties in capitalist countries and their subversion work. The seventh and final cause was the simple extermination of the best farmers, skilled workers and the greater part of the scientific and technical intelligentsia.

The level of popular consumption has fallen far behind the potentials of contemporary productivity. It is five or six times lower than in the capitalist countries and, most significant of all, the level of consumption of the populace in the USSR is less than in pre-revolutionary tsarist Russia.

The Communist form of ownership is deeply reactionary. It is harmful in the economic sphere and results in all-possible sorts of oppression of the individual and society. The historical development of forms of ownership [in Russia] was leading unswervingly to a free national economy; Communism represents an abnormal economic formation. The statist system did not develop naturally from the historical forms of the economy; it was artificially and forcibly created and adapted to the interests of a predatory exploiting class. A legal development of ownership should lead not to its monopoly by one social group or class but to its universal differentiation. Only a mixed economy can truly liberate labor and condition broad economic democracy.

While the historical development of society has been directed toward increasingly greater civil liberty and more advanced ethical relations among men, the Communist dictatorship in its very essence represents lawlessness, deprives both the individual and society of all rights, establishes a regime based on serfdom and morally corrupts the populace. Its temporary existence is maintained exclusively through deceit and coercion. But deception cannot continue forever, and coercion will be overthrown by force.

While there is a world-wide tendency toward the greater unification of mankind and toward mutual ties between peoples, the Communist regime has artificially isolated nations from one another and threatens to involve them in senseless war. Communist politics are a source of constant tension in the world.

The attempt forcibly to unite the world into a Communist International and to extend the system of totalitarian oppression to the whole world was doomed to failure from the very beginning. Only through freedom and voluntary cooperation among nations can the world be united.

While the development of human knowledge leads to an increased comprehension of truth, Communist ideology, with its dogmas of materialism and its fanatical intolerance for the spiritual experience of all humanity, represents the sectarian world-view of a predatory class which has broken away from the ideals common to all mankind.

The true nature of this class is becoming increasingly apparent to all. It can no longer conceal its egoism and has no goals which could justify its rule. Its only aim is to hold on to its possessions and power at any cost. This class is spiritually dead; its milieu is disintegrating, its policies are becoming vacillating and openly adventuristic, it is incapable of leading anyone anywhere. While at the beginning of the Revolution a part of the working class and landless peasantry mistakenly put their hopes on the coming to power of the Communist Party, at present the antagonistic contradictions between the interests of the Communist bureaucracy and the needs of all social groups of the populace have become obvious to the majority. Since it must wage an unceasing struggle with its own people, the Communist class is isolated and alone. The situation of this class, its psychology and behavior, are very similar to the position and psychology of occupying forces. The absence of any legal opposition renders the people's struggle for freedom difficult. Extensive spy networks and punitive secret police organs are attempting to smother the growing underground forces of revolution, but the people are united in a striving for liberation, and their victory has been historically predetermined.

SECTION V

The Inadequacy of Marxist-Leninist Doctrine in the Face of History

The International Anti-Communist Liberation Movement

A half century of life has shown the fallacy of the majority of Marxist predictions and the untruthfulness of the promises emblazoned on the flags of the Communist revolution.

Contrary to the basic thesis of Marxism, Communist revolution did not take place in industrial nations with a high concentration of capital and a large working class, where the Marxist "law" of a definite relationship between the level of production and the character of social relationships should have been in effect. It occurred in countries which had not yet undergone industrialization and which had an absolute predominance of agrarian population. The absence of a sizable and stable middle class, the tense situation resulting from the accumulated dissatisfaction of the masses, widespread disorganization caused by military failures, and the political illiteracy of the populace—these were the conditions under which the small but well-organized Bolshevik Party seized power. The establishment of Communist regimes in other countries has been the direct or indirect result of aggression from the international Communist center. A Marxist-Leninist revolution, meaning the socialization of the economy and the establishment of a Communist dictatorship, would be unthinkable in industrially developed countries, which testify to the capitalist system's capacity for further development. At the same time the Communist countries, in which labor productivity is comparatively low, are not in a position to defeat the West in peaceful competition. In view of this, it is obvious that Communism will never become a world-wide system. The capitalist countries, which are developing in an evolutionary manner, did not see, as the Marxists predicted they would, a fatal impoverishment of the proletariat and a concentration of the means of production and national wealth into the hands of a narrow group of monopolists. The advanced capitalist national economies have already provided their population with the food-stuffs and essential industrial goods in abundance which Communism has been promising in vain for half a century. In these countries there has been formed a large and constantly growing middle class, which is gradually absorbing the former proletariat. In this world engaged in self-renewal the shape of a free society where there will be no poverty and all will have rights is already becoming evident.

The former colonial countries of Asia and Africa have begun an independent development, having chosen a non-Communist path. The principles of Afro-Asian socialism are incompatible with Communist doctrine. Thus, the hopes of Marxist leaders and ideologists, who expected these countries to become an inexhaustible Communist reserve, have not materialized. At the same time, serious differences of opinion are becoming apparent in the socialist camp, and its much-vaunted unity is visibly crumbling before our eyes. Thus we see an attempt by China to create a separate Communist movement under its leadership and the striving of East European countries to carry out increasingly independent national policies. In some countries (Yugoslavia, Poland) the peasant economy has not been collectivized despite strong pressure from the Central Committee of the CPSU. In general, in spite of the bureaucratic class's striving toward total socialization and toward the concentration of the socialized economy in its own hands, something which would complete the Communist revolution, such a Communism has yet to be established anywhere. In practice, the system always exists with deviations from the "ideal." The attempts at complete socialization in communes (Russia, China) have inevitably led to a rapid collapse of the whole economy, and the fanatics have been immediately forced to retreat.

Communism has exhausted its potential strength, its aggressiveness is petering out, and it has already lost its nimbus. The old policies, which are carried on by inertia and because they are inseparable from the system itself, are becoming contradictory. The struggle between the CPSU and the Chinese Communist Party for hegemony over the world Communist movement and the Chinese leadership's desperate favoring of a world war in the name of Communist victory represent the final act in the prolonged Marxist-Leninist experiment on the peoples of the world.

Although Communism has never been imposed on a nation without encountering opposition, once it has ascended to its zenith it successfully suppresses any unrest. Decaying Communism has already been shaken by popular revolution. In the 'fifties a wave of liberation movements swept East Germany, Poland, Hungary and China.

The first successful people's revolution broke out in 1956 in Hungary. The elementally inflamed resentment of the populace destroyed a tyrannical system within a few days. The stage sets were removed and reality revealed. All social strata of the populace were united. A real national front consisting of all fighters for freedom was formed. The false myth of the unity of the Communist bureaucracy and the people was unmasked in open combat. Only a few agents of the secret political police defended the Party oligarchy. The intelligentsia, student youth and workers comprised the *avant-garde* of the people's revolution. Although, because of its dispersement and the brevity of the revolutionary clashes, the peasantry did not have time to get involved in the struggle, it openly expressed its attitude toward the events transpiring. The army manifested in deeds its full unity with the populace. Not only regular soldiers but also graduates of military schools and officers went over *en masse* to the side of the insurgents. The Communist Party fell apart. After the first days of the revolution, its numbers had been reduced from 900,000 to scarcely 100,000. The former rank-and-file Party members well understood that a chasm separated them from the Party bureaucracy and that they now had a real chance to serve the people in the struggle for its rights. Two other comparatively small groups, important for their social significance, participated in the revolution: political exiles and the opposition within the Party apparatus. Although the opposition in the Party-state apparatus and political émigrés were not capable of independently leading a struggle for liberation, they facilitated the people's path to victory and averted potential casualties.

The Hungarian revolution flared up under especially unfavorable circumstances—at a time when the country was filled with Communist bloc troops. Free Hungary survived several days and then was crushed as a result of direct foreign intervention. Nevertheless, the Communist regime which was reinstated was forced to make large concessions, allowing the peasants certain rights in the buying and selling of immoveable property, permitting private trade, significantly decreasing the bureaucratic apparatus and purging it of its most criminal elements.

Although the new order did not, because of the brevity of Hungary's interlude of freedom, have time to acquire a definite shape, an outline could already be clearly discerned in the programs of the numerous parties which arose and which represented the interests of all social groups. The common will of the populace rejected both the Communist path and capitalism. Even in the West the latter is gradually being transformed into a new democratic economic system. The principal demand of the populace in the agricultural sphere was that the peasantry be granted the right of free use of the land. Industry, it was felt, should develop according to self-governing and cooperative principles; an extant prototype for this were the workers' soviets which had been created by the revolution. The basic slogans of the revolution were: freedom of labor, a government of law, civil liberties, a renaissance of national religio-cultural tradition. These are the main features of the program of the anti-Communist people's liberation revolution.

The Hungarian Revolution of 1956 has enormous worldwide significance. It marked the initial awakening of the people from Communist hypnosis. It showed the entire world the weakness and worthlessness of the totalitarian class once it is deprived of the possibility of masking itself and oppressing the people by means of the people and in the name of the people. It became the prelude to the liberation of all peoples enslaved by Communism.

The exposure of the bloody Stalinist era throughout the whole world, anti-Communist uprisings and protests in a series of countries, rebellions in Russia's concentration camps—all this has forced the Communist leadership verbally to acknowledge the crimes committed in the process of the construction of socialism. This step was dictated by its need to disassociate itself from the nightmarish weight of the past before world opinion, international Communism and its own people. The hypocritical condemnation of past "errors" took place in an atmosphere of confusion, fear and internal conflict within the Communist leadership. The leadership's admissions contained only a small fraction of the full list of crimes, and none of those responsible for these acts of lawlessness were brought to trial.

Historical crimes, consciously committed by the class of the Communist bureaucracy, were labelled "errors" and the responsibility for the misfortunes of entire nations was ascribed to one man. After "principled" Marxist analysis, it was explained that the aberrations which occurred over the entire period of socialist construction had been alien to socialism and Communism and represented chance events conditioned by the negative traits of one man. The world Communist camp split on the question of how to evaluate Stalinism. While one segment hypocritically acknowledges the "accidental errors" of one individual, the other accuses them of being "outright revisionists" and "traitors to Communism" and continues to term the methods of Stalinism "truly revolutionary" and "verily Marxist-Leninist." Indeed, manifestation and essence are one. There existed a Marxist-Leninist socialism, and it was constructed by Marxist-Leninist methods. There was not and could not in the future be any other kind of "construction."

The period of the 'fifties and 'sixties is characterized by an especially rapid growth of popular awareness. Revolution first occurs in the mind. A liberation from illusions is taking place; Party propaganda and agitation have lost all influence. Peasants, workers and the intelligentsia are becoming aware of the basic unity of their interests and of the irreconciliability of these interests with those of the class of the Party bureaucracy. This conflict can only be resolved by the liquidation of this class's monopoly over all spheres of life. In Russia such forms of protest as demonstrations and strikes are already from time to time turning into open clashes with the authorities.

Revolutionary liberation tendencies definitely manifest themselves in the literature of the 'fifties and 'sixties.

Because the whole people is solidly united for a decisive struggle for liberty, the ruling bureaucracy has no other paths before it than gradually to retreat and maneuver under pressure from popular opposition or fully to reintroduce the methods of Stalinism. In vacillating between these two extremes, the dictatorship of the class of the Party bureaucracy is in process of disintegration. While the regime disintegrates, new revolutionary organizations are being formed and the forces of liberation are growing. The closer the revolution approaches, the more rapidly do splits occur in the Party. This process is historically inevitable. Two groups are formed: the dogmatists and revisionists. The struggle between them is being carried on within the world Communist movement and at times assumes extreme forms. Neither of these groups can emerge victorious or grow in strength. Revisionism is a negative and half-way movement; it is incapable of producing a program for the construction of a new free society. As a teaching, Marxism-Leninism is completely unknown to the people. A philosophical system can never serve as a popular world-view. Such a world-view can only be organic and religious. A temporary obscuring and weakening of spirituality only means that a people is living in a twilight which cannot continue for long. A people itself creates those new forces which will enable it to solve its basic problems. The Party opposition will be forced to join these forces, to accept popular ideology and dissolve itself in the ranks of liberators and creators.

The dogmatic wing of the Communist class lacks a broad social base among the populace which could give it support in organizing serious resistance. Its complete destruction is predetermined.

The fate of the world anti-Communist movement will be decided in Russia.

The All-Russian Social-Christian Union for the Liberation of the People calls for cooperation with any organized force which is struggling for the common cause. While promoting a Social-Christian program as the basis for the future organization of social relations in the country, the Union for the Liberation of the People is not hostile to programs which are different but close in spirit. The final choice [concerning Russia's future] must be made only after the overthrow of the Communist dictatorship and the destruction of the statist system, under conditions of freedom and peace.

PART TWO

Section VI

The Basic Principles of Social-Christianity

Conflict in today's world is not determined or exhausted by the economic interests of social classes. It is a much broader and deeper phenomenon: it involves a decisive confrontation between two contradictory conceptions of man— the Christian and the anti-Christian.

A spiritual battle is being waged for the personality [*lichnost'*]. Two courses are open to humanity: either a free turning to God and an acceptance of His commandments, which will lead to a revealing of the strength and beauty of Man, or a falling away from God, which will result in a Satanocracy, the dissolution of the personality into primordial forces, enslavement to matter and a degeneration of consciousness caused by a loss of true goals and of the meaning of life.

Both capitalism and its sickly offspring, Communism, can be overcome only through a Christianization of the entire life of society. Although the Christian religion is not bound to any transient social structure, its ethical principles can and should be embodied in economic and political practice. Christianity discloses the meaning of existence and points to the temporary goals toward which mankind should strive. Being the highest criterion, Christianity re-establishes the correct hierarchy of values in the world.

The Christian religion attributes the highest and most absolute value to the human personality and to brotherly relations between men. By rehabilitating the personality, Social-Christianity also re-establishes the people [*narod*] as a complex spiritual entity capable of creative self-expression.

The ideal of Christianity is a diversity of individuals in free unity. Christianity opposes both egoistical individualism and personality-less collectivism. The goal of the Social-Christian movement is to transform innerly the faceless Communist collective into a personalized collective, one which is inspired, free, independently active and united by brotherly ties.

While Communism demoralizes both the individual and society by alienating man from his own "I," Social-Christianity recognizes that man possesses certain inalienable rights arising from his nature. It [Social-Christianity] reestablishes the balance between the individual, society and the state. Denouncing totalitarianism in all its forms, Social-Christianity strives to confine all power within its natural limits. Totalitarianism—the greatest evil known to history—arises whenever society is absorbed by the state or, something which amounts to the same thing, whenever the state is dissolved into society, thus becoming a false-church.

The Social-Christian view of the state does not confuse it with society. The state has certain specific and irreplaceable functions, which serve the common good and cannot be passed on to anyone else. The strength of a state should always correspond to those tasks which it is called upon to perform. On the other hand, only in exceptional cases can the state be permitted to interfere in those broad areas which are the domain of social forces and individuals. Attempts on the part of the state to interfere with the rights of society and man and pretensions on the part of social elements to state prerogatives represent equally harmful abuses. The real rights of the citizen, both spiritual and material, are guaranteed when there exists a separation of the spheres of activity of the state and of private individuals. The political sphere, considerably limited, should primarily belong to the state. The Social-Christian doctrine of state sees as positively evil any system in which power becomes a prize for competing parties or is monopolized by one party. In general, the organization of state power along party lines is unacceptable from the point of view of Social-Christianity.

Society should be able to participate directly in the life of the country through local self-government and the representation of peasant communes and national corporations (the latter being large unions of those engaged in physical and mental labor) on the highest legislative body of the country. Political currents and movements may be permitted to be formed without hindrance (without, however, taking on the character of parties) in order to allow open expression of opinion and to exert a beneficial influence on everyday decision-making.

The economy and culture should primarily be areas of social and individual concern.

Social-Christianity strives to create a society in which man will not be exploited by man and where mutual relations will be based on common solidarity.

As the expression of man's creative spirit, labor must be emancipated so that it can fully serve the well-being of the individual, the family and society. Freedom of labor is only possible under a new, personalized form of property which would bind labor and the means of production into one and place them at the disposal of the individual. Each toiler has the right to own the implements of his labor. The Social-Christian system creates conditions under which each worker is provided the means of production with the help of special institutions. To accomplish this, a mixed economy must be created. And the widest possible personalization of capital and land must be carried out so that the national wealth will be accurately distributed among the populace and personalized property will be put to the service of social goals. The transfer of the means of production into the hands of the workers—something which preserves inviolate the fundamental condition of civilization: division of labor—leads to high productivity, unleashes popular initiative and liquidates proletarianization. Self-governing, personalized collectives, organized into national corporations, will become the decisive force in the economic life of the country. The obligatory result of such an economic order will be a balance between productivity and consumption and the distribution of the greater part of the national income in the interests of the majority. Only a Social-Christian economics can insure a decent standard of living for all, liberate labor and remove material obstacles on the road to man's spiritual development.

In contrast to Marxism, which looks upon the family as an economic category, Social-Christianity views it as a spiritual category. According to this view, the family is not a product of economics but rather performs the sacred mission of educating and perfecting the individual. It is instrumental in the development of spiritual culture and supports its foundations. Nothing can replace the family in this regard.

Social-Christianity assigns a special role to woman as preserver of the home. Her deeply beneficial influence on the moral life of society, chiefly through the family, is of unsurpassed value to a nation. Because of their irreplaceable role, women must be given special rights to make the performance of their duty less onerous. Social-Christianity would lead to a system in which women would not economically be forced to participate directly in social production.

While Social-Christianity recognizes the seriousness of the problem of education and does not decline actively to influence the spiritual, intellectual and physical moulding of man, it at the same time protects the right of each individual freely to develop his personality and grants the family the basic role in the initial education of children.

Social-Christianity reserves an important place for the Church as a free community of believers inspired by the highest ideals which bypasses all boundaries and gathers men into one whole. Social-Christianity also considers that the Church can carry out its spiritual mission only when it is independent of the state and striving toward global unity.

In its cultural policy, Social-Christianity affirms that living culture is a means of national self-knowledge and self-expression and that it can flourish only in an atmosphere of freedom. At the same time, Christian culture bears an inherently supra-national character which will play a decisive role in our era in the task of bringing peoples together into one pan-human family.

SECTION VII

On Property

POINT 1. The collective class property of the Communist bureaucracy, which has been gained as a result of the expropriation of the whole nation, must be taken under the people's control and personalized.

Through personalization, the people will regain direct control over the national economy, which has been alienated from them. In order for a mixed economy and a free, democratic economic system to be created, the following forms of ownership must be established: national, state, communal and personalistic.

SECTION VIII

Land Ownership

POINT 2. The land must belong to the entire people as national property not subject to sale or any other form of alienation. Citizens, communes and the state may use it only on the basis of limited holding.

POINT 3. The lands of the country must be divided into a citizens' fund, communal fund and state fund. The citizens' fund will consist of partitioned and reserved parts.

POINT 4. The lands comprising the citizens' fund must, once justly partitioned, be given over for individual use to all citizens of Great Russia [*Velikaia Rossiia*] desiring to work them. They will have the right to farm them either individually or in free union with other landholders. And they will have the right freely to dispose of the products of their labor. The right to transfer the basic land allotment through inheritance within the family must be guaranteed by law. The quantity of poultry and livestock on a farm should not be subject to limitation.

POINT 5. All general problems concerning land use, including the establishment of maximum norms of ownership and of the dimensions of a progressive tax, must be decided by the highest legislative body of the nation. Individual problems are to be left to local organs of self-government.

POINT 6. The state must grant new farmers long-term credit and technical and scientific aid to assist them in setting up their holdings.

POINT 7. The state must possess the exclusive right to exploit mineral resources, forests and water, all of which have a national significance.

SECTION IX

Industry and Service

POINT 8. Industrial enterprises and service industries must be owned and directed by collectives which work or finance them.

POINT 9. Depending on the size of its basic capital and on its significance for the national economy, an enterprise may be transferred

    (a) into the full ownership of the collective which works on it

(b) into the partial ownership of the collective which works on it and partially into the hands of free shareholders, so that profits from industry may be extended to all levels of the populace.

POINT 10. The collective of each independent enterprise forms a single shareholding company (association).

For each category of worker and engineer a normative share of the profits derived from an enterprise must be established. This should be gradated in accordance with their professional qualifications. This individual portion of the property is expressed in personalized shares, which are consolidated for each member of the company. Personalized property will be guaranteed by law and a national credit system.

POINT 11. In accordance with economic and cultural demands in industry and commerce, small, medium and large-scale ownership must be created. As distinct from private property, personalized property is available to all and regulated by the state.

POINT 12. Scientists and technicians in planning and construction bureaus and in scientific research institutes must, upon the personalization of their enterprises, be included in the shareholding companies of those branches of industry which they serve.

POINT 13. To coordinate the entire economy, all individual companies must be organized, without any harm being done to their autonomous rights, into single corporations according to the branch of industry to which they belong. Through these corporations the state will be able to perform its social functions: to thwart the formation of monopolies, to safeguard honesty of competition, to regulate taxation, to even out the distribution of goods among the population and to offer financial help to needy enterprises.

POINT 14. The highest body of industrial management

should be the Corporation Chamber (National Council of Commercial-Industrial Unions) in which both individual corporations and the state will be represented.

POINT 15. The state must support and encourage individual craft production, which has retained its importance despite the complex technology and high concentration of the contemporary economy. This should be accomplished through a favorable tax policy, special legislation and a system of credit.

POINT 16. Urban housing must in part be transferred, as state property, to the control of municipal self-government and in part personalized.

The state must rapidly provide individual housing for the entire population through offering credit and taking other necessary measures.

POINT 17. Neither energy, mining and military industry nor any rail, maritime and air transport which is of national significance should be personalized. The state must retain the right to exploit and administer them.

POINT 18. In the future the state will be able to own ordinary businesses only when the initiative of citizens is insufficient to create enterprises vital to the populace. The state may also involve itself in the direction of enterprises to which it gives financial help.

SECTION X

Credit, Banking, Commerce

POINT 19. A broad system of national credit must become the basis of social-economic policy.

Credit should be offered in the first instance to citizens involved in industry and the service professions to enable them to acquire personalized shares, which would give them the right to partake of the profits of their enterprise. And credit should be tendered to peasants for the acquisition of farm machinery and for a raising of the level of agriculture.

POINT 20. Credit for laborers, which would permit them to acquire the means of production, must in part be derived from the profits of national enterprises. These financial operations must be controlled by a National Bank. Moreover, each expanding enterprise must create a fund of personalized credit for new workers, who would immediately become full members of the company (association).

POINT 21. Banking should not be a government monopoly. It should also not be in the hands of private individuals.

Corporation Banks should function side by side with the State Bank in the handling of corporation and private funds.

POINT 22. Commerce must be free.

POINT 23. In the interests of society, the state must retain the right to set a ceiling on the price of basic commodities and to maintain control over foreign trade.

POINT 24. A free market restores to goods their natural value. This contrasts with the closed market of a Communist dictatorship, which turns price fixing, banknotes and exchange into an instrument for maintaining its supremacy and for exploiting labor.

The gold standard must be introduced under a system of personalized economics.

SECTION XI

Culture, Science, Education, Health

The people's cultural development and the activity of cultural and scientific institutions must be independent of any compulsory control by administrative organs of the state. The government is obligated to support and encourage cultural and scientific activity in every possible way, without interfering in the work of individuals or free associations of writers, musicians, artists and actors who maintain the traditions of national and universal art and contribute to the spiritual renewal of society.

The principle of the "Party-mindedness" of science and art reflects the ideological monopoly of the Communist bureaucracy. Its falsity and harmfulness are obvious. No single method, no single direction should henceforth be declared obligatory for all. Similarly, no method or direction should be prohibited unless it poses a threat to public safety or is contrary to good morals.

The constraint of an official methodology must be destroyed, as must the political favoritism which inevitably follows in its wake and impedes the development not only of the humanities but of technical research as well. Free experimentation and competition between different points of view, currents and scientific schools must be permitted, since their development must be ruled by a disinterested striving for truth.

The disciplines of law and history are faced with the special task of exposing the distortions and falsifications of the era of the Communist dictatorship and of restoring a just legal order and genuine history to our homeland.

POINT 25. The state must give material support to associations of persons active in culture.

POINT 26. Academies of science and their institutes should be maintained by the state.

POINT 27. While a free secondary school education should be guaranteed for all, the state should simultaneously offer citizens the right to found private and social [*obshchestvennye*] schools, thus insuring freedom of instruction and learning. The state should maintain overall control over the tenor and quality of instruction.

POINT 28.   Universities must be granted autonomy.

POINT 29.   The state should not monopolistically control the means of information (radio, newspapers, publishing, etc.). Censorship must be abolished. Freedom of communication, however, presupposes full responsibility [for the information conveyed].

POINT 30.   While insuring a system of public health care embracing the entire population, the state should permit the supplementary founding of private medical institutions.

SECTION XII

Religion and the Church

The Christian religion has proclaimed man's highest freedom in the Truth and the value of the human personality and has called all peoples to spiritual unity. This religion of heroic service, elevated morality and ideal human relationships communicates the meaning of life and points the way both for the individual and society. A society which preserves its faith in purity and keeps the Christian commandments is protected against moral degeneration, a decline in spiritual strength and social and military suicide.

Social justice and freedom can be supported only by the growing religious awareness of a society. The Christian Church, which preaches the religion of Love, Mercy and Salvation, serves to unite men in good works and great hope.

During a half century of rule by a Communist dictatorship seeking the destruction of the Church and the uprooting of religious awareness, the Christian peoples of Great Russia have accomplished the exploit of preserving their Church.

The Christian Church has performed its duty of spiritual service to the populace. During years of great trial in the nation's history, a period of extreme moral oppression, it remained a refuge and preceptress for believers.

POINT 31. A renewed Church must enjoy independence from the state and possess full sovereignty in its sphere.

POINT 32. Since the full independence of the Church from the state can be achieved only on condition that the Church is not materially dependent on the state, the Church must receive sufficient support for its needs from common national funds.

POINT 33. All known religions must have the right to preach without hindrance and the freedom to perform religious ceremonies publicly.

SECTION XIII

Law

POINT 34. The independence of the judiciary from any other part of government must be *de facto* established as a guarantee of the rights and liberties of citizens and society.

POINT 35. Judges must be irremoveable and answerable only before the law.

POINT 36. Judges must comprise a special category which would preclude their belonging to any other profession or participating in political movements.

POINT 37. Judges must possess moral authority, which gives them the moral right to dispense justice.

POINT 38. Trial by jury must be introduced.

POINT 39. All judicial norms which were imposed by the

dictatorship and served as a means for its supremacy over the people must immediately be abolished.

A new legal system must be introduced which would conform to the spirit and letter of Social-Christianity.

POINT 40.   Capital punishment must be declared incompatible with the Christian attitude toward man.

SECTION XIV

The State

POINT 41.   In accord with the view which sees the state as a natural body expressing the highest interests of the people in their unity and creating the conditions for the free development and broad expression of the personality within the limits of the law, the state must be constituted as a theocratic, social, representative and popular entity.

Theocratic, inasmuch as the state must be built on a moral foundation and is obligated to follow religious principles in its activity. These principles are common to all Christian peoples, conform to man's inner perception of the world and represent the most humane of commandments.

Social, inasmuch as the state is obligated to guarantee economic, political, civil, family and individual rights to all citizens. It is likewise obligated to regulate and harmoniously combine general, group and individual strivings, without sacrificing anyone's lawful interests.

Representative and popular, inasmuch as political power must not be the monopoly of an individual, caste, class or party but must be harmoniously distributed among the populace through communal self-government in administrative units and through the participation of the people in the highest legislative body of the country by means of freely elected deputies.

POINT 42. Legislative, executive, supervisory [*bliusti-tel'naia*] and judicial power must be separated.

Supreme authority must be divided thus:

legislative—The Popular Assembly and Head of State

executive—The Head of State and Cabinet of Ministers

supervisory—The Supreme Council

judicial—The Supreme Court

POINT 43. The Popular Assembly—the highest legislative body—must be elected both from village and urban communes on the basis of proportional representation. It should also be elected from industrial and commercial corporations, associations of the free professions and from the organizations of political movements.

POINT 44. As with this central body, village, urban and district councils, representing local self-government, must be elected. Their powers must be clearly defined in the constitution.

POINT 45. The Head of State—the representative of national unity—must be elected by the Supreme Council and confirmed by popular vote.

POINT 46. The Head of State must be supreme commander of the armed forces of the country and have the right to appoint and remove the government administration.

POINT 47. The post of Head of State is incompatible with membership in the organizations of any political movements.

POINT 48. The Head of State must appoint a Prime-Minister and, on his recommendation, members of the Cabinet. The government must be responsible to the Popular Assembly and the Head of State.

POINT 49. Specific conditions must be stipulated to insure the unhindered emergence of a lawful opposition in the Popular Assembly. This opposition would be able legally to criticize the government.

POINT 50.   The Supreme Council—the spiritual voice [literally: authority] of the people—not possessing administrative functions or legislative initiative, must have the right to veto any law or government action which does not accord with the basic principles of Social-Christian order. This is to prevent the misuse of political power.

POINT 51.   The Supreme Council must consist of one-third members of the Church upper hierarchy and of two-thirds outstanding representatives of the people, elected for life.

POINT 52.   Points of contention between the government and a corporation, the government and an individual, a corporation and an individual and betwen corporations must be resolved by a Constitutional Court.

SECTION XV

The Rights of Man and the Citizen

The principles of Social-Christianity, when placed at the foundation of the entire social life of the people, represent the sole trustworthy guarantee of the real freedom which every man has a sacred right to possess.

The constitution must fortify the following basic rights of man and the citizen:

POINT 53.   The life and dignity of every man are inviolable.

POINT 54.   The home is inviolable.

POINT 55.   The rights of the family may not be infringed upon. This includes the right of parents to give their children a physical, intellectual and moral upbringing and education according to their own free choice in the bosom of the family and in private and state educational institutions.

POINT 56.   All citizens are equal before the law.

POINT 57. All citizens enjoy the freedom to select their profession or form of vocation, industry or trade.

POINT 58. Freedom of labor is safeguarded for all by each citizen's right to have land and to obtain credit enabling him to acquire the means of production.

POINT 59. Personal, group and family property is not subject to requisition without full prior compensation and without it being according to law.

POINT 60. All citizens can inherit and bequeath belongings.

POINT 61. All handicapped have the right to state social security sufficient to insure a dignified form of existence.

POINT 62. No form of forced labor can be permitted in relation to free citizens.

POINT 63. Personal liberty is inviolable.

POINT 64. All means of disseminating thought are free [i.e. unrestricted].

POINT 65. The development of science and the arts is free.

POINT 66. Instruction and teaching are free.

POINT 67. Meetings and demonstrations are free.

POINT 68. The formation of unions, associations and societies is free.

POINT 69. Private correspondence and all other forms of communication are inviolable.

POINT 70. All citizens have the right of free movement within the country and of unhindered exit beyond its boundaries.

POINT 71. Every citizen has the right to elect and be elected to all elective government posts.

POINT 72. Every citizen has the right to use the courts in

defense of his constitutional rights and lawful interests no matter in what manner they have been violated.

PART THREE

POINT 73. The Union for the Liberation of the People considers itself a patriotic organization consisting of selfless representatives of all the nationalities of Great Russia. It is struggling for the interests of the entire populace and is not a party, either in the class or totalitarian sense of the word.

POINT 74. Following the overthrow of the Communist dictatorship, state power must pass into the hands of a provisional popular-revolutionary government, which will immediately carry out all urgent radical reforms, work out a constitution securing [social] transformation and present it to a national referendum. After this, normal state order must ensue.

POINT 75. The provisional government must root itself in the local representative bodies which will be formed by the workers, peasants, intelligentsia, student youth and military. For the defense of national liberty, each enterprise and institution will form detachments of a citizens' guard.

POINT 76. The national armed forces must be freed from political party influence so that they might serve the people as a whole and not the interests of any single party which has placed them under its control. Fundamental improvements must be made in the situation of the regular armed forces and, in particular, the officer corps.

POINT 77. The Communist Party, which has lost all moral right to existence, must be disbanded. Collective responsibility is inadmissible. Responsibility for crimes against the populace and humanity must be borne only by those directly guilty of them.

POINT 78. All totalitarian organizations formed under the leadership of the CPSU and serving as its instrument for oppressing and suppressing the populace must be disbanded.

POINT 79. The secret political police must be disbanded.

POINT 80. The organs of the Communist judiciary must be disbanded.

POINT 81. The Communist state apparatus must be disbanded.

POINT 82. While the personalization of property is being carried out, the rights of those temporarily not linked to production (the military, political prisoners, etc.) must be taken into account. Special measures must be speedily taken to insure the well-being of the families of victims of the regime and of heroes who perished or were disabled in the Great Fatherland War [WWII] as well as all handicapped citizens.

POINT 83. Those foreign countries in which Soviet forces are temporarily stationed can be offered help to initiate their own national self-determination on the basis of Social-Christianity.

POINT 84. Millions of countrymen living in political exile outside the borders of Russia must, after their return, be ,granted normal rights and opportunities in the Social-,Christian union of the entire populace.

POINT 85. A statute of Distinguished Citizenship must be established. The rights and obligations of Distinguished Citizenship must be extended to the entire flower of the nation, in the first instance to strugglers for national liberation.

Adopted February 2, 1964

APPENDIX III

The VSKhSON Library

The following list includes all books and articles known to have been used in VSKhSON libraries or reported to have influenced the thought of the organization's members prior to their arrest in 1967. Although the list cannot be considered complete, it does provide an indication of the interests and tastes of the underground union. After giving the name of the author of an item and its Russian title, I have appended as much additional information as could be gathered in the limited time available for bibliographical research. Where known to be extant, English translations have been listed.

Items catalogued as "VSKhSON classics" are works which were used extensively for recruitment and "self-education" purposes. "Potential classics" are works which were beginning to assume widespread usage at the time the organization was broken up by the KGB. "Tactical handbooks" are books which were primarily employed as military-conspiratorial manuals.

I. VSKhSON DOCUMENTS

1. *Programma* [Program]
2. *Ustav* [Statute]
3. *Nastavlenie No. I "VSKhSON"* [A conspiracy manual]

4. *Prisiaga* [Oath form]
5. *Anketa* [Questionnaire]

II. WRITINGS AUTHORED BY VSKhSON MEMBERS

1. Bochevarov, Georgii. "Kratkii ocherk istorii KPSS" ["A Short History of the CPSU"], pt. I.
2. _____. "Leninizm, trotskizm i stalinizm" ["Leninism, Trotskyism and Stalinism"].
3. _____. "Osushchestvimy li tseli Oktiabr'skoi revoliutsii?" ["Are the Goals of the October Revolution Realizable?"]
4. _____. "Prichiny proiskhozdeniia kul'ta lichnosti Stalina" ["The Reasons for the Origin of Stalin's Cult of the Personality"].
5. _____. "Sovremennoe polozhenie v kommunisticheskikh partiiakh Evropy" ["The Contemporary Situation in the Communist Parties of Europe"].
7. Goncharov, Vladimir. "Delo NIISI" ["The NIISI Case"—on the arrest and trial of the Ronkin-Khakhaev neo-Marxist group].
8. Konosov, Mikhail. "Admiral Kolchak." [A Poem]
9. _____. "Dva protsessa" ["Two Trials"].
10. _____. "Proekt listovki k rabochim" ["Project for a Leaflet to the Workers"].
11. _____. "Uroki Novocherkasska" ["The Lessons of Novocherkassk"].
12. _____. "Vengerskaia lirika" ["Hungarian Lyric"—a poem].
13. _____. "Vestnik pobedy" ["Messenger of Victory"].
14. Sudarev, Anatolii. "Po povodu zhertv" ["Concerning the Victims"].
15. _____. "Prizrak brodit po Evrope" ["A Specter Is Haunting Europe"].

III. *VSKhSON "CLASSICS"*

1. Berdiaev, Nikolai. *Novoe srednevekov'e* [*The New Middle Ages*]. Berlin: Obelisk, 1924.
2. _____. *Russkaia ideia*. Paris: YMCA-Press, 1946. English translation: *The Russian Idea*. Boston: Beacon, 1962.
3. Djilas, Milovan. *Novyi klass*. English translation of Serbo-Croatian original: *The New Class*. New York: Praeger, 1957.
4. Meray, Tibor. *Trinadtsat' dnei kotorye potriasli Kreml'*. English translation of Hungarian original: *Thirteen Days That Shook the Kremlin*. New York: Praeger, 1959.
5. Solonevich, Ivan. *Begstvo iz sovetskogo ada*. A Russian edition disseminated by the German authorities on occupied territory during WWII. English translation: *Escape from Russian Chains*. London: Williams & Norgate, 1938.
6. Von Rauch, Georg. *Istoriia sovetskoi Rossii*. Russian edition published in USA. English translation of German original: *A History of Soviet Russia*. New York: Praeger, 1957.

IV. *POTENTIAL "CLASSICS"*

1. Berdiaev, Nikolai. "V zashchitu khristianskoi svobody" ["In Defense of Christian Freedom"]. *Sovremennye zapiski* [Paris], 24 (1925).
2. _____. "Neogumanizm, marksizm i dukhovnye tsennosti" ["Neo-humanism, Marxism and Spiritual Values"], *Sovremennye zapiski,* 60 (1936).
3. _____. "Khristianstvo i opasnost' ateisticheskogo materializma" ["Christianity and the Danger of Atheistic Materialism"]. *Pravoslavnoe delo* [Paris], 1 (1939).

4. Burnham, James. *Vosstanie menedzherov.* English original: *The Managerial Revolution.* New York: John Day, 1941.

5. Fedotov, G. P. *Khristianin v revoliutsii: Sbornik statei* [*The Christian in a Revolution: A Collection of Articles*]. Paris: Author Publication, 1957.

6. Frank, Semen. *Dukhovnye osnovy obshchestva* [*The Spiritual Foundations of Society*]. Paris: YMCA-Press, 1930.

7. Il'in, Ivan. *Put' dukhovnogo obnovleniia* [*The Way of Spiritual Renewal*]. Belgrade: Izdatel'skaia komissiia, n.d. [1935?]. VSKhSON used a later reprint of this book, published in France.

8. "Mat' i nastavnitsa" [*"Mater et Magister"*—Papal encyclical of May 15, 1961]. English translation of Latin original in: Anne Fremantle, ed., *The Papal Encyclicals in Their Historical Context* (New York: The New American Library, 1963), pp. 337-387.

9. Ortega y Gasset, Jose. *Vosstanie mass.* English translation of Spanish original: *The Revolt of the Masses.* New York: W. W. Norton, 1957.

10. "Pis'mo sviashchennikov N. Eshlimana i G. Iakunina" ["Letter of the priests N. Eshliman and G. Iakunin"]. English translation in: *St. Vladimir's Seminary Quarterly,* 10, No. 1-2 (1966) and *A Cry of Despair from Russian Churchmen* (New York: Russian Orthodox Church Outside of Russia, 1966). Lengthy excerpts in: Michael Bourdeaux, ed., *Patriarch and Prophets: Persecution of the Russian Orthodox Church Today* (New York: Praeger, 1970), pp. 194-221.

11. Röpke, Wilhelm. *Chelovecheskoe obshchestvo.* English translation of German original: *Civitas Humana: A Humane Order of Society.* London: William Hodge, 1948.

12. _____. *Po tu storonu sprosa i predlozheniia.* English translation of German original: *A*

Humane Economy: The Social Framework of the Free Market. Chicago: Henry Regnery, 1960.

13. Shingarev, A. I. *Kak eto bylo. Dnevnik. Petropavlo- skaia krepost'. 27.XI.17-5.I.18* [*How It Was. A Diary. The Peter-Paul Fortress. Nov. 27, 1917-Jan. 5, 1918*]. Moscow: 1918, 68 pp.

14. Solonevich, Ivan. *Poteriannye*. A Russian edition disseminated by the German authorities on occupied territory during WWII. English translation: *Russia in Chains*. London: William & Norgate, 1938.

V. TACTICAL HANDBOOKS

1. Malaparte, Curzio. *Taktika gosudarstvennogo pere- vorota*. English translation of Spanish original: *Coup D'Etat: The Technique of Revolution*. New York: Dutton, 1932.

2. Middeldorf, Eike. *Rukovodstvo po taktike* [*Tactical Handbook*]. By a West German author of numerous handbooks on military tactics.

VI. OTHER WORKS IN VSKhSON LIBRARY

1. Berdiaev, Nikolai. "Dnevnik filosofa" ["Diary of a Philosopher"]. Probably refers to one of his contributions under that heading in *Put'*, 4 (1926), 6 (1927) or 16 (1929).

2. _____. *Istoki i smysl russkogo kommu- nizma*. VSKhSON possessed only a French translation. English translation of Russian original: *The Origin of Russian Communism*. Ann Arbor: U. of Michigan, 1966.

3. _____. *Opyt eskhatologicheskoi metafiziki*. English translation: *The Beginning and the End*. London: Geoffrey Bles, 1952.

4. _____. *Mirosozertsanie Dostoevskogo*.

Prague: YMCA-Press, 1923. English translation: *Dostoevsky.* Cleveland & New York: World, 1965.

5. _____. "Rossiia i era novogo mira" ["Russia and the Era of a New World"]. Said by sources to be from an English original.

6. Clarkson, Jesse D. *Istoriia Rossii.* English original: *A History of Russia.* New York: Random House, 1961.

7. Daniel', Iulii. *Govorit Moskva.* Washington, 1963. English translation in: Yuli Daniel, *This Is Moscow Speaking and Other Stories* (New York: Collier, 1970).

8. Datta. "Ekzistensializm i indiiskaia mysl'" ["Existentialism and Indian Thought"].

9. Denikin, General A. I. *Memuary* [*Memoirs*—unspecified].

10. Dostoevskii, Fedor. [Unspecified works]

11. Ginzburg, Evgeniia. *Krutoi marshrut.* English translation: *Journey into the Whirlwind.* New York: Harcourt, Brace & World, 1967.

12. Gor'kii, Maksim. *Nesvoevremennye mysli.* English translation: *Untimely Thoughts.* New York: P. S. Eriksson, 1968.

13. Kerenskii, Aleksandr. *Delo Kornilova* [*The Kornilov Affair*]. Moscow: 1918.

14. Maclean, Fitzroy. *Na podstupakh k Vostoku.* English original: *Escape to Adventure.* Boston: Little, Brown & Co., 1950.

15. Maritain, Jacques. "Korni sovetskogo ateizma" ["The Roots of Soviet Atheism"].

16. "Mir na zemle" [*"Pacem in Terris"*—Papal encyclical of April 10, 1963]. English translation of Latin original in: Anne Fremantle, ed., *The Papal Encyclicals in Their Historical Context* (New York: The New American Library, 1963), pp. 392-424.

17. Mueller, G. *Ispol'zovanie (primenenie) proshlogo* [*The Use (Application) of the Past*].
18. Northrop, F. S. C. *Vstrecha Zapada i Vostoka*. English original: *The Meeting of East and West*. New York: Macmillan, 1946.
19. Pipes, Richard. *Obrazovanie sovetskogo soiuza*. English original: *The Formation of the Soviet Union: Communism and Nationalism 1917-1923*. Cambridge, Mass.: Harvard U. Press, 1954.
20. Russell, Bertrand. *Praktika i teoriia bol'shevizma*. English original: *Bolshevism: Practice and Theory*. New York: Harcourt, Brace and Howe, 1920.
21. Solov'ev, Vladimir. [Unspecified works]
22. Sorokin, Pitirim. *Sotsial'naia ... alitika*. [*Social ...*].
23. Stenogram of the Moscow Trial of Writers Iulii Daniel' and Andrei Siniavskii. Transcribed from a BBC broadcast in April, 1966.
24. *The Times* [London]. Three articles on Soviet economics from the period March-April, 1965.
25. Ware, Timothy. *Pravoslavnaia tserkov'*. English original: *The Orthodox Church*. Harmondsworth, Middlesex: Penguin, 1963.
26. Wilson, Edmund. *K finliandskomu vokzalu*. English original: *To the Finland Station*. New York: Doubleday, 1940.
27. Wrangel, General Petr. *Memuary* [*Memoirs*—unspecified]. Probably: *Always with Honor*. New York: Robert Speller & Sons, 1957.

Note: Leonid Borodin's contribution to *Veche* No. 8 (AS 1665), written in 1973 after his release from prison, is amply footnoted and provides a number of new titles.

Notes

NOTES TO CHAPTER I

[1]From the organization's "Program." See Appendix II for the text.

[2]In Russian: Vserossiiskii sotsial-khristianskii soiuz osvobozhdeniia naroda.

[3]On occasion the organization's members have been referred to as "Social-Christians" or "peterburzhtsy" [from St. Petersburg, the pre-revolutionary name for Leningrad]. They have also been called the "Russian Party."

[4]Three of the seventeen were sentenced to the amount of time spent awaiting trial (Soviet terms of imprisonment are calculated from the date of arrest) and immediately released. Seven rank-and-file members were not tried.

[5]In his "The Berdiaev Circle in Leningrad" Vladimir Osipov tells us how this document reached the West: "In January, 1967, [VSKhSON leader] Vagin handed over the VSKhSON program, which had been photographed on film by [VSKhSON leader] Mikhail Sado, to the Frenchwoman L'vova for transmission to the representative of the Russian emigration N. Struve." See *Posev*, 11 (1972), 7. The *Messenger of the Russian Student Christian Movement* [*Vestnik R.S.Kh.D.*] was recently renamed *Messenger of the Russian Christian Movement* [*Vestnik R.Kh.D.*].

[6]The Russian original was first published in the collection *VSKhSON* (Paris: YMCA-Press, 1975), pp. 31-79. On this volume, see note 24.

[7]*Samizdat* means "self-publishing" and refers to the reproduction and circulation of written materials not approved by the Soviet government. For a definition of *samizdat* and a description of how it functions, see Andrei Amalrik, *Will the Soviet Union Survive until 1984?* (New York: Harper & Row, 1970), pp. 6-10 and Julius Telesin, "Inside 'Samizdat'," *Encounter*, 40, No. 2 (1973), 25-33. For an extensive bibliography of the history, mechanics and background of *samizdat,* see Michael Nicholson, "Solzhenitsyn and *Samizdat*" in John B. Dunlop, Richard Haugh and Alexis Klimoff, eds., *Aleksandr Solzhenitsyn: Critical Essays and Documentary Materials* (New York: Collier, 1975), 2nd rev. ed., p. 65, note 3.

[8]The Russian texts of *Chronicle* No. 1-20 appeared in Posev "spetsial'-nye vypuski" [special issues] No. 1-9 (1969-1971). Numbers 21-27 were published in *Vol'noe slovo* (Posev), No. 1-6 (1972), while issues 28-34

have been published by Khronika Press in New York (505 8th Ave., N. Y., N. Y. 10018). Number 35 has reached the West and is currently in press. For copious English selections from the *Chronicle*, see Peter Reddaway, ed., *Uncensored Russia* (New York: American Heritage, 1972). This volume contains a valuable introduction and notes. *Chronicles* 16-31 have been published in their entirety in English by Amnesty International Publications (53 Theobold's Road, London WC1X 8SP). Issues 32 and 33 are scheduled for English publication in the autumn of 1975. That the regime has not welcomed the *Chronicle's* coverage of VSKhSON came out at the recent trial of dissenter Gabriel Superfin (see *Vestnik*, 114 [1974], 276).

[9]"Vserossiiskii sotsial-khristianskii soiuz osvobozhdeniia naroda: sostav, programma, metody raboty, ideologicheskie pozitsii, prichiny porazheniia," *Posev*, 1 (1971), 38-43.

[10]*Chronicle* No. 33 (10 December 1974) provides a short sketch of Petrov-Agatov's prison biography, "In 1947, for several critical remarks about Stalin, Petrov-Agatov was charged with anti-Soviet propaganda...Five times he escaped from the camps. Each escape was termed 'counter-revolutionary sabotage'; for each attempt he received an additional sentence. In 1956, Petrov-Agatov was released and rehabilitated...In 1960, [he] was once again arrested. He was freed in 1967...On July 26, 1968 Petrov-Agatov was again arrested." (p. 15)

[11]"Rossiia, kotoroi ne znaiut," *Posev*, 3 (1971), 20-27.

[12]"Arestanskie vstrechi" in *Grani*, 82 (1971), 99-126, 83 (1972), 47-78 and 84 (1972), 56-96. For other recently-published *samizdat* works by Petrov-Agatov, see: "Otkrytoe pis'mo Borisu Polevomu" ["Open Letter to Boris Polevoi"], *Posev*, 6 (1970), 10-12, "Iz tsikla 'Snachala Kolyma. Potom Mordoviia.'" ["From the Cycle 'First Kolyma, then Mordovia'"], *Grani*, 80 (1971), 103-106 and "Rossiia, kotoroi ne znaiut: iz tsikla 'Snachala Kolyma. Potom Mordoviia.'" ["The Russia They Don't Know: From the Cycle 'First Kolyma, then Mordoviia'"], *Posev*, 5 (1971), 54-56.

[13]*Chronicle* No. 32 (17 July 1974) (New York: Khronika Press, 1974), p. 49.

[14]"Berdiaevskii kruzhok v Leningrade," *Posev*, 11 (1972), 3-10. This article was also published in *Vestnik*, 104-105 (1972), 153-65, but the *Posev* edition is textually superior. For biographical information on Osipov, see his "Ploshchad' Maiakovskogo, stat'ia 70-aia" ["Moscow Square, Article 70"], *Grani*, 80 (1971), 107-162 and "V poiskakh kryshi" ["In Quest of a Roof"], *Posev*, 1 (1971), 44-50. He gives his date of birth as 1938 in "K chitateliam Samizdata" ["To Readers of *Samizdat*"], *Grani*, 85 (1972), 188. For Osipov's writings which discuss VSKhSON in any detail, see the notes to this volume. Other writings of his which are of related interest: "Tri otnosheniia k rodine" ["Three Attitudes to the Homeland"], *Vestnik*, 103 (1972), 216-222, "Trus ne igraet v khokkei" ["A Coward Does Not Play Hockey"], *Posev*, 5 (1974), 37-38, "Piat' vozrazhenii Sakharovu" ["Five Rebuttals to Sakharov"], *Russkaia mysl'*, 27 June 1974, p. 5, "K voprosu o tseli i metodakh legal'noi oppozitsii" ["Concerning the Goals and Methods

of the Legal Opposition"], No. 1760 in the Radio Liberty Arkhiv samizdata [*Samizdat* Archive], 9 pp. and "Poslednii den' Moskvy" ["Moscow's Last Day"], *Vestnik*, 111 (1974), 220-32. See also Osipov's interview with two Western correspondents, "Beseda redaktora zhurnala 'Veche' s korrespondentom assoshieited press Stivinzom Bronningom i s korrespondentom gazety 'Baltimor san' Dinom Milzom" ["The Conversation of the Editor of the Journal *Veche* with Associated Press Correspondent Stephens Broening and Correspondent Dean Mills of the Newspaper *The Baltimore Sun*"], *Vestnik*, 106 (1972), 294-303. For the 10 issues of *Veche* which appeared, consult the Arkhiv samizdata. This valuable collection will hereafter be cited as AS plus the approapriate document number. Osipov ceased editing *Veche* after No. 9 and founded a new publication, *Zemlia*. For the text of *Zemlia* No. 1, see AS 1909.

[15]"Svedeniia ob Ogurtsove Igore Viacheslavoviche /r. 1937/," AS 1827, 5 pp. This document was eventually published in *Posev*, 4 (1975), 11-13.

[16]Osipov, "Ber. kr. . . . ," p. 6, footnote.

[17]Petrov-Agatov, "Ar. vstr.," *Grani*, 84 (1972), 72.

[18]AS 1555, described as "Official Text of Sentence in the Trial of 17 Leningraders Belonging to 'The All-Russian Social-Christian Union for the Liberation of the People' (VSKhSON), 4-5 April, 1968, 17 pp."

[19]What I possess is a partial photo-reproduction of the original. Probably due to faulty photo-copying, a considerable portion of the text is missing. Nonetheless, the sixty-four pages which survive serve as an invaluable source. In subsequent citations this document will be referred to as Z.S. (for *zakliuchenie sledstviia*).

[20]E.g. the stenogram and sentence for the trial of the four VSKhSON leaders, mentioned by Petrov-Agatov. See *Grani*, 84 (1972), 72-73.

[21]These are the English spellings of their names which they personally prefer. In Library of Congress transliteration, their names would be: Iurii Gendler and Iurii Lur'i.

[22]"Imi dvigala bol' za rodinu." In addition to defending Bochevarov and Konstantinov, Luryi also represented neo-Marxist dissident Valerii Ronkin in 1965 and Leningrad "hijacker" Eduard Kuznetsov at his trial in 1970.

[23]Vospominaniia uchastnika" in the collection *VSKhSON*, pp. 204-209.

[24]*VSKhSON: Programma, sud, v tiurmakh i lageriakh* [*VSKhSON: Program, Trial, In the Prisons and Camps*] (Paris: YMCA-Press, 1975), 217 pp. In 1972-73, at the request of an editor of YMCA-Press, I assembled the materials in this collection and wrote an 18-page introduction. Although I was the "compiler" of this volume, I was neither its editor nor proofreader. This led to several minor but lamentable errors, of which I will mention one: the omission of a portrait of VSKhSON member Leonid Borodin. Also, since the book was in press for almost two years, my introduction was, understandably, outdated by the time the volume appeared in 1975. Despite such flaws, this collection should nonetheless be of real assistance to those interested in VSKhSON and knowing Russian,

and I am personally grateful to YMCA-Press for having undertaken to publish it.

[25]The only significant written sources absent from the collection are the "zakliuchenie sledstviia" and Luryi's "Imi dvigala..."

NOTES TO CHAPTER II

[1]The Russian Bible follows the Septuagint numbering of the psalms, while the King James Version follows the Hebrew numbering. Psalm 91 in the *KJV* would be Psalm 90 in the Russian Bible. See "The Psalter" in Mother Mary and Archimandrite Kallistos Ware, trs., *The Festal Menaion* (London: Faber & Faber, 1969), p. 530. That a reading of this psalm was a regular feature of the rite of initiation into VSKhSON is mentioned by Petrov-Agatov in "Rossiia, kotoroi ne znaiut," *Posev*, 3 (1971), 23.

[2]Ogurtsov and Sado were in the Eastern Faculty, Vagin was in the Philological Faculty and Averichkin in the Faculty of Jurisprudence. According to Iurii Handler, each year in the camps the members of VSKhSON solemnly observed February 2nd, the date of their organization's founding.

[3]Boris Pasternak, *Doctor Zhivago* (New York: Signet, 1960), pp. 279-80.

[4]From Handler Interview and Petrov-Agatov, "Rossiia...," p. 22.

[5]Ogurtsov and Averichkin. See Osipov, "Berdiaevskii kruzhok v Leningrade," *Posev*, 11 (1972), 4, Petrov-Agatov, "Arestanskie vstrechi," *Grani*, 83 (1972), 56 and A., AS 1827, p. 1.

[6]Petrov-Agatov, "Rossiia...," p. 21.

[7]A., pp. 2-5.

[8]Osipov, "Ber. kr....," p. 4.

[9]A., p. 1.

[10]Bernard Karavatskii, "Vospominaniia uchastnika," in *VSKhSON* (Paris: YMCA-Press, 1975), pp. 208-209. Iurii Handler told me that Ogurtsov practiced Yoga while in Vladimir Prison. Karavatskii (p. 206) reports that Sado, like Ogurtsov, was a Yoga adept. One assumes that both became interested in Yoga through their academic speciality: Eastern Studies. Presumably, neither was aware that an engaging in Yoga is proscribed by the reigning school of Eastern Orthodox spirituality, Hesychasm. Like many contemporary Soviet intellectuals, they seem to have been somewhat eclectic in their religious views.

[11]Petrov-Agatov, "Ar. vstr.," *Grani*, 84 (1972), 72.

[12]*Ibid.*, p. 88.

[13]See Solzhenitsyn's August 23, 1973 interview with two Western correspondents in *Index*, 2, No. 4 (1973), 40 and Sakharov's appeal to L. I. Brezhnev and Richard Nixon on the occasion of their summer, 1974 summit meeting in *Russkaia mysl'*, 4 July 1974, p. 2.

[14]Handler Interview. The Leningrad "hijacker" Eduard Kuznetsov spent

time with Ogurtsov in Vladimir Prison and refers to him as "the 'Führer' of the demo-Christians." But his opinion of Ogurtsov is far from totally negative. See his *Dnevniki* [*Diaries*] (Paris: Les Editeurs Reunis, 1973), p. 253.

[15]Handler Interview.

[16]A., p. 1.

[17]Petrov-Agatov, "Rossiia...," p. 21.

[18]Bochevarov, Iovaisha and Fakhrutdinov.

[19]Balaian and Raginian.

[20]Petrov-Agatov, "Rossiia...," p. 21.

[21]S., "Vserossiiskii sotsial-khristianskii soiuz osvobozhdeniia naroda," *Posev*, 1 (1971), 38.

[22]Petrov-Agatov, "Rossiia...," p. 22.

[23]*Ibid.*

[24]*Ibid.*, p. 21.

[25]*Ibid.*

[26]Yevgeny Yevtushenko, *A Precocious Autobiography* (New York: Dutton, 1963), pp. 84-87.

[27]Petrov-Agatov, "Rossiia...," p. 22.

[28]For Leningradskii Gosudarstvennyi Universitet.

[29]See Vladimir Dudintsev, *Not by Bread Alone* (New York: Dutton, 1957).

[30]For F. F. Raskolnikov's 1939 "Open Letter to Stalin," see AS 376a. English editions of the other two works mentioned are: Evgenia Ginzburg, *Journey into the Whirlwind* (New York: Harcourt, Brace & World, 1967) and Aleksander Solzhenitsyn, *One Day in the Life of Ivan Denisovich* (New York: Praeger, 1963).

[31]Petrov-Agatov, "Rossiia...," p. 22.

[32]Handler Interview. See also "V Pot'me" ["In Pot'ma"], *Posev*, 4 (1973), 26. Karavatskii (p. 208) provides the name of Sado's wife but mistakenly states that the couple had three children.

[33]Karavatskii, p. 208.

[34]Petrov-Agatov, "Rossiia...," p. 20. P.-A. italics.

[35]Handler Interview.

[36]Petrov-Agatov, "Rossiia...," p. 23. As will be seen in Chapter V, most VSKhSON funds came from dues regularly paid by the membership.

[37]See F. M. Dostoevskii, *Tom pervyi: Bednye liudi, Povesti i rasskazy 1846-1847* [*Volume One: Poor Folk, Tales and Stories for 1846-1847*], (Leningrad: "Nauka," 1972). The editor of this volume is listed as G. M. Fridlender.

[38]Handler Interview.

[39]*Ibid.*

[40]*Ibid.*

[41]*Ibid.*

[42]Karavatskii, pp. 207-208.

[43]Petrov-Agatov, "Ar. vstr.," *Grani*, 83 (1972), 62. P.-A. italics.

[44]*Ibid.,* pp. 67-68. P.-A. italics.

[45]*Chronicle of Current Events* No. 19 (30 April 1971) states that Article 43 of the Criminal Code of the RSFSR ("Assignment of Milder Punishment Than That Provided by Law") was applied to Vagin (and Averichkin as well). See *Posev: Deviatyi spetsial'nyi vypusk* (1971), p. 8. For the Criminal Code, see Harold J. Berman, ed., *Soviet Criminal Law and Procedure* (Cambridge, Mass.: Harvard U. Press, 1972), 2nd ed.

[46]Osipov, "Ber. kr....," pp. 9-10.

[47]*Ibid.,* p. 4.

[48]Handler Interview.

[49]Petrov-Agatov, "Ar. vstr.," *Grani,* 83 (1972), 56.

[50]Mentioned by *Chronicle of Current Events* No. 35 (31 March 1975), the text of which will shortly be published by Khronika Press (New York).

NOTES TO CHAPTER III

[1]Petrov-Agatov, "Rossiia, kotoroi ne znaiut," *Posev,* 3 (1971), 21.

[2]S., "Vserossiiskii sotsial-khristianskii soiuz osvobozhdeniia naroda," *Posev,* 1 (1971), 38.

[3]Handler Interview.

[4]See the appendix, prepared by the *Grani* editorial staff, to V. Osipov's "Ploshchad' Maiakovskogo, stat'ia 70-aia" in *Grani,* 80 (1971), 145-46.

[5]Osipov, "Berdiaevskii kruzhok v Leningrade," *Posev,* 11 (1972), 9.

[6]Petrov-Agatov, "Arestanskie vstrechi," *Grani,* 84 (1972), 78.

[7]*Ibid., Grani,* 83 (1972), 71.

[8]*Ibid.,* p. 76.

[9]*Ibid.,* p. 71. Noting in the *Prigovor* [Sentence] against the VSKhSON rank-and-file (AS 1555, p. 6) that one of the charges against Ivanov was that he had received a copy of Richard Pipes' "anti-Soviet" book *The Formation of the Soviet Union* from "the author," I wrote the Harvard historian seeking more information. In his kind answering letter of 11 June 1974 Dr. Pipes explained that Ivanov had been assigned to him as a guide and personal assistant by the University of Leningrad during his visit there in the spring of 1962 to give a series of lectures on Russian intellectual history. Although Pipes saw a great deal of Ivanov, he was unable to make out what his politics were since he [Ivanov] was very guarded in his speech.

[10]See *Grani,* 80 (1971), 142-43.

[11]*Ibid.,* p. 143.

[12]Osipov, "Ber. kr....," p. 3.

[13]*Ibid.*

[14]Petrov-Agatov, "Rossiia...," p. 26.

[15]*Grani,* 80 (1971), 143.

[16]Handler Interview.

[17]*Zakliuchenie sledstviia,* p. 83 and Handler Interview.

[18]On the former point, see *Z.S.,* p. 142; on the latter, see *The Chronicle of Current Events, passim* and the anonymously-edited *Istoriia odnoi golodovki* [*History of One Hunger Strike*] (Frankfurt/Main: Possev Verlag, 1971).

[19]Fragments of his poems are quoted by Petrov-Agatov in "Rossiia...," pp. 24 & 26-27.

[20]Petrov-Agatov, "Rossiia...," p. 26.

[21]*Ibid.*

[22]*Ibid.,* p. 24.

[23]Information received from a recent Soviet émigré.

[24]See *Chronicle* No. 19 (30 April 1971) in *Posev: Deviatyi spetsial'nyi vypusk* (1971), p. 9.

[25]Petrov-Agatov, "Ar. vstr.," *Grani,* 83 (1972), 56.

[26]Handler Interview.

[27]Osipov, "Ber. kr....," p. 3.

[28]Petrov-Agatov, "Ar. vstr.," *Grani,* 83 (1972), 56.

[29]From Yuri Luryi's unpublished manuscript "Imi dvigala bol' za rodinu" ("They Were Moved by a Painful Love of Homeland").

[30]Handler Interview.

[31]Osipov, "Ber. kr....," p. 5.

[32]*Z.S.,* p. 120 and *Prigovor,* p. 16.

[33]See Petrov-Agatov, "Ar. vstr.," *Grani,* 84 (1972), 70 and *Posev,* 9 (1974), 10.

[34]See Appendix I for a more detailed listing.

[35]The names of twenty-three candidates are supplied by Z.S. and by Osipov in "Ber. kr...." See Appendix I. The information that Kulakov's father was the deputy commander for political affairs of a naval district comes from Yuri Luryi.

[36]From ZS., *Prigovor,* Osipov's "Ber. kr...." and *Chronicle* No. 1 (30 April 1968) in *Posev: Pervyi spetsial'nyi vypusk* (1969), p. 12.

NOTES TO CHAPTER IV

[1]*Prigovor,* AS 1555, p. 4.

[2]Osipov, "Berdiaevskii kruzhok v Leningrade," *Posev,* 11 (1972), 6.

[3]*Zakliuchenie sledstviia,* p. 48.

[4]*Ibid.,* p. 49. On the trial of writers Andrei Siniavskii and Iulii Daniel', see Max Hayward, ed., *On Trial* (New York: Harper & Row, 1967), rev. ed.

[5]*Z.S.,* p. 64. See Appendix III ("The VSKhSON Library") for full bibliographic information on the books mentioned in this and subsequent citations.

[6]*Prigovor,* p. 12.

[7]*Ibid.,* p. 7.

[8]Osipov, "Ber. kr....," p. 7.

[9]*Ibid.*

[10]*Ibid.* The regime took its revenge on L'vova when she arrived in Bulgaria in October, 1973 to attend a congress of sociologists. Accused of disseminating Solzhenitsyn's Nobel Lecture and other works, L'vova was sentenced by a Bulgarian court to four years' imprisonment. Other foreign delegates to the conference who distributed such literature were not touched. See *Posev*, 3 (1974), 16. I have been told that L'vova was eventually released by the Bulgarian authorities.

[11]S., "Vserossiiskii sotsial-khristianskii soiuz osvobozhdeniia naroda," *Posev*, 1 (1971), 40.

[12]*Z.S.*, p. 89.

[13]*Ibid.*, p. 44.

[14]*Ibid.*, p. 99.

[15]*Ibid.*, p. 111.

[16]S., p. 40.

[17]I deduce this from information supplied by A. (AS 1827), p. 1.

[18]*Z.S.*, p. 108.

[19]*Prigovor*, p. 8.

[20]*Z.S.*, p. 58.

[21]*Prigovor*, p. 12 and *Z.S.*, p. 89.

[22]*Prigovor*, pp. 7-8 and *Z.S.*, p. 99.

[23]Julius Telesin, "Inside 'Samizdat'," *Encounter*, 40, No. 2 (1973), 25.

[24]*Ibid.*, p. 31.

[25]In the early 1970s some Soviet dissidents began advocating the use of "home-made" mimeo machines, to be designed by members of the technical intelligentsia. See the interesting article by S. Topolev [pseud.] in the *samizdat* journal *Svobodnaia mysl'* [Free Thought], published in *Vol'noe slovo* (Posev), 7 (1973).

[26]Telesin, p. 30.

[27]*Ibid.*, p. 32.

[28]Osipov, "Ber. kr....," p. 6.

[29]*Z.S.*, p. 96.

[30]Telesin, p. 30.

[31]In *Vol'noe slovo* (Posev), 7 (1973), p. 75.

[32]Osipov, "Ber. kr....," pp. 6-7.

[33]*Z.S.*, p. 50.

[34]*Ibid.*, p. 56.

[35]*Ibid.*, p. 94.

[36]*Ibid.*, p. 57.

[37]*Ibid.*

[38]Andrei Dubrov, "A vse-taki 'Khronika' vykhodit" ["And Nevertheless the *Chronicle* Comes Out"], *Novoe russkoe slovo*, 23 May 1973. On July 2, 1973 Mukhamed'iarov was judged insane by the Moscow Municipal Court and sentenced to confinement in a mental hospital. See *Chronicle* No. 29 (31 July 1973), p. 63.

[39]*Z.S.*, p. 68.

[40]*Ibid.*, p. 58.

[41]*Ibid.*, pp. 73-74.

[42]*Ibid.*, p. 74.

[43]*Ibid.*, p. 35.

[44]*Ibid.*, p. 96.

[45]*Ibid.*, p. 40.

[46]The bibliographic history of this book is quite complex. It was first published under the title *Rossiia v kontslagere* [*Russia in a Concentration Camp*] in Bulgaria in 1936. This large book became two volumes in the English translation: *Russia in Chains* and *Escape from Russian Chains* (both published in 1938 by Williams & Norgate, London). The Germans published the Russian original of the work to aid their propaganda activities among the Soviet populace during World War II. This edition, however, was divided into two volumes: *Poteriannye* [*The Lost*] and *Begstvo iz sovetskogo ada* [*Flight from Soviet Hell*]. It should be added that *Rossiia v kontslagere* was initially published in two instalments and divides naturally into two parts. Although VSKhSON clearly appreciated both sections, it seems to have preferred part two. The *zakliuchenie sledstviia* tells us how the revolutionary organization acquired the book, "In October, 1966, the accused Ivanov, having received from Leningrad State University student O. L. Dugaev two anti-Soviet books by I. Solonevich, *Flight from Russian* [sic] *Hell* and *The Lost,* published and disseminated by the German Fascist authorities on temporarily occupied Soviet territory, gave these books to Sado for filming and photo-reproduction with the aim of using them in 'VSKhSON' propaganda activity." (p. 49) Osipov also mentions the two volumes in "Ber. kr....," p. 6.

[47]Milovan Djilas, *The New Class* (New York: Praeger, 1968), p. 45.

[48]*Ibid.*, p. 69.

[49]*Ibid.*, p. 45.

[50]*Ibid.*, p. 87.

[51]*Ibid.*

[52]*Ibid.*, p. 99.

[53]See Bukovskii's statement to William Cole of CBS in *Survey,* 77 (1970), p. 139.

[54]Tibor Meray, *Thirteen Days That Shook the Kremlin* (New York: Praeger, 1959), p. 131.

[55]*Ibid.*, p. 212.

[56]*Ibid.*, p. 213.

[57]Georg von Rauch, *A History of Soviet Russia* (New York: Praeger, 1957), p. v.

[58]*Ibid.*, p. vii.

[59]*Ibid.*, p. 442.

[60]*Ibid.*, p. 119.

[61]*Ibid.*, p. 368.

[62]Bernard Karavatskii, "Vospominaniia uchastnika" in *VSKhSON* (Paris: YMCA-Press, 1975), pp. 206-207 and Handler Interview.

[63]Ivan Solonevich, *Escape From Russian Chains* (London: Williams & Norgate, 1938), p. 138.

[64]*Ibid.*, p. 133.

[65]*Ibid.*, pp. 197-98.

[66]*Ibid.*, pp. 194-95.

[67]*Ibid.*, p. 339.

[68]*Ibid.*, p. 347.

[69]Nicolas Berdyaev, *The Russian Idea* (Boston: Beacon, 1962), pp. 252-53. It should be pointed out that it was Berdiaev's writings on the philosophy of Russian history and not his strictly philosophical or neo-Gnostic religious writings which attracted the interest of VSKhSON. For a systematic discussion of Berdiaev's views on Russia, see N. Poltoratskii's helpful study *Berdiaev i Rossiia* [*Berdiaev and Russia*] (New York: Obshchestvo Druzei Russkoi Kul'tury, 1967).

[70]*The Russian Idea*, p. 253.

[71]*Ibid.*, p. 254.

[72]*Ibid.*

[73]*Ibid.*, p. 255.

[74]Nikolai Berdiaev, *Novoe srednevekov'e* (Berlin: Obelisk, 1924), p. 5.

[75]See footnote 46 to this chapter.

[76]Osipov, "Ber. kr....," p. 6.

[77]See Appendix III for a full listing of these works.

[78]Berdiaev, *Nov. sr.*, p. 78.

[79]*Ibid.*, pp. 79-80.

[80]*Z.S.*, pp. 66-67.

[81]*Ibid.*, p. 56.

[82]*Ibid.*, p. 58.

[83]*Ibid.*, p. 76.

[84]*Ibid.*, p. 73.

[85]*Ibid.*, p. 108.

[86]*Ibid.*, pp. 97-98.

[87]Osipov, "Ber. kr....," p. 4.

[88]*Z.S.*, pp. 55-56.

[89]*Ibid.*, p. 56.

[90]*S.*, p. 40.

[91]*Z.S.*, p. 42.

[92]*Ibid.*, p. 111.

[93]*Ibid.*, pp. 42-43, 94 & 96.

[94]*Ibid.*, p. 43.

NOTES TO CHAPTER V

[1]Osipov, "Berdiaevskii kruzhok v Leningrade," *Posev*, 11 (1972), 3.

[2]*Zakliuchenie sledstviia*, p. 36.

[3]*Ibid.*

[4]*Ibid.*, p. 108.

[5]*Ibid.*, p. 99.

[6]*Ibid.*, p. 103. Orlov-Chistov had not officially been inducted into VSKhSON before the organization was broken in February, 1967.

[7]*Ibid.*, p. 93.

[8]*Ibid.*, p. 95.

[9]*Ibid.*, p. 108.

[10]*Ibid.*, p. 100.

[11]*Ibid.*, pp. 37 & 108.

[12]*Ibid.*, p. 97.

[13]*Ibid.*, p. 37.

[14]*Ibid.*

[15]From Luryi's unpublished article "Imi dvigala bol' za rodinu."

[16]*Z.S.*, p. 90 and Petrov-Agatov "Rossiia, kotoroi ne znaiut," *Posev* 3 (1971), 23.

[17]*Z.S.*, p. 35.

[18]Osipov, "Ploshchad' Maiakovskogo, stat'ia 70-aia," *Grani*, 80 (1971), 127-28.

[19]*Prigovor*, AS 1555, p. 4.

[20]*Z.S.*, pp. 93, 95 & 105.

[21]*Ibid.*, pp. 97, 95 & 111.

[22]*Ibid.*, p. 85.

[23]*Prigovor*, p. 8.

[24]*Ibid.*, p. 6.

[25]*Ibid.*, p. 9.

[26]*Ibid.*, p. 10.

[27]S., "Vserossiiskii sotsial-khristianskii soiuz osvobozhdeniia naroda," *Posev*, 1 (1971), 40.

NOTES TO CHAPTER VI

[1]S. sees this as one of VSKhSON's three major theoretical and tactical errors in his "Vserossiiskii sotsial-khristianskii soiuz osvobozhdeniia naroda," *Posev*, 1 (1971), 41.

[2]This information, and that which follows, is taken from Albert Boiter's valuable article, "When the Kettle Boils Over," *Problems of Communism*, 13, No. 1 (1964), 33-43.

[3]Petrov-Agatov, "Rossiia, kotoroi ne znaiut," *Posev*, 3 (1971), 22.

[4]Karavatskii, "Vospominaniia uchastnika" in *VSKhSON* (Paris: YMCA-Press, 1975), p. 204. K. italics.

[5]*Ibid.*, pp. 204-205.

[6]*Ibid.*, p. 205.

[7]*Ibid.*

[8]*Ibid.*

[9]*Ibid.*

[10]S., p. 41. The *Prigovor* (AS 1555, p. 5) gives a slightly different listing of the unit progression.

[11]*Zakliuchenie sledstviia*, p. 112 and *Prigovor*, p. 11.

[12]*Z.S.*, pp. 75-76 and *Prigovor*, p. 8.

[13]Osipov, "Berdiaevskii kruzhok v Leningrade," *Posev*, 11 (1972), 3. Osipov also lists Kozichev as a member of this unit, but this must be an error.

[14]Petrov-Agatov, "Rossiia...," p. 26.

[15]*Z.S.*, p. 80.

[16]*Ibid.*, p. 81.

[17]*Ibid.*, p. 36.

[18]Osipov, "Ploshchad' Maiakovskogo, stat'ia 70-aia," *Grani*, 80 (1971), 127.

[19]Osipov, "Ber. kr....," p. 7 and "K chitateliam Samizdata," *Grani*, 85 (1972), 190.

[20]Osipov, "Ploshchad'...," p. 128.

[21]*Z.S.*, p. 82.

[22]*Ibid.*, p. 81.

[23]*Ibid.*, p. 82.

[24]*Ibid.*, p. 84.

[25]*Ibid.*, p. 83.

[26]*Ibid.*, p. 92.

[27]*Ibid.*, p. 84.

[28]*Ibid.*, p. 92.

[29]*Ibid.*

[30]Osipov, "Ber. kr....," p. 6.

[31]*Z.S.*, p. 37.

[32]*Ibid.*, p. 40.

[33]Osipov, "Ber. kr....," p. 6.

[34]*Z.S.*, p. 83.

[35]Handler Interview.

[36]Osipov, "Ber. kr....," p. 5.

[37]See *Grani*, 80 (1971), 157-160.

[38]*Z.S.*, p. 72.

[39]*Ibid.*, p. 64.

[40]*Ibid.*

[41]*Ibid.*, p. 75.

[42]*Ibid.*

[43]*Ibid.*, p. 76.

[44]*Ibid.*

[45]*Ibid.*, p. 100.

[46]*Ibid.*, p. 99 and *Prigovor*, p. 5. Konstantinov seems to have only nominally belonged to this squad. It is significant that he did not even

attend the meeting at which was formed. (See *Z.S.*, p. 74).

[47]*Z.S.*, p. 74.

[48]*Ibid.*, p. 77.

[49]*Ibid.*

[50]*Ibid.*

[51]*Ibid.*, p. 79.

[52]*Ibid.*, p. 80.

[53]*Ibid.*, p. 84. The information that Konstantinov's pistol was defective comes from Yuri Luryi's unpublished article "Imi dvigala bol' za rodinu."

[54]*Z.S.*, p. 80.

[55]From the *zakliuchenie sledstviia* it seems abundantly clear that VSKhSON was contemplating a coup in Leningrad, to be spearheaded by an expanded Konosov "platoon." Of course, arms would have had to be obtained and recruitment accelerated before this could have been possible. As far as the date of the coup is concerned, we know that Konosov drafted a leaflet to the workers to be used as part of the "anti-Soviet actions" Ogurtsov intended to carry out "during the period of the celebration in Leningrad of the 50th anniversary of the Great October Socialist Revolution..." (*Z.S.*, p. 58) This period would understandably have had strong symbolic attraction for the revolutionary organization.

[56]*Z.S.*, p. 100.

[57]*Ibid.*, p. 78.

[58]*Ibid.*

[59]Osipov, "Ber. kr....," p. 3.

[60]*Z.S.*, p. 104.

[61]*Ibid.*, p. 79.

[62]*Ibid.*, p. 78.

[63]Curzio Malaparte, *Coup D'Etat: The Technique of Revolution* (New York: Dutton, 1932), p. 32.

[64]See Chapter IV ("Russian Kenoticism") in G. P. Fedotov, *The Russian Religious Mind* (New York: Harper Torchbook, 1960), pp. 94-131.

[65]E.g. his statement in *Winter Notes on Summer Impressions* that, "voluntary, fully conscious self-sacrifice utterly free of outside constraint, sacrifice of one's entire self for the benefit of all is...a sign of the supreme development of individuality, of its supreme power, absolute self-mastery and freedom of will. Voluntarily to lay down one's life for others, to crucify oneself or be burnt at the stake for the sake of all—all that is possible only at the most advanced stage of individuality." (New York: McGraw Hill, 1965, p. 111)

[66]In John B. Dunlop, Richard Haugh & Alexis Klimoff, eds., *Aleksandr Solzhenitsyn: Critical Essays and Documentary Materials* (New York: Collier, 1975), 2nd rev. ed., p. 555. A.S. italics.

[67]Handler Interview.

[68]Osipov, "Ber. kr....," pp. 4 & 5.

[69]*Z.S.*, p. 37. The fact that Klochkov was not sentenced suggests that he had become a relatively inactive member by February, 1967. Others

apparently in this category were Goncharov and Iovaisha. Shestakov had been in the organization only slightly over a month when the arrests came.

[70]S., pp. 40-41 and Petrov-Agatov, *passim.*

[71]Luryi, "Imi divigala..." L. italics.

[72]*Ibid.* When I wrote Luryi that I suspected that Bochevarov might not have told him the whole truth about VSKhSON's military intentions, he answered, in his written reply of 24 January 1975, that he was willing to admit that this could have been so. And when I directed his attention to passages in the *zakliuchenie sledstviia* seeming to point to concrete military plans in Leningrad, he did not deny that they could be based on fact. But he emphasized that VSKhSON was far too small to have posed a serious military threat to the regime. I, of course, agree but feel that, nonetheless, VSKhSON was seriously contemplating a military coup in the city of Leningrad.

[73]Osipov, "Ber. kr....," pp. 6 & 5.

[74]Osipov, "Trus ne igraet v khokkei" ["A Coward Doesn't Play Hockey"— the title is ironic], *Posev,* 5 (1974), 38.

[75]Osipov, "Ber. kr....," p. 6, footnote.

[76]*Ibid.,* p. 5. V.O. italics.

[77]*Ibid.,* p. 6.

[78]S., p. 40. In his "Berdiaevskii kruzhok...," p. 9, Osipov includes a list of those VSKhSON members who were Russian Orthodox. There are grounds for doubting this list is complete.

[79]S., p. 41.

[80]*Ibid.*

[81]*Ibid.,* p. 40.

[82]Osipov, "Ber. kr....," p. 9.

[83]S., p. 41.

NOTES TO CHAPTER VII

[1]*Prigovor, AS* 1555, pp. 16-17.

[2]Osipov, "Berdiaevskii kruzhok v Leningrade," *Posev,* 11 (1972), 7.

[3]Osipov, "K chitateliam Samizdata," *Grani,* 85 (1972), 190.

[4]*Zakliuchenie sledstviia,* p. 79.

[5]*Ibid.,* p. 56.

[6]*Ibid.,* p. 86.

[7]S., "Vserossiiskii sotsial-khristianskii soiuz osvobozhdeniia naroda," *Posev,* 1 (1971), 42. S. italics.

[8]In a letter dated January, 1975, Yuri Luryi writes that he suspects Petrov's denunciation may not have been the real reason for the downfall of VSKhSON. Petrov's letter—which was put on public display at the trial of the rank-and-file—could have been used by the KGB to "cover up"

another source or channel of information. According to Luryi, this is a widespread device employed by the security organs: they arrest an individual (in this case, Petrov), show him that the regime has evidence against him and then give him the chance to play the role of unmasker to avoid punishment. Even the "unmasker" does not understand in what his true service consists. Since, however, there is at present no hard evidence to support Luryi's hypothesis, I would continue to favor Osipov's explanation for VSKhSON's downfall, one which, moreover, seems to be backed up by the timing and pattern of the arrests of the revolutionary organization's membership and the behavior of the KGB after their arrest.

[9]Osipov, "Ber. kr....," p. 9.

[10]*Ibid.*, p. 7.

[11]*Ibid.*

[12]*Ibid.*

[13]*Ibid.*

[14]Z.S., p. 74.

[15]Osipov, "Ber. kr....," p. 7.

[16]*Ibid.*

[17]*Ibid.*

[18]Z.S., p. 83.

[19]*Ibid.*

[20]*Ibid.*, p. 73.

[21]*Prigovor*, p. 16.

[22]*Ibid.*, pp. 16-17. The *Prigovor* (p. 17) also informs us that Konstantinov was sent to a psychiatric ward for examination on March 6th and remained there until April 11th. In his letter to me of January, 1975, Luryi, who was Konstantinov's defense attorney, writes that Konstantinov was given a psychiatric examination after numerous requests from his mother, who made reference to his various departures from normal development since childhood. Konstantinov was ruled to be "a psychopathic personality, but sane."

[23]Harold J. Berman, ed., *Soviet Criminal Law and Procedure: The RSFSR Codes* (Cambridge, Mass.: Harvard U. Press, 1972), 2nd ed., p. 240.

[24]Osipov, "Ber. kr....," p. 8.

[25]Petrov-Agatov, "Rossiia, kotoroi ne znaiut," *Posev,* 3 (1971), 23.

[26]Z.S., pp. 120 & 142.

[27]Handler Interview.

[28]Osipov, "Ber. kr....," p. 8.

[29]Petrov-Agatov, "Rossiia...," pp. 20-21.

[30]Osipov, "Ber. kr....," pp. 7-8.

[31]*Ibid.*, p. 8.

[32]*Chronicle of Current Events* No. 1 (30 April 1968) in *Posev spets. vyp.,* 1 (1969), 13 and Osipov, "Ber. kr....," pp. 5-6. The Mauser is discussed by Luryi in his unpublished article "Imi dvigala bol' za rodinu."

[33]Osipov, "Ber. kr....," p. 8.

[34]In his "Imi dvigala..." article Luryi voices the opinion that, both during the investigation and trial, Ogurtsov involuntarily exaggerated the

real, practical significance of VSKhSON. This Luryi ascribes to two factors: "the overestimation of an organization by its *founder*, a phenomenon frequently encountered in life, and Ogurtsov's *fearlessness*, which made it possible for him to be revolted by the idea of attempting to diminish the significance of what had been done, something which would also have given grounds for accusing him of cowardice." (Luryi italics) I see the matter differently. Rather than exaggerating the importance of VSKhSON, Ogurtsov, I suspect, simply stated what his organization's plans and intentions were. The other VSKhSON members—out of understandable self-preservational instincts or, perhaps, due to devotion to their families—succumbed to what must have been a powerful temptation to downplay the revolutionary union's military-political significance.

[35]Handler Interview.

[36]Petrov-Agatov, "Arestanskie vstrechi," *Grani*, 84 (1972), 72.

[37]Petrov-Agatov, "Rossiia...," p. 23.

[38]Osipov, "Ber. kr....," p. 3.

[39]S., p. 42.

[40]*Ibid.*

[41]Osipov, "Ber. kr....," p. 6.

[42]*Ibid.*

[43]Handler Interview.

[44]Berman, ed., p. 152.

[45]Luryi, "Imi dvigala..."

[46]A., "Svedeniia ob Ogurtsove Igore Viacheslavoviche /r. 1937/," AS 1827, p. 1. Yuri Luryi provided Kheifets' first name and patronymic in a letter.

[47]A., p. 1 and Osipov, "Ber. kr....," p. 8.

[48]From Luryi's letter to me of January, 1975. Luryi italics.

[49]Osipov, "Ber. kr....," p. 8.

[50]*Prigovor*, p. 14.

[51]Osipov, "Ber. kr....," p. 8.

[52]*Prigovor*, p. 14.

[53]Petrov-Agatov, "Ar. vstr.," *Grani*, 84 (1972), 72.

[54]*Chronicle* No. 19 (30 April 1971) in *Posev spets. vyp.*, 9 (1971), 8. The text of the article reads: *"Article 43. Assignment of Milder Punishment Than That Provided by Law.* If the court, taking into consideration the exceptional circumstances of a case and the personality of the guilty person, deems it necessary to assign a punishment less than the lowest limit provided by law for the given crime or to resort to another, milder type of punishment, it may permit such mitigation but shall be obliged to indicate its reasons." (Berman, ed., p. 140)

[55]Handler Interview.

[56]Berman, ed., p. 153.

[57]*Ibid.*, p. 154.

[58]A. reports (pp. 2-3) that lawyers, acting on behalf of Ogurtsov's parents, twice lodged appeals arguing that he had been incorrectly sentenced

under Article 64. Both times a written answer was received stating that Ogurtsov's sentence "had been correct."

[59]*Z.S.,* p. 84.

[60]*Prigovor,* p. 1.

[61]Luryi, "Imi dvigala..." Luryi italics.

[62]*Ibid.*

[63]*Chronicle* No. 1, p. 13. The April, 1968, No. 43 issue of the neo-Marxist *samizdat* journal *A Political Diary* also mentions the second and third of these points. See *Politicheskii dnevnik, 1964-1970* (Amsterdam: Herzen Foundation, 1972), pp. 310-11.

[64]AS 140, p. 1. Other protests, signed by Handler and others, against the trial of the VSKhSON rank-and-file may be found in Pavel Litvinov, ed., *Protsess chetyrekh [The Trial of the Four]*(Amsterdam: Herzen Foundation, 1971), pp. 267-269.

[65]See the account of Handler's trial by L. P. Nestor in *Posev spets. vyp.,* 5 (1971), 23-34. The jurist Nikolai Danilov was employed by the Sakhalin regional procuracy from 1960-1963. According to the *Chronicle,* "The decision on his insanity and his internment in the severe conditions of a special psychiatric hospital were probably the result of his firm behavior at the investigation, and also of the particular hatred of the K.G.B. organs for a former investigator who had voluntarily left his work in the investigation organs. At the moment Danilov is being given potent 'treatment'—insulin shocks, which have resulted in him genuinely being reduced to a serious condition." (Cited in Peter Reddaway, ed., *Uncensored Russia* [New York: American Heritage, 1972], pp. 382-83.) I have been informed that Danilov was released from the psychiatric hospital in 1972.

[66]Luryi, "Imi dvigala..."

[67]Osipov, "Ber. kr....," p. 8.

[68]Luryi, "Imi divigala..." Luryi italics.

[69]*Chronicle* No. 1, p. 13.

[70]*Prigovor,* p. 15.

[71]*Ibid.* Luryi writes in "Imi dvigala...": "At the trial the criminal examiners were forced, in answering a question from the defense, to admit that this 'Mauser' revolver—of pre-World War I vintage (and perhaps earlier, I cannot recall precisely)—was not *suitable* for firing. Incidentally, Stanislav Konstantinov acquired this revolver a year before becoming acquainted with VSKhSON...In the 'sentence' a 'Mauser' revolver is mentioned, but it is not said that the gun was not suitable for firing." Luryi italics. Osipov ("Ber. kr....," p. 6) gives the gun's year of manufacture as 1898.

[72]Luryi, "Imi dvigala..." Luryi italics.

[73]Article 71 concerns the "evaluation of evidence," articles 301-303, the "legality and well-founded nature of judgment," "the secrecy of the judges' conference" and "questions resolved by the court when decreeing judgment." Article 317 deals with "other questions to be decided in the resolutory part of judgment." See Berman, ed., pp. 225, 294 & 299.

[74]Petrov-Agatov, "Rossiia...," p. 27.

NOTES TO CHAPTER VIII

[1]*Grani,* 89-90 (1973), 192.

[2]Petrov-Agatov, "Arestanskie vstrechi," *Grani,* 82 (1971), 104-105.

[3]*Ibid.,* pp. 106-107.

[4]Peter Reddaway, *The Forced Labor Camps in the U.S.S.R. Today* (Brussels: International Committee for the Defense of Human Rights in the U.S.S.R., 1973), pp. 5-6.

[5]Anatoly Marchenko, *My Testimony* (Harmondsworth, Middlesex: Penguin, 1971), p. 51.

[6]Reddaway, pp. 5-6.

[7]See note 5.

[8]Alexander Solzhenitsyn, "Interview with Two Western Correspondents," *Index,* 2, No. 4 (1973), 41.

[9]Reddaway, p. 8.

[10]Handler Interview.

[11]Petrov-Agatov, "Ar. vstr.," *Grani,* 83 (1972), 56-58. P.-A. italics.

[12]Solzhenitsyn, "Interview...," pp. 40-41.

[13]*Chronicle* No. 4 (31 October 1968) in *Posev spets. vyp.,* 1 (1969), 39.

[14]*Chronicle* No. 6 (28 February 1969) in *Posev spets. vyp.,* 1 (1969), 59.

[15]*Ibid.*

[16]*Ibid.*

[17]*Chronicle* No. 8 (30 June 1969) in *Posev spets. vyp.,* 2 (1969), 31-32.

[18]*Istoriia odnoi golodvki* [*The History of One Hunger Strike*] (Frankfurt/Main: Possev Verlag, 1971), p. 91. This volume is a collection of materials relating to Ginzburg's hunger strike.

[19]*Ibid.,* p. 92.

[20]*Ibid.,* p. 103.

[21]*Ibid.,* pp. 106-107.

[22]*Chronicle* No. 11 (31 December 1969) in *Posev spets. vyp.,* 3 (1970), 46. The full text of this letter appeared in *Posev,* 6 (1970), 12-14.

[23]*Chronicle* No. 11, p. 34.

[24]*Chronicle* No. 17 (31 December 1970) in *Posev spets. vyp.,* 8 (1971), 23. Galanskov's and Ivanov's hospitalization was reported in *Chronicle* No. 18 (5 March 1971) in *Posev spets. vyp.,* 8 (1971), 44.

[25]*Chronicle* No. 18, pp. 42-43.

[26]*Chronicle* No. 22 (10 November 1971) in *Vol'noe slovo* (Posev), 2 (1972), 14. Anatolii Radygin, a cellmate of Ogurtsov in Vladimir Prison (and, it seems, of Borodin as well), writes concerning the mentally deranged Tarasov, "...Nikolai Tarasov, the fetid specter of Vladimir Prison, roamed for years from cell to cell. He was specially 'dandled' [by the authorities] in the cells of newcomers, and his sinister and gloomy marasmus fitted well into the picture of 'educational influence'." (*Posev,* 5 [1975], 43)

[27]Reddaway, appendix 4, p. 7.

[28]*Ibid.*

[29]*Ibid.*, pp. 3 & 6. See also *Chronicle* No. 25 (20 May 1972) in *Vol'noe Slovo*, 4 (1972), 100.

[30]Petrov-Agatov, "Ar. vstr.," *Grani*, 83 (1972), 56 & 64.

[31]*Ibid.*, p. 64.

[32]*Ibid.*

[33]*Ibid.*, *Grani*, 84 (1972), 58.

[34]*Ibid.*, p. 70.

[35]*Ibid.*, pp. 70-71. P.-A. italics.

[36]Handler Interview.

[37]E.g. the "Interv'iu 11-ti politzakliuchennykh Permskogo lageria VS 389/35" ["An Interview of Eleven Political Prisoners of the Perm' Camp 389/35"], which comes to 28 pages in the Arkhiv samizdata edition (AS 2090). This interview occurred in the fall of 1974.

[38]See the two documents "Permskii lager'" ["The Perm' Camp"] and "Den' pamiati zhertv" ["Memorial Day for the Victims"] in *Russkaia mysl'*, 31 January 1974, p. 6.

[39]*Chronicle* No. 30 (31 December 1973), published by Khronika Press (New York) in 1974, p. 97.

[40]*Chronicle* No. 32 (17 July 1974) (New York: Khronika Press, 1974), p. 80.

[41]*Chronicle* No. 35 (31 March 1975). To be published shortly by Khronika Press.

NOTES TO CHAPTER IX

[1]*Russkaia mysl'*, 4 July 1974, p. 2.

[2]Anatoly Marchenko, *My Testimony* (Harmondsworth, Middlesex: Penguin, 1971), pp. 116-17.

[3]Iurii Ivanov, "Gorod Vladimir" ["The City of Vladimir"], *Vestnik R.S. Kh.D.*, 99 (1971), 126. Compare Marchenko, p. 120.

[4]Marchenko, p. 122.

[5]Ivanov, p. 126.

[6]Marchenko, p. 207.

[7]*Ibid.*, p. 161.

[8]*Ibid.*, pp. 160-61.

[9]*Ibid.*, p. 185.

[10]*Ibid.*, p. 124.

[11]Vladimir Osipov, "V organizatsiiu 'Mezhdunarodnaia Amnistiia' g-nu Shonu MakBraidu" ["An Appeal to Mr. Sean MacBride of the Organization 'Amnesty International'"], AS 1761, p. 2.

[12]A., "Svedeniia ob Ogurtsove Igore Viacheslavoviche /r. 1937/," AS 1827, p. 2.

[13]Osipov, "V organizatsiiu...," p. 2.

[14]A., pp. 1-2.

[15]I have not had an opportunity to interview Radygin, but Iurii Handler spoke with him at length about his experiences in Vladimir Prison.

[16]See, for example, *Chronicle of Current Events* No. 18 (5 March 1971) in *Posev spets. vyp.*, 8 (1971), 43.

[17]Eduard Kuznetsov, *Dnevniki* (Paris: Les Editeurs Reunis, 1973), p. 253.

[18]In the camps VSKhSON member Mikhail Konosov asked that he be addressed "not only by his first name but by his patronymic as well." See Petrov-Agatov, "Arestanskie vstrechi," *Grani*, 83 (1972), 56.

[19]Eduard Kuznetsov told this to his defense attorney Yuri Luryi.

[20]Anatolii Radygin, "Po obitaemym ostrovam Arkhipelaga" ["Along the Inhabited Islands of the Archipelago"], *Posev*, 3 (1975), 51. Radygin italics.

[21]A., p. 3.

[22]*Ibid.*

[23]*Chronicle* No. 32 (17 July 1974) (New York: Khronika Press, 1974), p. 49.

[24]The Committee on the Judiciary's 257 page collection was published by the U.S. Government Printing Office (Washington, D.C.) in 1972, Stock Number 5270-01653. The journal materials appeared in *Survey*, 21, No. 1-2 (1975), 176-99 and *Index*, 4, No. 2 (1975), 61-71.

[25]A., p. 3.

[26]*Ibid.*, pp. 3-4.

[27]*Ibid.*, p. 4.

[28]*Ibid.*, pp. 4-5.

[29]*Ibid.*, p. 5.

[30]*International Herald Tribune* (Paris), 16 May 1974.

[31]*Russkaia mysl'*, 29 August 1974, p. 2. An English translation of Sakharov's statement appeared in *Survey*, 20, No. 4 (1974), 111-12.

[32]Osipov, "V organizatsiiu...," p. 1.

[33]*Chronicle*, No. 33 (10 December 1974) (New York: Khronika Press, 1975), p. 29.

[34]*Ibid.*, p. 30.

[35]Petrov-Agatov, "Ar. vstr.," *Grani*, 84 (1972), 73.

[36]*Grani*, 89-90 (1973), 195.

[37]*Ibid.*, p. 176.

[38]Petrov-Agatov, "Ar. vstr.," *Grani*, 84 (1972), 86.

[39]Petrov-Agatov, "Rossiia, kotoroi ne znaiut," *Posev*, 3 (1971), 23.

[40]*Ibid.*

[41]Petrov-Agatov, "Ar. vstr.," *Grani*, 84 (1972), 86.

[42]*Ibid.*, p. 87.

[43]In an "Open Letter to Gennadii Shimanov," dated April 29, 1973,

Osipov asserts that "at the end of his life Iurii Galanskov became a Russian patriot . . ." (AS 1732).
[44]See "Ot redaktsii zhurnala 'Veche' " ["From the Editors of the Journal *Veche*"], AS 1791.
[45]Petrov-Agatov, "Ar. vstr.," *Grani,* 84 (1972), 87-88.
[46]Petrov-Agatov, "Rossiia. . .," p. 23.

NOTES TO CHAPTER X

[1]Vladimir Osipov, "Berdiaevskii kruzhok v Leningrade," *Posev,* 11 (1972), 8.
[2]In *Sakharov Speaks* (New York: Vintage, 1974), pp. 135-150. The out-of-print Sakharov volume *Progress, Coexistence and Intellectual Freedom* (New York: Norton, 1968) contains copious notes to the Memorandum by Harrison Salisbury.
[3]*Programma demokraticheskogo dvizheniia sovetskogo soiuza* [*Program of the Democratic Movement of the Soviet Union*] (Amsterdam: Herzen Foundation, 1970). See also the analysis of this document by Albert Boiter: "A Program for Soviet Democrats," Radio Liberty Dispatch, April 6, 1970, 16 pp.
[4]Aleksandr I. Solzhenitsyn, *Letter to the Soviet Leaders* (New York: Harper and Row, 1974).
[5]Boiter, pp. 2-3.
[6]Program, Introduction & Section IV.
[7]*Ibid.,* Introduction.
[8]S., "Vserossiiskii sotsial-khristianskii soiuz osvobozhdeniia naroda," *Posev,* 1 (1971), 39.
[9]Program, II.
[10]*Ibid.*
[11]*Ibid.,* V.
[12]*Ibid.,* II.
[13]*Ibid.,* I.
[14]*Ibid.*
[15]*Ibid.,* Introduction.
[16]*Ibid.,* III.
[17]Solzhenitsyn, *Letter,* p. 30.
[18]See his response to Solzhenitsyn's *Letter:* AS 1874, p. 13.
[19]Program, I.
[20]*Ibid.,* IV.
[21]*Ibid.,* III.
[22]*Ibid.,* II.
[23]*Ibid.,* III.
[24]*Ibid.,* V.
[25]In *Iz-pod glyb: Sbornik statei* (Paris: YMCA-Press, 1974), pp. 29-72.

This collection was published in the U.S. by Little, Brown and Company in 1975 with the title *From Under the Rubble*.

[26]Program, Introduction.

[27]*Ibid.*

[28]*Ibid.*, III.

[29]*Ibid.*

[30]*Ibid.*

[31]See, for example, "Solzhenitsyn Denounces Serfdom in Russia," *The Times* (London), 6 April 1974, p. 1.

[32]Program, III.

[33]*Ibid.*

[34]*Ibid.*

[35]*Ibid.*

[36]*Ibid.*, II.

[37]*Ibid.*, III.

[38]*Ibid.*, I.

[39]*Ibid.*, VI.

[40]*Ibid.*, II.

[41]*Ibid.*

[41a]*Ibid.*, III.

[42]*Ibid.*

[43]*Ibid.*, IV.

[44]*Ibid.*, III.

[45]Ibid.

[46]*Ibid.*

[47]*Ibid.*

[48]*Ibid.*

[49]*Ibid.*

[50]*Ibid.*

[51]*Ibid.*

[52]*Ibid.*, I.

[53]*Ibid.*, III. On the Lysenko affair, see: Zhores Medvedev, *The Rise and Fall of T.D. Lysenko* (New York: Columbia U. Press, 1969).

[54]Program, I.

[55]*Ibid.*, Introduction.

[56]*Ibid.*, II.

[57]*Ibid.*

[58]*Ibid.*

[59]*Ibid.*, Introduction.

[60]*Ibid.*

[61]*Ibid.*, V.

[62]*Ibid.*

[63]*Ibid.*

[64]*Ibid.*

[65]*Ibid.*, IV.

[66]*Ibid.*

[67]B. V. Talantov, "Sovetskoe obshchestvo, 1965-68," *Posev,* 9 (1969), 40. Talantov perished in a concentration camp in 1971. On Talantov, see my article: "Dissent Within the Orthodox Church: Boris Vladimirovich Talantov (1903-1971)," *The Russian Review,* 31, No. 3 (1972), 248-259.
[68]"Sov. ob.," pp. 40-41.
[69]Program, V.
[70]*Ibid.*
[71]S., pp. 41-42.
[72]Program, III.
[7⁻]*ʳbid.*

NOTES TO CHAPTER XI

[1]Program, Section V.
[2]See Röpke's and Fedotov's works listed in Appendix III ("The VSKhSON Library"). At present, I have no evidence concerning when precisely the organization came into possession of these writings. Hence I cannot with certainty claim that Röpke's and Fedotov's thought influenced the Program. Osipov's report, on the other hand, that the VSKhSON leaders decided to photocopy Berdiaev's *The New Middle Ages* in 1964 supports internal evidence that this work played no small role in influencing the Program. See his "Berdiaevskii kruzhok v Leningrade," *Posev,* 11 (1972), 6-7.
[3]Program, II.
[4]*Ibid.,* V.
[5]VSKhSON's "personalism" derives—via Dostoevskii, Berdiaev and other mediators—from a major doctrinal emphasis of the Eastern Orthodox Church. Both Orthodox Triadology and Christology stress the supreme importance of the concept of "person." See chapters 3 and 7 in Vladimir Lossky, *The Mystical Theology of the Eastern Church* (London: James Clarke, 1957) and the chapter devoted to "lichnost' " in S. Verkhovskoi, *Bog i chelovek* (New York: Chekhov Publishers, 1956).
[6]Program, VI.
[7]*Ibid.*
[8]*Ibid.,* V.
[9]Nikolai Berdiaev, *Novoe srednevekov'e* (Berlin: Obelisk, 1924), pp. 29-30.
[10]*Ibid.,* p. 85.
[11]Program, IV.
[12]Berdiaev, pp. 139-140.
[13]Wilhelm Röpke, *Civitas Humana: A Humane Order of Society* (London: William Hodge, 1948), pp. 10 & 154.
[14]Program, VI.
[15]*Ibid.,* VII.

[16]*Ibid.*, VIII, point 4.

[17]*Ibid.*, pt. 2.

[18]*Ibid.*, pt. 5.

[19]*Ibid.*, pt. 4.

[20]*Ibid.*, XV, pt. 58.

[21]*Ibid.*, IX, pt. 8.

[22]*Ibid.*, pts. 9 & 18.

[23]*Ibid.*, VI.

[24]*Ibid.*, IX, pt. 10.

[25]The term "free market" is used in Section X, point 24.

[26]Program, IX, pt. 13.

[27]*Ibid.*, X, pt. 21.

[28]Berdiaev, p. 33.

[29]A recent right-wing Russian nationalist *samizdat* manifesto "Slovo natsii" (translatable as either "The Nation Speaks" or "A Word to the Nation") proclaims, "The catastrophically low productivity of labor will grow only in instances when the workers are given the opportunity to participate directly in the management of enterprises and the distribution of profits, when the workers feel themselves to be, and really are, the masters." (*Survey*, Summer [1971], p. 194.) Toward the other end of the political spectrum, the liberal *samizdat* "Program of the Democratic Movement of the Soviet Union" is also receptive to the idea of worker management. (*Programma demokraticheskogo dvizheniia sovetskogo soiuza* [Amsterdam: Herzen Foundation, 1970], p. 44.)

[30]Program, VI.

[31]*Ibid.*, XIV, pt. 43.

[32]See, for example, his "Slovo razrushit beton" ["The Word Will Destroy Concrete"] in *Vestnik Russkogo Khristianskogo Dvizheniia*, 114 (1974), p. 196.

[33]Program, VI.

[34]Paul Avrich, *Kronstadt 1921* (Princeton, N. J.: Princeton U. Press, 1970), p. 162.

[35]Berdiaev, pp. 50-51.

[36]G. P. Fedotov, *Khristianin v revoliutsii: Sbornik statei* (Paris: Author Publication, 1957), p. 64.

[37]*Ibid.*, p. 153.

[38]Georges Nivat, *Sur Soljenitsyne: Essais* (Lausanne: Editions L'Age d'Homme, 1974), p. 194.

[39]Alexander Solzhenitsyn, *August 1914* (New York: Farrar, Strauss and Giroux, 1971), p. 582. In the same historical novel he appears to advocate the idea of a "union of engineers," a professional organization which would enjoy considerable social and political influence (p. 572). And in his *Letter to the Soviet Leaders* he counsels the granting of "real power" to the soviets. (*Pis'mo vozhdiam sovetskogo soiuza* [Paris: YMCA-Press, 1974], p. 46. The published English translation of the passage in which these words occur [*Letter*, p. 54] is inaccurate.)

[40]Berdiaev, p. 53 and Fedotov, p. 153.
[41]Berdiaev, p. 53.
[42]Program, XIV, pt. 45.
[43]*Ibid.*
[44]*Ibid.*, pt. 48.
[45]*Ibid.*, pt. 49.
[46]*Ibid.*, pt. 50.
[47]*Ibid.*
[48]Julien Benda, *The Treason of the Intellectuals (La Trahison des Clercs)* (New York: Norton, 1969).
[49]Röpke, pp. 117-118.
[50]Program, XIV, pt. 52.
[51]*Ibid.*, XIII, pt. 34.
[52]*Ibid.*, VI.
[53]*Ibid.*, XI.
[54]*Ibid.*
[55]*Ibid.*, XV, pt. 61.
[56]*Ibid.*, IX, pt. 16.
[57]*Ibid.*, XI, pt. 29.
[58]*Ibid.*, XII, pt. 32.
[59]Berdiaev, p. 38.
[60]S., p. 42.
[61]Program, Introduction.
[62]*Ibid.*, XII.
[63]*Ibid.*, Part III, pt. 83.
[64]Bernard Karavatskii, "Vospominaniia uchastnika" in *VSKhSON* (Paris: YMCA-Press, 1975), pp. 206-207.
[65]On the East Europeans, see Osipov, "Ber. kr....," p. 7 and *Zakliuchenie sledstviia*, p. 64.
[66]Program, Part III, pts. 74 & 75.
[67]*Ibid.*, pt. 77.
[68]*Ibid.*
[69]*Ibid.*, pt. 85.
[70]*Ibid.*, XV.
[71]*Ibid.*, pt. 55.

NOTES TO CHAPTER XII

[1]Vladimir Osipov, "Berdiaevskii kruzhok v Leningrade," *Posev*, 11 (1972), 9.

[2]*Ibid.*

[3]*Ibid.*

[4]*Ibid.*

[5]AS 1706, p. 2 and *Chronicle* No. 32 (17 July 1974) (New York: Khronika Press, 1974), p. 62.

[6]Osipov, "Ber. kr...," p. 10 and *Chronicle* No. 19 (30 April 1971) in *Posev spets. vyp.*, 9 (1971), 8-9.

[7]AS 1627, p. 6 and *Russkaia mysl'*, 20 June 1974, p. 5.

[8]Editor's afterword to Borodin's article in *Veche*, No. 8 (AS 1665).

[9]*Russkaia mysl'*, 20 June 1974, p. 5.

[10]*Chronicle* No. 34 (31 December 1974) (New York: Khronika Press, 1975), p. 80.

[11]*Ibid.*

[12]In fact, even Ivoilov's release from prison has not been reported by the *Chronicle*. One simply assumes that he was freed at the same time as Borodin and Ivanov, who were released at the conclusion of their six year sentences (*Chronicle* No. 29 [31 July 1973], 61.).

[13]*Chronicle* No. 32, p. 80.

[14]*Chronicle* No. 35 (31 March 1975). In press at the present time.

[15]Besides neo-Slavophilism, which places great stress on the role of the Russian Orthodox Church, there exists a variant of contemporary Russian nationalism which is violently anti-Christian: neo-national socialism. One also is in something of a quandary as to how to categorize the tendency known as "National Bolshevism" (e.g., the now-defunct Fetisov group). Solzhenitsyn sees its adherents as irreligious, if not anti-religious (*Iz-pod glyb* [Paris: YMCA-Press, 1974], pp. 128-129.). The writings of M. Antonov, an influential member of the group, however, manifest at least some degree of acceptance of Russian Orthodoxy. See *Veche*, Nos. 1-3.

[16]From conversations held with persons who emigrated from Soviet Russia during the Second World War.

[17]The release during the 1950s of some ten million persons—many of them religious—from the concentration camps was a contributing factor to this upsurge. Helpful general studies of the Russian Church under the Communists are: Matthew Spinka, *The Church in Soviet Russia* (New York: Oxford, 1956) and Nikita Struve, *Christians in Contemporary Russia* (New York: Scribners, 1967). On the underground or "catacomb" Orthodox Church, see William C. Fletcher, *The Russian Orthodox Church Underground 1917-1970* (London: Oxford University Press, 1971). For the period 1945-1960, see Fletcher's *Nikolai* (New York: Macmillan, 1968). On the Khrushchev

persecution of 1959-1964, see Michael Bourdeaux, ed., *Patriarch and Prophets: Persecution of the Russian Orthodox Church Today* (London: Macmillan, 1969), John B. Dunlop, *The Recent Activities of the Moscow Patriarchate Abroad and in the U.S.S.R.* (Seattle: St. Nectarios, 1974), 2nd ed., Fr. Dimitrii Konstantinov, *Gonimaia tserkov'* [*The Persecuted Church*] (New York: Vseslavianskaia Izd., 1967), Donald A. Lowrie and William C. Fletcher, "Khrushchev's Religious Policy, 1959-1964" in Richard H. Marshall et al., eds., *Aspects of Religion in the Soviet Union, 1917-1967* (Chicago: U. of Chicago Press, 1971), pp. 131-155, Peter Reddaway, "Freedom of Worship and the Law" in Abraham Brumberg, ed., *In Quest of Justice* (New York: Praeger, 1970), pp. 62-75. For the post-Khrushchev period, see Fr. Konstantinov, *Zarnitsy dukhovnogo vozrozhdeniia* [*Lightning Flashes of Spiritual Renewal*] (London, Ontario: Zaria, 1973).

[18]From Solzhenitsyn's open letter to Patriarch Pimen in John B. Dunlop, Richard Haugh and Alexis Klimoff, eds., *Aleksandr Solzhenitsyn: Critical Essays and Documentary Materials* (New York: Collier, 1975), p. 553.

[19]From an open letter to Patriarch Aleksii by a group of Orthodox believers in Kirov Province. In *Vestnik R.S.Kh.D.*, 83 (1967), 38.

[20]Dimitry Pospielovsky, "The Resurgence of Russian Nationalism in *Samizdat*," *Survey*, 19, No. 1 (1973), 52.

[21]The scenario appeared in *Isskustvo kino*, 4 & 5 (1964). According to Soviet poet Naum Korzhavin, who recently emigrated to the West, the film was shown solely in Moscow and that only for several days. (*Posev*, 11 [1974], 19.)

[22]Pospielovsky, pp. 52-53 and Thomas E. Bird, "New Interest in Old Russian Things," *Slavic Review*, 32, No. 1 (1973), 22-23, ft. 29.

[23]Petr Dudochkin, "Kak cheloveku sdaet ekzamen prirode" [How Man Will Pass Nature's Exam"], *Veche* No. 4, AS 1140, p. 115. See also Dudochkin's address to the Second Kalinin Conference of the All-Union Society for the Preservation of Historical and Cultural Monuments in *Veche* No. 6, AS 1599, pp. 94-100.

[24]Gleb Rar, "Skol'ko pravoslavnykh v Rossii" ["How Many Orthodox Are There in Russia"], *Posev*, 3 (1973), 39-42. According to the recent émigré Anatolii Levitin, who is well-informed about church life in the USSR, Furov, the deputy of the chairman of the Soviet for Religious Affairs, in his report to the government for 1971-1972 stated that "more than forty million" Soviet citizens adhere to the Russian Orthodox Church. Citing such factors as unregistered baptisms, Levitin considers this figure to be too conservative and suggests that fifty million would be more appropriate. But his own estimate may suffer from over-caution. If one were to lump all those "somehow" attracted to or interested in Russian Orthodoxy together, the figure could approach Rar's seemingly high estimate. (Levitin's information appeared in an interview in *Russkaia mysl'*, 5 December 1974, p. 5.)

[25]Aleksandr Solzhenitsyn, "Tret'emu soboru zarubezhnoi russkoi tserkvi" ["To the Third Council of the Russian Church Abroad"], *Novoe russkoe slovo*, 27 September 1974.

[26]On the *Molodaia gvardiia* episode, see Vl. N. Pavlov, "Spory o slaviano-
fil'stve i russkom patriotizme v sovetskoi nauchnoi literature, 1967-1970"
["The Disputes Concerning Slavophilism and Russian Patriotism in Soviet
Journals, 1967-1970"], *Grani,* 82 (1971), 183-211, esp. 189-195. The five
pieces which most displeased the regime were two by V. Chalmaev in No. 3
and No. 9 (1968), two by Iu. Ivanov in No. 6 and No. 12 (1969) and
one by S. Semanov in No. 8 (1970). See *Veche* No. 1, AS 1013, p. 140.
A number of attacks on the journal, all claiming to represent Marxist orthodoxy, appeared in the Soviet press. See, for example, A. Dement'ev, "O
traditsiiakh i narodnosti" ["Concerning Traditions and National Character"],
Novyi mir, 4 (1969), 215-235 and A. Iakovlev, "Protiv antiistorizma"
["Against Anti-historicism"], *Literaturnaia gazeta,* 15 November 1972, pp.
4-5. For Solzhenitsyn's comments on the episode, see his *Bodalsia telenok s
dubom* [*The Calf Butted the Oak*] (Paris: YMCA-Press, 1975), pp. 266-274.

[27]Vladimir Soloukhin, *Searching for Icons in Russia* (New York: Harcourt,
Brace and Jovanovich, 1971). This work, plus Soloukhin's interesting "Letters
from a Russian Museum," appeared in the collection *Slavianskaia tetrad'*
[*Slavic Notebook*] (Moscow: Sovetskaia Rossiia, 1972).

[28]Georgie Anne Geyer, "A New Quest for the Old Russia," *Saturday
Review,* 25 December 1971, p. 16.

[29]Jack V. Haney, "The Revival of Interest in the Russian Past in the
Soviet Union," *Slavic Review,* 32, No. 1 (1973), 3.

[30]*Veche* No. 1, p. 140. Since the purge of *Molodaia gvardiia,* the journal
Nash sovremennik [*Our Contemporary*] has become the leading officially-
permitted tribune of neo-Slavophile thought.

[31]A concise guide to the thought of the 19th century Slavophiles is:
A. Gratieux, *A. S. Khomiakov et le Mouvement Slavophile: Les Doctrines*
(Paris: Cerf, 1939). This is the second of two volumes devoted to Khomiakov
and the Slavophiles.

[32]Vladimir Osipov, "Ploshchad' Maiakovskogo, stat'ia 70-aia" ["Moscow
Square, Article 70"], *Grani,* 80 (1971), 131 & 135.

[33]See the text of the interview in *Vestnik R.S.Kh.D.,* 106 (1972), 301-302.

[34]AS 1583.

[35]AS 1627.

[36]See, for example, his protests in *Veche* No. 6, pp. 3-5 and AS 1845.

[37]See his letter to the Procurator of the City of Moscow in *Russkaia
mysl',* 9 August 1973, p. 3.

[38]See "Kriticheskie zametki russkogo cheloveka o patrioticheskom zhurnale
'Veche' " ["Critical Remarks of a Russian Man about the Patriotic Journal
Veche"] in *Novyi zhurnal* (New York), 118 (1975), 219-227. Internal
evidence strongly suggests that the anonymous author of this chilling *samizdat*
document moves in high places in the regime. The letter is produced as an
appendix to Melik Agurskii's "Neonatsistskaia opasnost' v sovetskom soiuze"
["The Neo-Nazi Danger in the Soviet Union"], pp. 199-204 in the same
number of *Novyi zhurnal.*

[39]Agurskii, p. 202.

Notes   331

⁴⁰For the charges and counter-charges, see AS 1705, 1706, 1787, 1790 and 1966. Those signing pro-Osipov statements were: **V. I. Il'iakov, G. F. Dudnikov, V. S. Rodionov, S. F. Seryi, V. F. Starikov, I. V. Pogorelov,** and **V. F. Gorlopanov.** Anti-Osipovites were: **A. Naidenovich, V. Repnikov, V. Ovchinnikov, G. Gusarova, I. Cherdyntsev, N. Bogdanov, A. Ivanov, Iu. Pirogov, M. Rogachev, V. Polenov** and **V. Sychev.** It is noteworthy that no former VSKhSON member signed documents emanating from either camp.

⁴¹L. Sergeeva, "V usloviiakh ugolovnogo presledovaniia" ["Under Conditions of Criminal Persecution"], *Posev,* 9 (1974), 24-27. By August, 1974 Osipov realized that his opponents were not linked with the KGB. He wrote at that time, "In March, 1974 an attempt was made by my [*Veche*] confederates to blacken my reputation at the same time as 'information' concerning my anti-government activities was fabricated [by the regime]." See his letter in *Russkaia mysl',* 12 December 1974, p. 2 (also AS 1908).

⁴²AS 1705. This "urgent press release" is dated March 7, 1974.

⁴³AS 1706 and 1787.

⁴⁴Declaration of July 9, 1974 (AS 1792).

⁴⁵*Chronicle* No. 32, p. 62.

⁴⁶*Ibid.* Osipov thinks that the regime began to prepare its case against himself and *Veche* as early as December, 1973 (*Russkaia mysl',* 12 December 1974, p. 2 and AS 1908).

⁴⁷*Chronicle* No. 32, p. 81.

⁴⁸*Ibid.,* p. 62.

⁴⁹*Zemlia* No. 1 appeared as AS 1909.

⁵⁰See Rodionov's declaration of December 15, 1974 (AS 2061), which describes the contents of *Zemlia,* No. 2. They are also listed in *Chronicle* No. 35.

⁵¹Rodionov, p. 1.

⁵²The protest was published in *Russkaia mysl',* 6 March 1975, p. 5.

⁵³See his open letter to world opinion in *Russkaia mysl',* 27 February 1975, p. 2. See also Anatolii Levitin's appeal "Zashchishchaite Vladimira Osipova!" ["Defend Vladimir Osipov!"] in *Russkaia mysl',* 19 December 1974, p. 2 and his interview on the subject of Osipov's arrest in *Novoe russkoe slovo,* 11 December 1974.

⁵⁴*Moskovskii sbornik* No. 1 will shortly be available from the Arkhiv samizdata.

⁵⁵For a more detailed discussion of contemporary neo-Slavophile currents, see my article, "The Eleventh Hour. An Account of Neo-Slavophilism. Is It the Emerging Ideology of a Post-Marxist Russia?" in *Frontier,* 18, No. 2 (1975), pp. 71-82.

⁵⁶*Zemlia* carried a piece by Anatolii Levitin, and *Moskovskii sbornik* one by Melik Agurskii. And *Zemlia* published a contribution by Gennadii Shimanov, who is closer to *Sbornik* in orientation, while Leonid Borodin, the compiler of *Sbornik,* protested Osipov's arrest.

⁵⁷*Chronicle* No. 35 reports the publication of a second number of *Moskovskii sbornik*—dated January, 1975—and lists its contents. *Chronicle*

No. 34 includes a short abstract of Borodin's recent *samizdat* essay "Protiv real'nosti vo imia istiny" ["Against Reality in the Name of Truth"]. (pp. 80-81) This four-page essay seeks to defend Solzhenitsyn's *Letter to the Soviet Leaders* against criticism. Solzhenitsyn recently showed that he is not indifferent to Borodin's fate. At his December 12, 1974 Stockholm press conference he remarked, "...in the Soviet Union today there exist many people who could give extraordinarily important interviews. However, these people, who are still unknown, do not interest Western correspondents. Thus, not long ago Borodin gave an interview to Western correspondents...and the agency itself said, 'We don't need your interview. Who is he [Borodin] anyway?' And so they did not print it." (*Russkaia mysl'*, 16 January 1975, p. 6)

[58]It hardly needs stating that I have every confidence in the veracity and accuracy of Handler's account.

[59]On Leont'ev, see Berdiaev's study *Leontiev* (Orono, Maine: Academic International, 1968). On Fedorov, see V. V. Zenkovsky, *A History of Russian Philosophy* (New York: Columbia, 1953), vol. II, pp. 588-604. Gogol's book was published in English in 1969 by Vanderbilt University Press. It contains an introduction by Jesse Zeldin, the translator.

[60]Aleksandr I. Solzhenitsyn, *Letter to the Soviet Leaders* (New York: Harper and Row, 1974), pp. 49-59. See also the clarifications made at the writer's April 10, 1975 press conference (*Russkaia mysl'*, 24 April 1975, p. 3).

[61]See Igor' Shafarevich's piece on the nationalities question in *Iz-pod glyb* (Paris: YMCA-Press, 1974), pp. 97-113 and Solzhenitsyn's comments on it in *Dve press-konferentsii* [*Two Press Conferences*] (Paris: YMCA-Press, 1975), pp. 42-46, esp. p. 46.

[62]The articles were: O. Altaev, "Dvoinoe soznanie intelligentsii i psevdo-kul'tura" ["The Dual Awareness of the Intelligentsia and Pseudo-culture"] (pp. 8-32), V. Gorskii, "Russkii messianizm i novoe natsional'noe soznanie" ["Russian Messianism and the New National Consciousness"] (pp. 33-68) and M. Chelnov, "Kak byt'?" ["What Shall We Do?"] (pp. 69-80). The *Messenger of the Russian Student Christian Movement* [*Vestnik R.S.Kh.D.*] metamorphosed into the *Messenger of the Russian Christian Movement* [*Vestnik R.Kh.D.*] with issue No. 112-113 (1974).

[63]For Osipov, "Ibragimov" and "Radugin," see *Vestnik*, 106 (1972), pp. 295, 309-319. For Shimanov, see *Vestnik* 104/105 (1972), pp. 319-322 and AS 1132. Solzhenitsyn's comments on the *Vestnik* 97 authors and their views can be found in his essay "Raskaianie i samoogranichenie" ["Repentance and Self-Limitation"] in *Iz-pod glyb*, pp. 130-136 and in *Vestnik*, 111 (1974), p. 7.

[64]The mutual polemics of neo-Slavophiles and neo-Westernizers usually make depressing reading. Rather than discourse and debate, abuse and contempt are all too often the order of the day. Both "Judophobia" (e.g., *Veche*, *passim*) and "Russophobia" abound (e.g., *zapadnik* Vasilii Grossman's disquisition on the "slave soul of the Russians" in chapter 22 of his novel *Forever Flowing* [New York: Harper & Row, 1972] or G. Pomerants' harsh

judgments in his *Neopublikovannoe [Unpublished Works]* [Frankfurt/Main: Possev, 1972], pp. 162-175). Personally, my admiration goes out to those such as Solzhenitsyn, Agurskii and Levitin, who attempt to cut through the cant and rhetoric and discuss *issues* instead of endeavoring to smother their opponents in righteous indignation.

[65]Pp. 181-182 of a photo-copy of the original of *Veche* No. 8. I have not been able to check if the Arkhiv samizdata edition (AS 1665) follows the pagination of the original. An advertisement for *Grani* No. 96 (1975) mentions an article by Borodin entitled "Concerning the Russian Intelligentsia." Presumably, this is the *Veche* No. 8 piece.

[66]*Ibid.*, p. 184.

[67]*Ibid.*, p. 186.

[68]*Ibid.*, p. 192.

[70]*Ibid.*, p. 193.

[71]*Ibid.*, p. 203.

[72]*Ibid.*

[73]*Ibid.*, pp. 206-207.

[74]*Ibid.*, p. 207.

[75]*Ibid.*, p. 209.

[76]Apparently this is a reference to the Orthodox Church's negative opinion of Masonry. But the Church's opposition to Masonry is based more on its doctrinal views than on its secrecy. Secret or semi-secret organizations of Orthodox believers have more than once played a role in Russian history, e.g., in the struggle against Uniate Catholic encroachments in south-west Russia in the 16th and 17th centuries.

[77]Borodin, p. 197.

[78]See *The Devils*, Part III, chapter 1. On Turgenev as the model for Karmazinov and *Merci* as a parody of his works, see Konstantin Mochulsky, *Dostoevsky* (Princeton: Princeton U. Press, 1967), pp. 468-469.

[79]*Moskovskii sbornik* No. 1, p. 197. I used a photo-copy of the original. Again, I am ignorant of whether or not the Arkhiv samizdata pagination will follow that of the original.

[80]*Ibid.* Incidentally, Borodin seems to be publishing his poetry and fiction in *Moskovskii sbornik* under the pseudonym Aleksandr Berezovskii. A poem cited by Petrov-Agatov (*Posev*, 3 [1971], p. 26) as Borodin's appears under Berezovskii's name in *Sbornik* No. 1.

[81]Borodin's infatuation with Russian maximalism, whether used for good or evil, could lead him into espousing a kind of racial supremacy theory. The stress, of course, should be on the *end* toward which the maximalism is directed.

[82]*Iz-pod glyb*, pp. 124-136.

[83]*Veche* No. 8, p. 193.

NOTES TO CONCLUSION

[1]Marc Raeff, *The Decembrist Movement* (Englewood Cliffs, New Jersey: Prentice-Hall, 1966), p. 29.

[2]Andrei Amalrik, *Will the Soviet Union Survive Until 1984?* (New York: Harper & Row, 1970), pp. 11-12.

[3]*Ibid.*

[4]*Ibid.*, p. 12, footnote and p. 39. Personally, I feel that what Amal'rik calls "Christian ideology" is best described as "liberal neo-Slavophilism." As we have seen, all strands of neo-Slavophilism are characterized by a commitment to the Russian Orthodox Church and the belief that Russia's future development should not be a slavish imitation of the West.

[5]Jacob S. Dreyer, "Soviet Intellectual Opposition," *New Politics,* 9, No. 2 (1971), 24.

[6]Pietro Sormani, "Dissidence in Moscow," *Survey,* 17, No. 2 (1971), 16.

[7]*Novoe russkoe slovo,* 11 December 1974.

[8]See *Posev,* 4 (1975), 17-18.

[9]Medvedev's essay on the first volume of *Gulag* appeared in *Index,* 3, No. 2 (1974), 65-74 and was reprinted in John B. Dunlop, Richard Haugh and Alexis Klimoff, eds., *Aleksandr Solzhenitsyn: Critical Essays and Documentary Materials* (New York: Collier, 1975), pp. 460-476. For the other two pieces, see AS 1874 and AS 1998.

[10]"How I Would Run the Soviet Union." An interview with Roy Medvedev and Valentin Turchin. *The Observer,* 15 June 1975, p. 23.

[11]It is also of course a factor that neo-Slavophiles would ignore to *their* peril. Most of them seem to realize this and offer various solutions to the "nationalities problem."

[12]On this, see *Veche, passim* and my essay "The Eleventh Hour" in *Frontier,* 18, No. 2 (1975), 71-82. *Zemlia* No. 2 is reported by the 35th issue of *Chronicle of Current Events* to contain an anonymous article concerning the necessity of creating a mutual assistance "Russian Fund" to aid participants in the "Russian national movement." The very existence of such an article shows (1) the degree to which some Russians have become aware of themselves as a "persecuted majority" and (2) the growing need they now feel for mutual assistance and solidarity. Surely this bodes ill for the regime.

[13]*Veche, passim* and Solzhenitsyn's "To Patriarch Pimen of Russia" in *Critical Essays,* pp. 550-555. Unfortunately, the demographic issue has become another important factor. The 1970 Soviet census shocked and alarmed many Russians by demonstrating that population growth in the Asiatic republics was far outstripping that of the Eastern Slavs. Great Russians will soon be a minority of the Soviet populace. (On the census, see Teresa Rakowska-Harmstone, "The Dialectics of Nationalism in the USSR," *Problems*

of Communism, 23, No. 3 [1974], 7-8.) For Russian nationalist reactions, see the anonymous "Dom, kotoryi my stroem" ["The House We Are Building"] in *Veche* No. 3, AS 1108, pp. 100-101 and K. Voronov, "Demograficheskie problemy Rossii" ["Russia's Demographic Problems"] in *Veche* No. 9 (19 December 1973), shortly to be published by the Arkhiv samizdata.

[14]See my article "Solzhenitsyn in Exile" (*Survey*, 21, No. 3 [1975], 133-154) which treats Solzhenitsyn's "program" for Russia's future.

[15]The view of Gennadii Shimanov (AS 1846) and, surprisingly, Aleksandr Petrov-Agatov (*Grani*, 83 [1972], 57-58).

[16]Bernard Karavatskii, "Vospominaniia uchastnika" in *VSKhSON* (Paris: YMCA-Press, 1975), p. 209.

[17]S., "Vserossiiskii sotsial-khristianskii soiuz osvobozhdeniia naroda," *Posev*, 1 (1971), 42.

[18]Karavatskii, p. 209.

POSTSCRIPT TO NOTES

This book was in press when I learned that Yuri Luryi's article "Imi dvigala bol' za rodinu" had appeared in the No. 119 (June, 1975) issue of *Novyi zhurnal* (New York), pp. 119-129. Retitled "Na protsesse VSKhSON" ["At the Trial of VSKhSON"], the printed version differs in a few minor ways from the earlier variant to which I refer in the notes.

From the bibliographical section of the May-June, 1975 *Khronika zashchity prav v SSSR* (English title: *A Chronicle of Human Rights in the USSR*), published by Khronika Press in New York, I discovered the existence of a *samizdat* article on Ogurtsov by Boris Skeisharov, a Soviet Jew. Khronika Press kindly supplied me with the text, and I made the acquaintance of a most interesting, if somewhat unrestrained, piece. Skeisharov claims to have known Ogurtsov from childhood and reports that the VSKhSON leader invited him to join the revolutionary organization, an act which he declined for personal reasons. Despite certain factual errors (e.g. the assertion that VSKhSON counted "several hundred members" before arrest) and an indiscriminate mysticism-mongering (e.g. the ascribing of profound importance to two prophecies, one by a Gypsy and one by a "gray-eyed old man" on a train, that Ogurtsov will be tsar of Russia), Skeisharov's article would seem to provide valuable information on Ogurtsov and his family. Skeisharov, incidentally, has an extremely high opinion of the VSKhSON leader and considers him a genius.

In May, 1975, Aleksandr Gidoni emigrated from the USSR; he now resides in Vienna, Austria, with his wife and two children.

On September 25, 1975, Vladimir Osipov was sentenced to eight years in a strict regime camp. The trial, which was not open to the public, was held in the city of Vladimir (*The New York Times*, September 28, 1975, p. 9).

An important article on former VSKhSON member Nikolai Ivanov appeared in the No. 11, 1975 number of *Posev*, pp. 18-19.

Index of Names

A

"A" [anonymous author of "Information Concerning Igor' Viacheslavovich Ogurtsov (b. 1937)."] 16, 21, 22, 158
Abramov, E. P., 44, 48, 52, 55, 56, 233
Agurskii, Melik, 208, 212
Alekhin, E. N., 45, 72, 234
Alekhin, S. N., 45, 72, 233
Altukhov, E. V., 124
Amal'rik, Andrei, 223, 224
Andreev, [student] 44, 69, 70, 234
Antipin, V. N., 234
Anufriev, Iu. E. [teacher] 44, 45, 72, 73, 234
Arbuzov, Colonel, 143
Arkhangel'skii, Iu. B., 72
Arkhangel'skii, [conspiratorial name of Sergei Sergeevich Ustinovich] 77
Astanovitskii, S. L. [attorney] 124
Averichkin, Boris Anatol'evich, 24, 35, 66, 80, 105, 109, 112, 113, 114, 125, 136, 138, 147, 200, 230, 234, 235, 236, 237, 238, 241

B

Balaian, D. G., 44, 73, 234
Bal'dysh, G. P., 116
Baliakina, V. S., 105
Baranov, Iurii Petrovich, 44, 66, 73, 91, 93, 104, 131, 136, 200, 232, 235, 236, 237, 240, 241
Belozerskii, Andrei Timofeevich, [conspiratorial name of Viacheslav Mikhailovich Platonov] 76
Benda, Julien, 192
Berdiaev, Nikolai Aleksandrovich, 16, 21, 32, 53, 56, 60, 61, 62, 63, 71, 85, 167, 168, 169, 180, 181, 182, 183, 187, 189, 190, 194, 214, 219, 220, 297, 299
Blok, Aleksandr, 30
Bochevarov, Georgii Nikolaevich [conspiratorial name is Nikolai Ivanovich Burmak] 17, 42, 43, 49, 50, 71, 76, 77, 84, 90, 91, 92, 95, 96, 97, 106, 107, 108, 111, 131, 136, 144, 196, 199, 200, 207, 209, 210, 211, 231, 235, 236, 237, 239, 241, 296
Boiter, Albert, 166
Bourdeaux, Michael, 298
Boris, St., 95

337